FORGOTTEN
AVIATOR

# HUBERT
# LATHAM

A HIGH-FLYING GENTLEMAN

# FORGOTTEN AVIATOR

# HUBERT LATHAM

## A HIGH-FLYING GENTLEMAN

BARBARA WALSH

TEMPUS

*Front cover:* Inspired by a depiction of Latham by the French cartoonist MICH, 1909 (courtesy Stephen H. King) combined with images from HLPP.

*Frontispiece:* Hubert Latham, 1883–1912. (HLPP)

First published 2007

Tempus Publishing
Cirencester Road, Chalford,
Stroud, Gloucestershire, GL6 8PE
www.tempus-publishing.com

Tempus Publishing is an imprint of NPI Media Group

British Library Cataloguing in Publication Data.
A catalogue record for this book is available from the British Library.

ISBN 978 0 7524 4318 8

Typesetting and origination by NPI Media Group
Printed in Great Britain

# Contents

# Acknowledgements

First of all, I must express my deep appreciation and thanks for the assistance and hospitality extended to me by the present-day descendants of the extended Latham family – especially Hubert Latham's nephew, the late Lionel Armand-Delille, and his daughter, Sylvie, who so kindly provided access to family papers, photographs and memorabilia. I am grateful, too, for the useful reminiscences of Latham's grand-nephews Matthew, Jeff and Oliver Murray and other surviving cousins. Sincere thanks is also due to Dr Guy Parmentier and members of the Parmentier family who were most generous with their time in providing me with insightful recollections, observations and access to their collection of photographs and family archives.

In addition, I would like to acknowledge all the authors of aeronautical history whose sources I have been able to cite, and the many other writers whose work has inspired me to add colour and depth to the Latham story. My appreciation goes also to all the patient librarians and archivists who provided me with incalculable help during the course of my research. In this regard, Brian Riddle, the Royal Aeronautical Society's librarian, proved to be particularly useful in providing access to aeronautical historiography and images. The support of affiliate RAS member, Ken Harman, also deserves a special mention and thanks for his permission to use images from his own private collection.

Finally, let me offer a heartfelt word of gratitude to my family and many good friends who read the work in progress with a critical eye. Their good advice and encouragement throughout the research process was of inestimable value. I would also like to thank Amy Rigg, and her colleagues Stephen Holford and Sophie Atkins at Tempus Publishing for the care taken in the final stages and for their foresight and belief that this is a story worth telling.

Every effort has been made to attribute illustrations and sources accurately. If there are any errors or misinterpretations which remain uncorrected these are entirely my own responsibility.

*Barbara Walsh, Kildangan, 2007*

# Introduction

'Hear the challenge, learn the lesson, pay the cost'. (R.W. Service)

If Hubert Latham is remembered at all today, it is for having been Louis Blériot's unsuccessful rival for the honour of making the first aeroplane flight across the English Channel in the summer of 1909. Little remains in historical records of Latham's background and personality – despite adulation and international public acclaim as one of the brightest stars of aviation which lasted for two further years of press coverage and eye-catching headlines on both sides of the Atlantic. Although usually dismissed in a couple of sentences in historical biographies which attribute his untimely death at the age of twenty-nine to a fatal encounter with a wild buffalo in the Congo, Latham's exceptional talent as a pilot of the new 'flying machines' was not his only noteworthy achievement. Before taking up aviation, like many of his generation he had looked to Africa for a vision of the future and, as a young sportsman, had already made his mark exploring unknown terrains in Abyssinia before embarking on a tour of the world in search of excitement and knowledge of Oriental art and culture. The privilege of unlimited access to a collection of family papers and memorabilia has allowed the author to present a new analysis of the controversies surrounding Latham's aviation career and the mysterious circumstances of his death.

Latham was wealthy, charming and good-looking. Accustomed to mixing easily within the higher circles of the social scene in Paris and London, his popularity as one of Europe's most eligible bachelors was underlined by a dapper sartorial style. This, then, is an account of a life which encompasses more than the tale of one traveller, sportsman and aviator – it follows the trail of the many unusual characters who peopled Latham's life: his friends, his colleagues and his loves. Here are the brave and unhesitant; the innovators, visionaries and entrepreneurs; the engineers, artists, craftsmen and businessmen with whom he came to be surrounded. Of these, some were creators of impossible dreams, some were lured by the scent of money, others by the power of influence in high places or the subtleties of behind-the-scenes politics. While stalwart friends remained supportive, there were also those who swirled with predatory intent on the fringes of this milieu: the spoofers, the charlatans and opportunists, the inept and the stupid. He was to suffer from colleagues who failed him and enemies who sought to destroy. Set in the volatile years of *Belle Époque*, the weft and warp of his life was as subtle with depth and colour as the ancient tapestries hanging in the grand corridors of his French château.

Latham's days ended in a violent incident in a remote outpost of the French Colonial Empire while ostensibly engaged in a big game hunting expedition. But might there have been a secret hidden agenda behind his sudden visit to this notoriously troubled region? Is it possible he had been engaged on a covert mission? There are many clues to raise uneasy questions.

Three small books – all written in English – were among the few personal effects repatriated to France with Latham's body. One was a small volume of popular poetry, *The Spell of the Yukon and other Verses*, by the Preston-born author Robert W. Service, who is more usually remembered for renditions of his famous poem, 'The Shooting of Dan McGrew'. A few lines extracted from one of the poems in this collection, entitled 'The Call of the Wild', may seem appropriate to preface Latham's life and times. Having asked his readers if they have: 'searched the Vastness for a something you have lost?' the poet goes on to ask:

> Have you strung your soul to silence? Then for God's sake go and do it;
> Hear the challenge, learn the lesson, pay the cost.[1]

To echo these sentiments, one can reflect that Latham was a young man who ultimately 'paid the cost' for the adventurous and independent streak that ruled his life. However, his search for that 'something lost in the Vastness' has not survived in the world's memory of those times. It makes a fitting epitaph to restore his life to its rightful place within history as one of the most intriguing forgotten stories of early twentieth-century heroic endeavour.

# ONE

# A Tale of Two Dynasties: Expectations of Excellence

The significance of the Latham dynasty, deeply embedded within the English establishment, and its effect on the life of Hubert Latham cannot be easily discounted. It lies like a slumbering giant in the shadows of this story; rarely stirring to make its presence felt, yet clearly a powerful influence when allied to the authority of the distinguished European links inherited through the maternal side of his family. For a number of generations his English forebears had flourished as successful shipping merchants and financiers, having risen in status to become well connected in the City of London, while his French mother's family, the Mallets, bore an even more distinguished pedigree which could boast of over two hundred years of prestigious banking interests that had survived several radical changes of economic fortunes and political regimes.[1] With the subsequent unfolding of events affecting Latham's short life, the influences generated by these two strong familial connections may be sensed as lurking with faint, but inexorable, menace in the background to this story; perhaps even to the extent of bringing about his ultimate undoing.

Latham was often deeply annoyed when British journalists focused too closely on his English ancestry, insisting that, in reality, he could lay claim to enjoying three-quarters' French blood and considered himself entirely French. Nonetheless, once having drawn attention to himself in the public eye through his exploits, he did indeed appear the quintessential French-born Anglophile, with his fluent and accent-less English, London-cut tweeds and fondness for whisky and soda. By contrast, his father and grandfather had made much of what they believed to be their deeply rooted Anglo-Saxon heritage, forgetting, perhaps, that the earliest Lathams were probably Normandy knights – military mercenaries – who had rampaged across the Channel with William the Conqueror.

Today, the roots of the Latham family can be traced back through a long and distinguished line to twelfth-century courtly circles, wherein the mediaeval knights of de Latham gained credit for the endowments of priories and churches in Lancashire and eventually came to hold positions of authority as High Sheriffs of Lancaster. Each passing century witnessed the fortunes of the de Lathams in Lancashire, rising and dipping in tune to local struggles for influence and power. In the mid-seventeenth century many Catholic Latham supporters of royalist causes lost their lands, became impoverished and slipped into obscurity, although there were a few inheritors of surviving gentrified branches of the family who clung onto modest estates in the rich Lancashire farming area known as the Fylde, having settled for tenancies as squires and farmers under the protection of one of the remaining Catholic landowning families, the Cliftons. Younger sons, the disinherited and those less well placed in the social scheme of things moved away to establish themselves elsewhere, and some of the less fortunate sought work in service or were engaged in more humble livelihoods. By then the expanding Latham family network had spread far southwards to London and the Home Counties, but it did not take long for those with an enterprising streak in the family to reassert themselves characteristically and, as a result of their efforts, they were soon on the rise again within the higher ranks of society.

Arthur Charles Hubert Latham, only son and second child of Lionel and Magdeleine Latham, was born in Paris on 10 January 1883. Known later only by his last name, Hubert, the baby was baptised into the Protestant faith in a ceremony which gave traditional precedence to the selection of at least two Christian names that recalled his maternal and paternal forebears. On his mother's side, the baby's grandfather, Arthur, was a scion of a prestigious French banking family, while his English paternal grandfather, Charles, a resident of Le Havre for over fifty years, had headed-up one of the many successful Latham overseas trading companies. The Lathams enjoyed solid foundations in London as enterprising merchant-shipping traders, bankers and professional men of wealth and influence with a history of commercial and social success which can be traced back to a rise in status of a wine merchant called Thomas Latham in the eighteenth century. Twice-married Thomas – whose antecedence as the enterprising son of a master blacksmith in Islington and grandson of a coachman from Holborn was modest enough – had fathered fourteen children, born between 1771–1804. As his business prospered, he had moved his family south of the river to the more salubrious surroundings of Camberwell in Surrey in the London borough of Southwark, where six sons and three daughters survived into adulthood. Thomas lived to see his family expanding their business expertise into worldwide markets and before his days drew to a close his contribution to commercial growth in the City had been noted by influential people. Nearing retirement as a long-standing member of The Clothworkers' Company, one of the oldest Livery companies in the City of London, his contemporaries marked their esteem by electing Thomas Latham as their Master. This office carried the highest and most sought after distinction – a crowing glory to a lifetime devoted to commerce – and one which brought his family social recognition in the world of business and finance.

By the time of old Thomas Latham's death in 1818, his sons and grandsons had created a network of business interests that spanned a whole spectrum of enterprise from commodity trading to merchant banking. In addition to the wine trade, the family owned and ran plantations in the West Indies and partnerships had been set up in firms which shipped cotton, indigo, hides, coffee and tea and other goods from abroad. These brought about links with Bombay, Madras, the East Indies and China. One son, Alfred, went on to be appointed as a director of the Bank of England, followed by a short period as Governor of the Bank. It was a post that carried high status but mixed blessings at the time. The competence – or indeed inexperience – of the directors of that great institution was often subjected to scathing criticism. As Walter Bagehot, the often acerbic Victorian commentator, once observed, these gentlemen were prone to pay more attention to their own money-making concerns than they did to the Bank's business.[2] It was a fair enough comment; the Bank's directors were mostly self-made men who, naturally, expected to gain something for themselves from these positions.

The increasing prosperity of this conglomerate of family businesses in the nineteenth century boosted the fortunes of a thriving third generation who were to be born into families that were now wealthy, well travelled and well educated. Latham sons developed careers as professional men in law and banking; Latham daughters married well and the established merchant princes in the family continued to engage in profitable overseas commercial trading. The personal qualities which drove the dynasty forward included keen sharpness of mind, fearless risk-taking and a hefty dose of individualistic determination – even stubbornness – all of which were notable characteristics that, three generations later, may be identified as having filtered down to emerge as useful, if sometimes idiosyncratic, traits deployed by Thomas's great-grandson Hubert Latham to achieve his own success.

Hubert's grandfather, Charles, had been one of the wine merchant's many children that arrived in quick succession to fill the Latham household in Camberwell. Born here in 1795, he was approaching thirty when he married an eighteen-year-old French Hugenot émigré from Nantes – a lady by the name of Pauline Marie Elise Cécile Delaroche. At first, the newly-wed young couple settled down within the Latham family circle in Camberwell, but the astute young husband may well have been already scheming to improve his prospects, because four years later, in 1829 – and just over sixty years before the birth of his famous grandson Hubert – he put London life behind him and moved his wife and three children across the English Channel to the port of Le Havre, where he set up his own trading company to specialise in importing indigo and other exotic goods from abroad. In the meantime, one of his brothers, Arthur, had founded the well-established Liverpool and Manchester operation which continued to flourish for another generation under the direction of his son, also named Arthur, and both ventures were typical of the many entrepreneurial mercantile-based commodity trading concerns developed by the family.

Despite his cunning move across the Channel, Charles Latham had steadfastly remained the typical English business gentleman and his advancement within French social and commercial circles may be greatly credited to his wife's family who became well-connected politically and prominent in local and national government. His brother-in-law, Michel, by then styled 'de la Roche', held office as Mayor of the city and served as the elected Deputy for Havre, where his valued contributions to public service prompted King Louis-Philippe to bestow on him the decoration *Chevalier de la Légion d'honneur*. Charles Latham also received a measure of recognition and respect in due course by becoming president of the port's Chamber of Commerce. The self-exiled Englishman's personal life had not been without its share of tragedy, for he and his wife were to mourn four fine sons and a daughter whom they lost either in childhood or in the years of their early youth and, when he died in 1875 at the great age of eighty, a second daughter and two sons were the sole survivors of a large and vigorous family. On his death, when the thriving business in Le Havre, *Latham et Cie*, passed into the hands of his sons, the French branch of the Latham family – notwithstanding the continuation of the close familial and business links to their English cousins – could now claim to be firmly established in its adopted country.

During his father's lifetime, Charles's eldest son, Edmond, had gradually slipped into taking over responsibility for the firm's administration – even to the extent of applying for French naturalisation papers in 1872. This calculated move had possibly been dictated more by political expediency than by any lessening of loyalty to the family's English roots. By contrast, his only brother Lionel, twelve years younger, who was to become Hubert's father, was given little chance for hands-on contact with company business. When he reached the age of twenty-one he had been duly despatched to finish his education at Magdalen College, Oxford, but it was unlikely that he entertained any serious intention of graduating with a degree under his belt. As was customary at the time, this short stint at Oxford would have been regarded merely in terms of adding a certain social cachet to his background and he developed no ambition to enter commercial life thereafter. Instead, he chose to distance himself from day-to-day involvement and a desk-bound job by eagerly undertaking any travel assignments that were required. Not only was it an old family tradition for the younger Lathams to gain first-hand experience of the firm's overseas commercial enterprises, it was also a valid excuse for Lionel to spend a great deal of his time away from France, for, in truth, he may well have found life in the shadow of his efficient older brother somewhat intimidating. Certainly, one of the outcomes of the firm's younger partner's frequent absences abroad was the affinity and passion Lionel soon acquired for Oriental art. During 1877–79 he completed an ambitious world tour by travelling in a westward direction across the United States and thence to a lengthy sojourn in Indochina and Japan. Enthusiasm for Japanese art forms was riding high on a tide of popularity in Europe at this time and it comes as no surprise to learn that Lionel took care to ship back an immense amount of *objets d'art* during his extended tours. These purchases subsequently formed an impressive and valuable collection which he installed in his home. In due course, this collection would become the inspirational base for Hubert's fascination with the concepts of Far Eastern art and design.

Lionel's travels could not go on forever. In 1879, he returned to France and in the following year he married Magdeleine Mallet, a daughter of one of the most prestigious banking families in France whose directors held considerable status among the elite ranks of the French *Haute Société Protestante*. For a Latham to gain entry into the inner ranks of these circles through marriage was a match *par excellence*.

The House of Mallet – a private bank – had been founded in Paris in 1713. Their adherence to the strict observance of their Protestant faith had brought advantages during the turbulent days of late eighteenth-century France and the family's reputation for impeccable tact, astuteness and integrity quickly forged links to powerful overseas trading and commercial enterprises. The Mallets held the privilege of managing the financial affairs of the French Royal family throughout its chequered history and, on the foundation of the *Banque de France* in 1800, it was a Mallet who received the honour of becoming its first *Régent*. Although avowedly non-political, *Régent* Guillaume Mallet was well favoured by the Emperor Napoleon, who subsequently conferred on him the title of Baron in 1810. At that time, Paris was being transformed with a spate of elaborate building programmes and the support of the directors of private banks like the *Mallet Frères et Cie* came to be much sought after by the boards of new companies engaged in construction or in the setting-up of infrastructures in transport and communications. The House of Mallet soon ranked foremost in the economic life of the capital.

For Lionel, gaining familial connection to such an exalted and highly powered circle had its drawbacks. The strictly upright Mallet family expected a high sense of decorum. There could be no more racketing around the world; no more dubious forays into the Far East in search of adventures and Oriental treasures. A lifestyle more in keeping with the couple's elevated standing in society was now required and, as plans for the wedding gained momentum, his first task would be to provide a suitable home for his bride-to-be. At the time of his engagement to Magdeleine, he had purchased – perhaps impulsively – a large villa in Le Havre which had been the former home of the exiled Queen Marie-Christine of Spain. The house was located in a very central position in the town with terraced gardens which faced the beach. However, according to one source, its situation did not appeal to Magdeleine and the anxious-to-please Lionel was forced to look elsewhere.[3] The newly-weds finally settled for a fine mansion in the Côte d'Ingouville in what was undeniably the best residential district of the town, overlooking the harbour. Even so, Lionel was still restless; he had other plans in mind.

Apart from his interests in Oriental art and fondness for travelling abroad, Lionel's consuming passion was his love of *la chasse* (the hunt) and he was soon plotting to set himself up in a country estate that could be made into a base for his horses and his large circle of like-minded friends. Such ambitions did not come cheap. Lionel was a wealthy man, but an investment in a property of this type needed an injection of extremely serious money and there was only one way he could go about getting it. This was by selling-out the bulk of his shareholding in the family firm to his brother, thereby raising enough capital to acquire Maillebois and its surrounding lands from the Vicomte de Maleyssie. Lying not far from the city of Chartres, in the present Eure et Loir region, south-west of Paris, the château attached to this ancient *demesne* enjoys a colourful history that can be traced back to the fourteenth century.

When Lionel took it on in 1882, the château had been altered, re-built and restored by its various noble *seigneurs* over several centuries. Although its seventeenth-century architecture was in need of much-needed refurbishment, Lionel's first priority was to make improvements to its outbuildings by adding an attractive new stable block and barns to accommodate all the needs of the hunt. With this done, he then threw himself whole-heartedly into rearranging the interior layout of the château itself. He changed the design of upper floors, installed plumbing and made the reception rooms into a showcase for his collection of Oriental artefacts. The couple finally set up home here shortly before the birth of their second child, and only son, Hubert.

Lionel found the life as a country gentleman very much to his taste. It was fortunate that he could turn his creative talents towards reinventing the imposing grandeur of Maillebois, with its acres of fertile land, its farms, river, park and feudal village nestling close-by, while at the same time his energies and ambition could be consumed by enthusiasm for the socially accepted endless round of hunting, shooting and fishing which made up the rural pursuits of the landed classes. Despite the fact that his mother had been a Frenchwomen, it may be recognised that Lionel still considered himself to be an entirely English sporting gentleman, through and through. Indeed, it had come to be a matter of pride for him to boast how the last two generations of the French-based branch of the Latham dynasty had managed to hold on tenaciously to their English ancestry – and their English passports. His portrait, in which he poses as the very archetype of a Home Counties squire in hunting pink, dominates one of the château's drawing rooms to this day.

Lionel and Magdeleine's anticipated idyllic life together in the impressive perfection of their château was not to last for long. Within a year or so, the legacy of Lionel's previously exotic lifestyle, the stress of constant travel and consequent exposure to foreign maladies – or a combination of all of these, perhaps – took their toll. When he died in 1885, reputedly from pneumonia brought on by getting a chill following a dramatic plunge into the icy waters of a lake to perform a *coup de grâce* on a wounded stag while out hunting, he had been a relatively young man in his mid-thirties and married barely five years. At the time of his fatal accident, his widow, Magdeleine, was twenty-seven and expecting the birth of their third child, a second daughter, Léonie. Their first-born daughter, Edmée, was four years old and their son, Hubert, a toddler only two months short of his third birthday.

*Opposite:* Château de Maillebois. (Harman Collection)

*Right:* Lionel Latham poses in hunting pink: portrait by Gustave Courtois, 1885. (Photograph taken by the author, 2005)

Hubert was to grow up having little or no memory of his father and if it had not been for his mother's keenly perceptive concern, he might have been destined to spend the days of his childhood as heir to Maillebois as the sole male in an all-female household where he would be surrounded by deeply affectionate and doting women, bereft of any other male companion or role model. Fortuitously, this potentially psychologically damaging scenario was off-set by Magdeleine Latham's close acquaintanceship with the wife of the eminent Judge Parmentier and his family of three young sons. They were the owners of the neighbouring château de Marcouville, which lay barely three miles distant. Mme Latham's decision had been a wise one. The two elder Parmentier brothers were destined to play an important role in Hubert's future life as friends and companions.

The owners of Marcouville were a devout Catholic family of lawyers, steeped in high moral tone and intellectual excellence and it may be seen that the friendship that developed between young Hubert and the elder sons of the Parmentier family was carefully nurtured by the two women so that, as they grew up together – Léon was a year older and Jean the same age as Hubert – they progressed from sharing boyhood adventures to becoming staunch friends and travelling companions. A younger brother, Maurice, being four years younger, was to some extent understandably left out of the trio's close relationship. As the three grew to maturity it was through their influence that

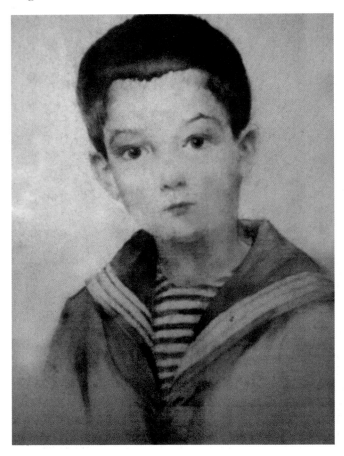

A study of Hubert Latham as
a small child by G. Dubuff, fils,
1889. (Photograph taken by the
author, 2005)

young Latham learned appreciation of academic prowess in addition to the importance of gaining exceptional proficiency in many of the tough and demanding gentlemanly sports and occupations suited to his upbringing and class.

It may be of some significance that Magdeleine Latham's own severely Huguenot religious background had not prevented her from holding the integrity of her neighbours' religious faith in high regard, and when the Catholic Geneviève Parmentier was also widowed in 1902, the affection and respect that existed between the two ladies was drawn even closer, especially in their mutual concern for the welfare of their sons.

To outsiders, it had seemed sadly clear that Magdeleine's efforts to cope with her widowhood had not been easy. Although cushioned by her late husband's wealth and the security of her own well-to-do family background, these were emotionally difficult years for her. Devastated by the loss of her husband, the young widow never wore anything other than black for the rest of her life, never re-married and, surrounded by Lionel's collection of Oriental art which he had so enthusiastically installed in Maillebois, kept everything in the château *in situ*, almost as if she believed she would one day see the return of her beloved. Soon afterwards she took to dividing her time between Maillebois

The young widow with her
family, 1885. (HLPP)

and an elegant Paris apartment in the fashionable 8th Arrondissement, close to the Arc
de Triomphe, a lease which her son later took over, probably on reaching his majority in
1904. In this restless adoption of the role of an inconsolable victim, her lifelong mourning
for the loss of her flamboyant young husband may well have cast an uneasy funereal
gloom on those closest to her. For Hubert Latham as a young boy, the opportunity to
escape into the more easy-going, if challenging, household of the Parmentier brothers
must have provided a veritable lifeline capable of drawing him into a more welcoming
normality, for one can detect a sense of cloying uneasiness surrounding the depth of
Latham's relationship with his mother which was to last for the remainder of his life. It
might be a provoking question, but it is not an unknown psychological manifestation
found in the background of other men of notable achievement. Moreover, perhaps it may
be also asked to what extent does this trait cast a reflective slant on Latham's later, gentle
empathy and patent preference for the companionship of older, more worldly women?

Yet let it be said that even the darkest days held some compensations for Magdeleine
Latham. She was accustomed to move in circles which enjoyed political connections of
significance. As a daughter of one of the senior members of the Mallet family prominent

within the *Banque de France*, she benefited from their links to high-ranking society and important Franco-German and Swiss financial and business institutions. Successive Mallets had become key figures in presiding over leading French insurance companies, the port and dock entrepôt development of Le Havre, several national railway networks, public transport systems in Paris and the expanding National Electricity Company An important point to note – for it will surface later – is that one of Mme Latham's Paris-born aunts – her mother's sister (their maiden name had been de Rougemont) – was the mother of a clever and ambitious German politician, Theobald von Bethmann Hollweg. He, too, had a powerful banking family background and was destined to reach the pinnacle of his career when the Kaiser appointed him to the post of German High Chancellor in 1909.

The two families had remained quite close. Having been brought up in circles which habitually spoke excellent English and German, as well as their native French, Mme Latham, in addition to employing reliable and formidable German nannies, regularly sent her children to spend part of their summer holidays to perfect their easy command of High German in the company of their cousins, the Bethmann Hollwegs. As the subsequent unfolding of events will reveal, the existence of family links of such significance may well have unwittingly provided a devastating drawback to Latham's future aviation career and prospects.

However, it should be made quite clear, nonetheless, that the loyalty of the Latham family always remained steadfast to the English/French *entente*. Many decades later, in the Second World War, Latham's elder sister, Edmée, would risk her life as a member of the French Resistance by sheltering British and American servicemen in the attics of château de Maillebois.

Young Latham's formal education began at the *École Alsacienne* in Paris, after which he went on to attend the fashionable *Lycée Janson de Sailly*. To judge from his academic qualifications, he had been a bright child and clever, if not totally dedicated to scholarship as manhood approached. School reports show him to have been proficient in his command of classical Greek and Latin – on occasion gaining the class annual first prize and the professor's comment that this scholar was capable of 'clear intellect and much energy'. By 1900 he had gained a qualification in classical philosophy and his Baccalaureate was awarded in 1903.

As a child, Hubert did not enjoy robust health, and around the turn of the century – by which time he was in his teens – he had been diagnosed as suffering from *albuminuria*, a liver complaint of varying severity, which meant that the final winter months of his education were spent in the fashionable, if *risqué*, Algerian health resort of Biskra under the eyes of professors in the *Académie D'Alger*. His summers saw him sent off to the Pyrenees or Alps in the company of a series of private tutors. These long absences established the habit of frequent letter writing home with news to his beloved *Chère Maman* – a practice which he was to continue throughout his life.

The delicacy of his constitution was an irksome burden for the boy to bear. By 1899 he was already showing signs of rebellious impatience with the cosseting it required. A tutor, obviously under some pressure, writes to Mme Latham from a Pyrenean Health Spa in early October 1899, begging her to remind her sixteen-year-old son that the doctors had advised him against going up to extremely high altitudes and would she also please tell his charge that 'he was wrong in thinking cigarette smoking was a good habit to acquire.' The tutor's concern was to no avail. Young Latham soon became an inveterate chain-smoker and, as an aviator, displayed disdain for the supposedly bad effects of extremely high altitudes by becoming the first aircraft pilot to break world records for height on many occasions. Whether or not his claim that no long-term ill-effects on his constitution ensued from this high flying remains a moot point.

It may be recognised that the pattern of Latham's earliest years was one that was filled with a regular shifting of scene. Among his private papers there exists a sheet of foolscap on which an unknown hand has plotted the ebb and flow of the socially imposed seasons which saw his family decamped to Paris for three or four months each year, followed by summers spent in Maillebois and interspersed with regular visits to Cannes, Jouy-en-Josas (with the Mallet grandparents), Biarritz, San Moritz, Schaden (near Salzburg), Innsbruck, Mont Doré and elsewhere. None of this regular change of location and activity was unlike the fluid lifestyle of many other families of similar class and background. The Parmentier family also took up residence in a Paris apartment during the winter months, and the Latham cousins – scattered across France, England and Germany – adopted very similar regimes with the aim of managing their own mixture of well-regulated business and leisure pursuits.

The final years of the nineteenth century and early 1900s had witnessed much greater openness within Europe. Travel restrictions had never been so relaxed and Europe was seen as welcoming to all comers. For the rising middle classes this had created a climate of greater intimacy and familiarity with other cultures. This was especially the case for upper-middle-class English families, many of whom enjoyed flourishing international trade and business operations and continued close association with Western-European-born kin. When King Edward VII of England cemented the inspired political *Entente Cordiale* between England and France in 1904 with his unashamed affection for *la vie Parisienne* and all things French, he created an even greater enthusiasm among his subjects for admiring and unquestioning collaboration with their French cousins. However, historically, the English nation had always nurtured a dark suspicion of the foreigners beyond its shores – especially those which lay just across the Channel. The closer they were, the more threatening they appeared and there had always been a special wariness of England's traditional enemy, France, since the Dark Ages. Such ingrained perceptions were hard to change and the fragile acceptance of the French nation in Great Britain came about through the increasing distrust of the military intentions of the Kaiser's Germany. As time went on, the barely concealed sabre rattling of Germany, the building up of its naval fleet, the aspiration to capitalise on its colonial territory in Africa and the concentration on industry and heavy engineering spoke loudly of an undisguised ambition to become the most powerful economic nation in Europe. It was an escalating situation that was becoming increasingly disturbing and threatening. Even England's extended royal family was hearing faint murmurs of public disapproval of its many close marriage links to foreigners. While it was accepted that these European-born first and second cousins were all grandchildren of the much loved old Queen Victoria, each and every one of these royal relatives had been raised in a tongue other than English and, therefore, in the public mind they were seen as potentially unreliable. Eventually, within a few years of Edward's death in 1910, such was the weight of gathering concern during the First World War, the ruling English Saxe-Coburgs would be forced to change their name to Windsor to silence those critics who were keen to harp on about their Germanic roots. This show of royal deference to public pressure was received with a great deal of general relief.

None of this would have yet bothered Latham as a young man ready to embark on the seas of higher education soon after the turn of the century. His first decision to read law at the University of Paris was possibly influenced by the high academic achievements of his childhood friends and close neighbours, Léon and Jean Parmentier, both of whom had studied Law in addition to gaining other scholarly distinctions. Léon qualified as an agricultural scientist and Jean, who while still a schoolboy had gained a national award of a gold medal in philosophy, graduated with a double first in humanities. Jean's scholarly brilliance had brought about his swift entry into the Department of Finance in 1903 at the age of twenty. Despite the good example of these companions, however, a career as a lawyer seems not to have grabbed Latham's enthusiasm overmuch. A short stint at the University of Paris was shortly to be replaced by matriculation at Balliol College in Oxford in the autumn of 1903. This choice was probably expected of him. Apart from that of his own father, the example set by a number of his English relatives, uncles and cousins, had made a short spell at Oxford almost *de rigueur*.

In 1903, Latham was still not completely free from serious problems with his health. During the spring he had embarked on an ambitious motoring trip with friends in Egypt. En route home the party incorporated a visit to Sicily and Naples and his letters from here speak of the good air and empty roads 'free from tourists'. Yet something was giving cause for concern, for by the time they reached the South of France in mid-April, a disappointed Latham was forced to abandon the car and seek medical attention, adding a plaintive note in a letter to his mother that, 'I do not want to get the reputation of always falling sick.'

He was to remain in Nice for several weeks, consulting specialists, resting and undergoing daily treatment for his albuminuria. He writes of receiving ultraviolet rays and of the strictly imposed diet – no red meat, two litres of milk a day and plenty of fruit and vegetables. The care he received must have proved successful. By 19 October 1903 he was able to take up his place at Balliol College in Oxford as planned. He took lodgings in Wellington Square and, if the entries in a small account book are anything to go by, frequently partook of a very British diet, which featured breakfasts of bacon and eggs during his sojourn there. As was the case with his father – and unlike his friends the ambitious Parmentiers – it may be surmised that Latham did not seriously aspire to an academic career at the college despite being under the tutelage of the redoubtable historian, A.L. Smith, one of the more lively and popular dons of his day, who would later make his name as one of the most outstanding Masters of Balliol.

Latham soon found life in Oxford could be convivial and intellectually undemanding. There were plenty of social activities to be enjoyed and his letters home, which date from October 1903 to the spring of 1904, are full of references to his English cousins and their network of friends.

Young bloods at Oxford – with Latham at the wheel, 1903/04. (HLPP)

He writes to tell of trips up to London, house parties and dances and, as might be expected, there were regular requests for money. His yearning to be back at Maillebois for the hunting season was palpable and he fixed to sneak back there for a few days' sport in mid-December. Apart from reporting that two of his essays were satisfactorily received, his letters have precious little to say about the progression of his studies. Instead, he complains about the English winter climate: '… rain every day' and buys himself 'a superb waterproof – a Burberry' by way of compensation for the 'execrable' weather.

January 1904 saw Latham reaching his majority, which brought him the inheritance of a considerable and well-invested fortune. He had settled into the routine of Oxford life without too much difficulty, although by February 1904 his mind was even less concerned with academic matters and rather more concentrated on the acquisition of a motorcar. His health was in good shape and by March he was telling everyone at home that he was having a good time and there was mention of a (presumably motor-) 'racing club'. Plans were being laid for a motoring trip with some college acquaintances in the coming vacation. The weeks passed quickly and pleasantly and, not pushed by any ambition or need to sit examinations at the end of the academic year, it was soon time for him to 'go down'. Like many others of that era he could now claim to have been educated at Oxford.

From this time onwards, it might be argued that Latham perfected the skill of compartmentalising his life so as to cope with the many shifting horizons of challenge that lay ahead. On the one hand here was the young sportsman who maintained close and affectionate links to family and home – the dutiful son who continued to display loving concern for his mother and two sisters and familial matters – while, conversely, here was a wealthy young man-about-town, freely demonstrating a careless ability to mix with perfect ease among some of the most eccentric and creative associates to be found in Paris at that time; a set which distinguished itself more for fast and racy behaviour than for sober success or financial wizardry.

Perhaps it was because this was Paris. And not just that; it was Paris at a particular moment in time. No question about it, this was the place to be in the first decade of the 1900s. Where else could people from every walk of artistic life, business entrepreneurs, gentlemen of leisure and titled society mix with such easy *élan*? If you were clever, amusing, dashing, decidedly odd or endowed with any form of outrageous behaviour, or even talent, the Parisian climate would nurture your natural ability to blossom, shock or intrigue. For the honestly enterprising, it was the place to flourish; for the charlatan, equally so. Titled heads of Europe graced the salons; the English landed gentry and American *nouveaux riches* met and mixed at the dinner tables and clubs; and the middle classes of all nations flocked to this re-discovered epicentre of the world's culture.

With Oxford behind him, Latham returned home in May 1904 and almost immediately set off with a group of friends to the South of France with no other intent than that of enjoying himself. Before the year was out, he was obliged to fulfil the customary short spell of service duty as a Reservist French Army private and, in due course, when he received the call to report for duty in Paris on 11 November 1904, he was posted to the 25th Battalion in St Cloud. His stint as a reservist seems to have passed without incident and by all accounts he must have made a good impression, perhaps because of his excellent marksmanship with a rifle – a skill acquired from early boyhood days spent shooting game on the family estate – or for his stoic ability to take things as he found them. Both attributes would stand him to good stead later in his life.

Knowing the state of his health to be questionable and now in receipt of a considerable fortune, it is doubtful whether he ever contemplated taking up a formal career and it would seem he did not have any great desire to join his uncles in the worlds of banking or commerce. Like many other privileged young men of his age, he had not made his mind up as to what he might, or could, do to make his mark in the world. In the meantime, he was young, he had money and was developing into a keen and expert sportsman. Then fate stepped in. His love affair with aeronautics was about to be launched by an adventure, not in a flying machine, but in a hot-air-balloon trip organised by his cousin Jacques Faure. The aim of the balloon voyage was to break the existing record for the time it took to make the journey across the English Channel from London to Paris. The adventure would be Latham's *baptême de l'air.*

Ten years older than Latham, Jacques Faure was a relation on his mother's side of the family as a result of Mallet marriages to two Oberkamf daughters from another prominent Huguenot family with Franco-German banking and business interests.[4] Faure was well known in France and international circles, not only as an athlete, hunter and sportsman *extraordinaire* but also as an expert balloonist and one of the founder members of the Aéro Club de France

The cousins in the balloon basket, prior to take-off from London, February 1905. (*La Vie au Grande Air*, No.336, February 1909)

Long-distance ballooning had become a popular sport in Europe and the accomplishment of balloon journeys across the English Channel was not unknown. The first ever crossing coast to coast from Dover to Calais had been undertaken back in 1785 by Joseph Blanchard, who had been accompanied by an American colleague, a physician called Jeffreys. Their journey took two hours. Now Faure was promising Latham the chance to accompany him on another history-making flight – one hundred and twenty years later – this time to create a new record for the longer crossing from city to city, London to Paris, in a craft supplied by the *Aéro Club de France*. Not only would they seek to set a new time record, the trip was to be accomplished at night. The occasion would be the first to mark Latham's name in association with world records for air flights – one of many to come.

Faure was later interviewed for an illustrated account of this exploit in *La Vie au Grand Air* recalling the preparations, the flight and the conversations between himself and his cousin Hubert.[5] A photograph shows the older man to have been an impressive figure sporting a large handle-bar moustache. He was a tall and well-built man and as he posed in the balloon basket, prior to take-off, his frame towered over his young cousin's slight figure.

At that time, Latham was barely into his twenty-second year. Decked out in a Norfolk jacket, stiff collar, tweed cap, gloves and polished brogues, he was already demonstrating something of the stylishness that would distinguish his good taste as a dashing sophisticate in later years. Latham sported a small moustache, which, being less impressive than his cousin's, failed to disguise the fact that, despite the seriousness of expression and the studied

The twenty-two-year-old Latham faces the camera on the eve of his famous ballooning adventure, February 1905. (*La Vie au Grande Air*, No.336, February, 1909)

formality of his dress as he posed for the photographer, he still looked much younger than his years. Three or four years later Latham's escapades in foreign lands, hunting and travelling alone through wild places, would bring about a sharpness and refinement of his features. His skin by then would have acquired its habitual pale sallow tan and his shoulders the slight stoop that would be later over-emphasised in many caricature drawings. By that time his careless good looks, elegant London tweeds and courageous disregard for personal safety would have created a reputation that was legendary in the eyes of an adoring public. Poised for his first aerial exploit, however, these days were still far ahead in the future for the young man.

# TWO
# A Sporting Young Tiger, 1905

The aspiration to fly has held a fascination for man since the dawn of history and there are many recorded accounts of experimentation in design and innovation: some imagined like the mythological story of Icarus, and others as real as the hundreds of detailed technical drawings produced by Leonardo da Vinci, the fifteenth-century Italian artistic genius. Success, albeit very limited in its extent, was not to be achieved for another two centuries and, when it did arrive, it brought world recognition of French superiority in skilled aeronautical experiment. By the eighteenth century, developments of the *Montgolfière*-type of hot-air ballooning had proved to be spectacular crowd-gathering entertainment in Europe. In 1782, one of the Montgolfier brothers' first successful experiments had carried a sheep, a rooster and a duck in a balloon basket, travelling upwards to a great height and for a distance of a mile. When the apparatus finally crash-landed, the sheep survived, although, strangely, the duck did not; but it was enough encouragement to bring about the next step one year later – the aerial transport of a man. When Blanchard completed his crossing of the English Channel in 1785, his triumph was greeted as a crowning glory for the French nation. However, realisation of the true worth of this innovative mode of communication did not come about until almost a hundred years later during the Siege of Paris in 1870, when the beleaguered and starving citisens broke the blockade by constructing balloons which sent a regular stream of messages sailing over the heads of the Prussian armies to reach French supporters in the provinces.

The interest of Latham's cousin, Jacques Faure, in aeronautics had been sparked off in 1899 when he had made an ascent as a passenger in a balloon piloted by the eminent balloonist, Comte Henri de la Vaulx. From that moment on, Faure was hooked. As many others had discovered, the freedom of being airborne was a life-changing experience and one that was to introduce him to the most exhilarating and challenging of sports. A year later he was one of the three competitors in the first long-distance balloon flight to Russia organised by the French Aero Club. In 1905, following the exploit which was to introduce his young cousin Hubert Latham to ballooning, he went on to win the *Grande Prix de l'Aéro Club de France* for piloting a balloon single-handed from Paris to Kirchdraft in Hungary, a distance of 1,314km.

For the next few years Latham and Faure's paths were to cross many times and on many important occasions.

Soon after the New Year 1905, Faure's plans for the record-breaking Channel crossing by balloon from London to Paris were all ready. His intention had been to make this trip even more sensational by using a small petrol-run engine to control their craft's steering devices. Almost immediately this proposal ran into difficulties, causing frustration and serious delays which did not auger well for a successful undertaking. When he and Latham arrived at Calais on Saturday 11 February, with their balloon *Aéro-Club II* and all its equipment carefully packed up for the journey across to Dover, they were to discover to their dismay that the Customs Office in the port was now claiming that their petrol engine would be subject to a high export levy. They insisted that the gentlemen could not embark until this was paid in full. Faure argued in vain that the engine would actually be re-imported within a matter of a few hours – by balloon – as it was an integral part of the apparatus to be used. The customs officials, as is their wont, remained unimpressed and unbending, but Faure was not a man prepared to back down. Equally stubborn, he had no intention of paying so much as a sou in tariff charges. There was nothing for it but to leave the engine behind.

In Dover, further frustration awaited. Intending to begin the flight that evening, they found there was an insufficient amount of gas available to fill the balloon there and it would be necessary to proceed on up to London as fast as possible. They found a secluded spot in the park beside the Crystal Palace, where preparations could begin without any further setback. The balloon was filled. The adventure was about to commence. Paris was 344km away. All was well. By 6.45 p.m. that evening, they were successfully up and away.

It had been a bright, moonlit night. Although the sky was clear, the journey over sea and land was to become a battle against winds and bitter cold. It took the aeronauts just over an hour to reach the coast at Hastings, travelling at the height of 1,500ft. As they left the English coast behind them they threw out enough weighting ballast to allow them rise to 3,000ft without difficulty. From then on, however, it proved a hard struggle to keep the balloon on course and steady over the water. As time went on, slowly and surely their height was diminishing to a dangerously low level. When landfall in France loomed on the horizon they found themselves travelling along so near to the water that the guide rope of the craft was being dragged along the wave tops. This was a time for cool nerves and confidence. Only when the French coast was reached could they afford to ditch more ballast to regain height. At last, the town of Dieppe came into sight. The Channel was conquered. It was done! They were now once more travelling over dry land. At this stage, cold and tired as they were, they could have made their descent with honour if they had so wished. But, having held what Faure describes as 'a council of war', they make a decision to proceed further – they would head for Paris. Nothing to lose and all to gain.

Finally, after what seemed an age aloft, Latham mistook the faint light in the sky on the horizon to be the breaking dawn. This was impossible – it was only one o'clock in the morning. With excitement, he quickly realised the brightness in the sky was the lights of Paris ahead of them.

Later, when writing an account of this adventure, Faure recalls the jokes and banter tossed between the pair as they approached the centre of the city. His young cousin, swept

Faure has signed a souvenir postcard of himself for his cousin, February 1905. (HLPP)

by the heady thrill of the moment was displaying a desire for a stylish splash of publicity. Latham had said: *'C'est admirable! Nous allons descendre sur la Place de la Concorde.'* (This is wonderful! We are going to land in the Place de la Concorde.) Obviously, the difficulty of descending in the middle of the city centre completely unfazed him. Faure teased him along for a bit, asking, *'Nous ne continuons pas?'* (You do not think we should continue?)

Latham's excitement was undiminished. Their journey was complete. They had done it! He was not in the least worried about landing – just excited at their having achieved the journey. *'Non! Londres–Paris c'est un record fameux!'* (Oh no! London to Paris is a famous record!) But by this time, the older man must have felt he had let the joke go far enough. It was time to assert his authority: *'Tu as raison. Nous allons descendre, mais pas sur la Place de la Concorde.'* (You're right. We are going to land – but not in the Place de la Concorde.)

Circumspection had prevailed in the end. An impressive night landing bang in the centre of Paris was not on. As Faure later explained, apart from the dangerous downwind, there were too many high buildings in the vicinity and they had already displayed enough risky heroics that night. Instead, the pair drifted on until they reached the outskirts of the city where they made a safe landing on the plain of Aubervilliers. The journey had taken six hours and thirty minutes. They had completed the journey in a new record time.

Their exploit was received with rapturous approval. Six and a half hours was a magnificent time to have achieved. The *Aéro Club de France* honoured them with a reception and the speeches on this occasion recalled famous names attached to aeronautical exploits – not forgetting the first-ever balloon Channel crossing in 1785 – and the many others who had marked progress by setting up historic, albeit notional and invisible, milestones in the air.

Parisian society, always ready to fête new heroes, picked up on their achievement without hesitation and the two young men found themselves the toast of several gatherings. Everybody wanted to meet them, to congratulate the pair – and the ladies, in particular, made a great fuss over them.

Perhaps conscious of his mother's highly tuned sensitivity to the position held by the family within the ranks of what she deemed to be select society, Latham tended to keep many of his romantic adventures strictly discreet and private. But, as might be expected, there was never any shortage of speculation doing the rounds in respect of the many eager young women who would come to flutter on the fringes of Latham's life, especially after he had made his name in international circles as a pioneer aviator. Many of these paramours are now only identifiable by their first names and remain shrouded in romantic mystery, but he must have retained recollections of these affaires with great affection – keeping letters and cards which carry tantalising evidence of his admirers' breathless appreciation of his attentions. 'Wish my thoughts would stop soaring and come down to earth...' writes one. 'I love you, dearest,' sighs another, while another jokes about the postcard she sends which shows the Mona Lisa with a printing flaw mark on the famous lady's neck, asking him if the blotch might not be a 'love bite?' – adding an obscure comment about Edward VII. One should be wary of not reading too much into these exchanges. Perhaps it was all very frothy and inconsequential – even quite innocent.

Or maybe not.

Artist Eileen Gray, *c.*1910. (The
National Museum of Ireland: Eileen
Gray Collection)

Peter Adams, in his biography of the Paris-based artist and designer, Eileen Gray,
suggests it was during a social reception held in honour of his famous first ballooning
exploit that Latham was formally introduced to this blue-eyed Irish lady of striking
appearance, eight years older than him and one of the several outstandingly interesting
females in his life with whom there may be evidence of a more long-term and possibly
intimate dalliance.[1] Latham's friendship with Eileen, as shall be seen, may have been not
so much a conventional romantic encounter as an attraction created by similar character
traits, interests and mutual friends, for here was a differently independent spirit with
whom he could share a deeper, yet undemanding empathy; someone who came and
went in a way which matched his own patterns of restlessness. Born in Wexford, Ireland,
into a family with links to minor nobility, Gray's lineage had opened many doors for her
within elite Protestant social circles in Paris. Although officially entitled to call herself an
'Honourable' as a result of her mother's inherited title to a Barony in Scotland, she had
an unpretentious attitude in regard to class rankings and, during her sojourn in Paris as
an art student, Gray had gained the reputation of being quite a shy person in company.
Latham may have found her quiet and reflective reticence a refreshing alternative to the

string of gutsy girls who were to become awestruck admirers, fellow aviators or would-be pupils. In any case, it may be speculated that the pair were already known to each other long before that recorded encounter in 1905 because they both enjoyed the friendship of René Raoul-Duval, a mining engineer whose father had been a director of the *Banque de France* and thus well acquainted with the Mallet and Latham families. Raoul-Duval was also a motoring enthusiast – one of Latham's passions since his Oxford days – and a colleague of Jacques Faure in the French Aero Club. Slightly older than Latham, he was married to one of Eileen Gray's closest *confidentes*, Jackie Gavin, a former fellow art school student. It is a connection on which there will be more to say, later.

It might be noted that Latham's attachment to Gray – no matter whenever or wherever they made their first acquaintance – may also have been based on a shared knowledge of Oriental art. In 1905, Gray was about to become engaged in a life-long fascination with the Japanese-inspired art form known as *urushi* and had started to learn the demanding technique of creating artefacts in lacquer. Latham had grown up surrounded by magnificent examples of these designs in Maillebois, which had been collected by his late father. One can speculate that the discovery of several mutual interests sparked off that special recognition that can only be kindled by an encounter of like minds and, in their case, it was fortunate that such friendships have the ability to survive the fractures formed by a lack of steady continuity. Latham was often far away from Paris on a series of expeditionary travels which kept him abroad for increasingly long periods of time. When he finally returned to France in 1908 to find himself unwittingly presented by the challenge of the *Daily Mail's* prize for an aeroplane flight across the English Channel, he and Eileen Gray quickly re-established contact. What ensued would seem to have been a relationship which was to contain a few teasing elements of ambiguity, not the least of these being Gray's notorious bisexuality and Latham's own sexual predilections, which appear to have contained some blurring at the edges.

That balloon trip in February 1905 – although exciting – must have had an unsettling effect on the twenty-two-year-old Latham. It had shattered his customary habit of spending some time pottering around Egypt or Algeria to avoid northern European winters. With the novelty of the aerial adventure behind him, the young sportsman must have found the days hanging heavy on his hands, especially as the early spring weather was still uninvitingly chilly. Jacques Faure had promised some fun at the Monaco Regatta and had arranged for him to participate as helmsman for him in some of the motor-yacht-racing competitions. None of this would be happening until April and, in the interim, what was he to do? Since Christmas, his mother had been hinting it was time he began to think ahead about a career, a lifestyle; something that would, perhaps, provide him with an interest worth total absorption. While a future in banking might not have been envisaged – he was much too volatile for this – there may have been hopes that he had the makings of a tough and astute entrepreneur in trade like his paternal grandfather and uncles. Bearing in mind that the Latham family fortunes had been based on decades of import and export dealings, some gainful experience in a shipping office in Bordeaux when he returned home for the summer months might be just the thing. In the meantime, February was no time for him to be hanging around France and an immediate escape

Latham's favourite sports car – a French-made Grégoire. (HLPP)

to the more salubrious surroundings of Algerian sunshine in Biskra was called for. From there, Latham would find it easy to nip back across to the South of France for the small interlude in Monaco.

The promise to help Faure with the trials of a new racing motor boat was to be a momentous turning point in his life – his first introduction to the Antoinette Motor Company, run by his cousin, Jules Gastambide, in partnership with the eccentric but clever engineer and graduate of *L'École des Beaux Arts*, Léon Levavasseur.

Jules Gastambide was a financier and businessman of some standing and a cousin of Latham's late father on his maternal grandmother's side of the family. During his business career, Gastambide had run several successful manufacturing enterprises in France and, like many others with an eye for the future, had recognised the potential for lucrative expansion of French commercial interests in North African territories. The businessman's first association with the engineer Levavasseur had come about around 1902 when he had sought him out to rectify some tricky technical faults in one of his companies, an electrical generating plant in Algeria.[2] At that time, the red-bearded engineer, Léon Levavasseur, who had earned himself the reputation of working with a very short fuse, had begun to make his name as a clever electrical technician who wanted to spread his talents into the wider arena of internal combustion engines. Considered eccentric in much of his design concepts, Levavasseur had skilfully combined his qualification as an electrician

Engineer Léon Levavasseur. (HLPP)

and specialist in generators with a latent artistic ability for technical innovation. He had become sufficiently successful to start up his own firm by 1901.

Gastambide had a keen eye for new business opportunities and he was not averse to taking risks. Recognising that many developing sporting activities were increasingly reliant on the performance of a light-weight internal combustion engine, he set up a partnership deal with Levavasseur to develop the engineer's ideas. Several disappointing and unproductive years passed and their first imaginative efforts to design a flying machine for Levavasseur's engine proved abortive; but they did not give up. The aeronautical historian and biographer of Blériot, Brian Elliott, has cited the views propounded by the distinguished commentator, Dollfus, who believed Levavasseur's background training in the arts gave his designs for his innovative engines an artistic quality and undoubted '*cachet d'élégance*' which was not found in other makes. However, Elliot takes care to add a dry caveat to this observation: '… elegant they were, but reliable they were not'.[3] By the end of 1903, the partnership had abandoned the thought of building an aeroplane chassis that could stay airborne and began to look at other uses for the engine.

Levavasseur had a connection to maritime life – born in Cherbourg in 1873, the son of a naval officer, he had been at one time keen to make a career at sea. With their earlier hopes dashed, the partners' decision to pursue a policy of selling the engine to owners of motor yachts would seem to have been a sensible turning point. The transition to adapt the engine for use on the water went smoothly and there were renewed hopes for the successful performances of the 'Antoinette' engine – named after Gastambide's young daughter – in some forthcoming yachting competitions .

Calling Levavasseur's engine the 'Antoinette' had come about quite early on in the partnership and it was said at the time that this was because her father had been charmed by the notion of Daimler's use of their chairman's daughter's name for a new product. But this German firm's choice had been no fashionable whim. With an appraising eye on the lucrative but sensitive French market they had decided on a Gallic-sounding female appellation, Mercedes, for their new model in a specifically calculated manoeuvre to deflect customers' attention away from the company's Teutonic origins. Such subtlety of thought would have never occurred to Gastambide and, when, some years later, the Antoinette Motor Company returned to the concept of producing a workable design for a flying machine which could expand the business into aeroplane manufacturing, no particular consideration would seem to have been afforded to the name by which their next new product might be sold. By 1908, their monoplane, which Latham would later fly into international fame, carried the same title as the original Levavasseur engine: 'Antoinette' and it was thus that the names of Latham and his cousin Antoinette came to be inexorably linked.

When Latham arrived at the 1905 Monaco Regatta in April, he was to find himself working alongside Gastambide and Levavasseur for the first time. He was to show off the paces of their latest refinement of the Antoinette engine, which they had installed in Jacques Faure's racing speedboat.

Monte Carlo in springtime was delightful. The regatta held there in the first two weeks of April were popular sporting events. Well established on the social circuit – and attended by Europe's most elegant elite – the venue could be relied upon to attract an interesting mixture of spectators and competitors. This stretch of Mediterranean coastline had always enjoyed a regular stream of visitors drawn from the inner circles of royalty, the seriously rich and other well-known faces who were made welcome, if not for their status or money, then for a reputation to be amusing or charming. Famously dubbed some years later as 'A sunny place full of shady characters' by writer W. Somerset Maugham, whispers of scandal and gossip filled the casino gardens and floated easily and unceasingly along the waterfront. What did the flamboyant French sportswoman, automobile and motor-yacht owner, Mme Camille du Gast, really get up to when her name was linked to the twenty-four-year-old Sultan of Morocco, Abd el-Aziz?[4] This young Arab ruler was rather better known as an enthusiastic Anglophile with a passion for bicycles, so how many there knew or cared that he was deeply and dangerously indebted to France, psychologically, politically

Latham at the helm: the Monaco Regatta, 1905. (HLPP)

and, indeed, literally, to the tune of many millions of francs owed to several French banks? It was a situation which pundits at that time might have recognised as a guarantee of trouble to come. Problems were already brewing over the vagueness of frontier lines in North Africa, and the Kaiser, mightily irritated by the French and British *entente cordiale*, had recently caused feathers to fly by the tenor of a speech in Tangiers which recognised the independence of the Sultan's kingdom (an incident which led to 'the first Moroccan crisis'). Such posturings by the Kaiser were a constant thorn of irritation for France and a worry to Britain. There was gathering suspicion of German aspirations in Africa, which was something that was to rumble on right up to the time of Latham's final visit to the French-held Equatorial territory in the Congo some years later.

Anticipation of such anxieties to come, however, were not likely to have caused many flutters of concern among the brittle socialites who had gathered to enjoy themselves in Monaco. Gossipers were more eager to learn who had gained the privilege of being entertained on the British Royal Yacht. The Duke of York, Prince George, who was now the new Prince of Wales, was a keen naval man and while punctilious in observing the niceties of social behaviour on such occasions, he was known to display far less hearty *bon vivant* than his father, the popular King Edward VII. When Prince George entertained, his parties were marked by substantially less amounts of alcohol and far fewer interesting women, and the only one intriguing question left hanging was: had anyone actually spotted the vulgar tattoos that it was rumoured adorned both arms of this younger royal personage?

As the top people mingled and socialised, the organiser of the occasion, Monaco Sporting Club's president, Camille Blanc, was happy to allow the racing events and viability of the competitions to be kept alive with the help of wealthy businessmen and newspaper moguls. The Prince of Monaco, a scion of the Polignac dynasty, graciously presented prizes and a trophy for the major event, and there were plenty of others willing to give their names and offer sponsorship. Among these were Alfred Harmsworth, the British newspaper proprietor – to be ennobled as Baron Northcliffe later that year – and the *outré* American newsman, James Gordon Bennett, owner of the *New York Herald*. Both gentlemen were not only renowned for their generosity, but for the rivalry and power they wielded in the press. Not altogether altruistic in their aspirations, much energy and time was spent vying with each other to provide prizes and trophies in sporting events around the world. This was the age to challenge speed and newspaper readers were avid for lively reports featuring motors, yachts and balloons which Harmsworth later liked to call 'splash stories'. Such sensation-generating tales of risks to life and limb kept newspaper sales figures nicely buoyant.

Well hidden within the froth, too, were the more serious intentions of European industrialists who vied determinedly with each other in their preparedness for future armed conflicts and the likelihood of war being reliant on the enhanced performance of internal combustion engines.

Gathered on the fringes of these dark shadows, the list of participants for the Monaco programme that spring presented a tight coterie of familiar sporting personalities from England, France and Italy for the readers of trade journals and newspaper reports. A great number of the combatants were already old friends and rivals – be it on the ground, on water or, increasingly, in the air. Among the French representatives well known to society in Paris were names long associated in international sporting exploits. All-rounders like Jacques Faure and Henri Farman and the Russian-born French nobleman Comte de Lambert provided good copy for eager journalists, while the antics of the flamboyant Brazilian–born Paris-based balloonist and flying machine fanatic, Alberto Santos-Dumont could be always relied upon for a story. That year, he did not disappoint, but added value to the content of sporting and society columns by ditching his latest aerial contraption down in the bay. The competition from Italy came in the form of a number of celebrated naval architects which included Gallinari and Vicente Florio. For England, there was the attendance of the Napier engineering firm's regular driver, the Australian-born Selwyn F. Edge, already the possessor of several Gordon Bennett trophies for motor-car racing, who would pilot a boat equipped with one of their marine engines. Another Napier boat was entered under the name of Lord Howard de Walden and a yacht owned by the Duke of Westminster was equipped with a Hotchkiss engine developed in France by an expatriate American engineer. The rising fortunes and social acceptance of the influential English middle-classes in sporting circles was typified by the owner of the Lowestoft Marine Yacht Yard, Mr Brooke, who had made his money from an iron and brassworks foundry.

Underlying the whole frippery of sociability and enjoyment for the well-to-do, however, there lay a far more dedicated and serious intent of the motor-manufacturing firms. It was not so much a showcase for their wares as a forum for hard-nosed business deals.

Under the auspices of a sporting event like this, every new advance being made in the production of light engines could be carefully scrutinised and assessed by the keen-eyed and the curious. That year, the makers of the Fiat, Mercedes, Panhard, Napier and Renault engines, who had regularly set themselves up against each other on previous occasions, were for the first time facing the challenge of a newcomer in the choppy waters of Monte Carlo Bay. Word was going around that Gastambide and Levavasseur's Antoinette engine had been successfully showing her paces throughout the week and Léon Levavasseur's hopes were high. The firm had already received an offer of 90,000 francs for their boat from an agent of Prince Henri [sic] of Prussia, 'brother of the Kaiser and Admiral of the German fleet', who wanted to sail it under his colours at the forthcoming regatta at Kiel.[5] When Faure's young protégé, Latham, took his turn at the helm of this craft, the Antoinette boat responded to his handling with gratifying success. To their delight, this helmsman displayed an instinctive touch. He coaxed displays of extraordinary speed and endurance in run after run. Finally, in a competitive race held in rough seas which spectators conceded as presenting the most difficult of conditions, Latham defeated the hopes of several major combatants by coming in third. Not surprisingly, the name of this new helmsman came to be noted by old hands as an up-and-coming young sporting tiger. Here was a chap worth watching out for, they told themselves.

Yet, it was not to be in maritime events that Latham would eventually be destined to gain the world's greatest accolades of fame. As soon as the Regatta was over, he quickly left behind the sophistication of Monaco and headed for Marseilles to catch a packet boat back to the Egyptian port of Alexandria.

Although we can recognise that he had grown very accustomed to spending the winter months away from France, there may have been more than one special reason why Latham was so eager to return to Egypt in late April 1905. Unsettled by the months of obligatory military service which had followed his time at Oxford, it is possible he had made up his mind it was time to break free from the strictures imposed by the expectations of a family whose adherence to the rules of polite society now increasingly bored him. Like so many travellers before him, once having tasted the pleasures of desert places he had allowed himself to became infected by impatient yearnings to return, time after time. In Africa one could succumb to the seductive mix of culture, sights, smells and undemanding simple living which proffered new horizons of possibility. In one sense here was the hope of release, in another the tempting danger his soul might be re-captured by an alternative dimension.

Another, more practical consideration may have prompted Latham's return to Egypt at the end of April 1905. This was to investigate the feasibility of an African exploratory expedition. The dying wish of Judge Parmentier, the father of his old friends and neighbours, had been that his sons should see something of the world before settling down and he had always hoped the two elder brothers might join forces with Latham if he agreed to lead a trek into unexplored territory – perhaps in North Africa or further southwards from the Sudan. This now seemed a real possibility and tentative plans were being formulated for an ambitious journey up the Nile into remote regions of Abyssinia – today's Ethiopia – in order to conduct exploratory surveys in this lesser-known corner of North East Africa. It would be partly adventure and partly an astute future career prospect for Jean Parmentier in a move to impress his superiors in his new job in the Department of Finance.

The academically brilliant Jean Parmentier had joined the French Civil Service two years earlier and was probably already being earmarked as a future candidate for top postings in the colonies. His request for several months' leave of absence to gain first-hand experience of conditions in Africa would have found much approval in the right quarters. His elder brother, Léon, meanwhile, had skills as a photographer and an approach to the French Geographical Society – a powerful and influential institution – with the promise of an illustrated account of their expedition and a collection of rare specimens of flora and fauna for the Natural History Museum in Paris would gain further official support. Setting in place an altruistic *raison d'être* for this journey was consistent with the Parmentier family tradition of public service but, realistically, it may be viewed that there was always an unspoken hidden agenda behind expeditions of this nature; the submission of a fresh geographical and ethnological survey of unexplored African territory for the French Colonial Office. Of singular worth was information which could be passed on to the French Ministry for War. (Several years later, a personal letter written by the Ministry to Latham's mother to thank her for presenting a set of her late son's 1906/07 original maps to the war department adds how 'very useful' his work in Abyssinia had proved to be for the '*Service Géographique de l'Armée.*'[6])

There were others within the French government and its associates concerned with commercial and communication opportunities who would find this kind of report great use and of great interest. Since the defeat of the Arab Dervishes by the British at the Battle of Omdurman in 1898, the Sudan had been administered under a joint British and Egyptian mandate, which gave the former all the control it needed along the Nile and effectively shattered French ambitions for further expansion of colonial influence. The compromise which was subsequently reached over Khartoum had allowed the possibility of serious conflict between the two nations to fade away with a modicum of face-saving dignity and the immediate outcome was that French priorities switched to establishing a firmer footing in the north-western desert territories bordering on the Sahara. Abyssinia, the last unconquered kingdom in Africa, was now being eyed by a number of European nations with increasing rivalry. The English saw the region as forging a link with existing mandated territory southwards as far as British Uganda; the French had not forsaken earlier aspirations to create a useful bridge to their colonial territories in the French Congo and the Italian and Germans wanted to keep their options open with an eye to the future.

Vast areas of Abyssinia's almost impenetrable high mountain ranges remained for the most part still unexplored and it was the policy of Emperor Menilek II (1889-1913) to welcome small expeditionary parties – such as one that might be mounted by Latham and his friends – to survey these uncharted territories. The Emperor was keen to modernise his country and any means which might obtain up-to-date findings and fresh cartography of unknown terrain was viewed as being of particular value to him. Fortunately, the relationship between the Emperor and the resident French consul in Addis Ababa was good. It would seem the time was right and the stage set. A suggestion to mount a French-funded Latham-Parmentier expedition to the Abyssinian Kingdom was sure to receive full approval.

'Hubert when he makes his tour of the world.' (Courtesy of Matthew Murray, 2006)

That Latham and his friends should look to Africa was almost predictable. European society's enthusiasm for wintering in North African resorts in Algeria and Tunisia had been unassailable for decades but, as Britain and France established a greater measure of control over the crumbling Ottoman Empire, regular seekers of winter sunshine now sought out new destinations. The more adventurous, whose imagination had been excited by the tales of popular fiction writers like Rider-Haggard, joined caravans which travelled south of the Sudan, drawn by the rumours of the immense gold and mineral wealth to be found in the legendary gold mines of the Queen of Sheba, consort of King Solomon.[7] A young Englishman, Herbert Weld Blundell, heir to a large Lancastrian landed estate and a name probably familiar to Latham, had just completed writing up a paper for the London Geographical Society to describe his recent tour of territory lying to the north of Addis Ababa.[8] French-born Baron Maurice de Rothschild, a notoriously wayward individual who preferred travelling to working in the family banking business, had trekked from the port of Djibouti in French Somaliland as far as the walled city of Harer, spiritual capital of the Abyssinian Islamic population. And within the next couple of years, an ambitious up-and-coming British politician, former war correspondent and army subaltern by the name of Winston Churchill would be seen making his own re-assessment of potential developments along this coastal area of East Africa.[9]

On leaving Monaco, Latham had not dallied long in Egypt. By the time springtime had slipped into the summer of 1905 he had returned to France to face decisions as to his long-term future. In his heart he must have known that family aspirations to introduce him to the experience of a normal work-a-day world in a Bordeaux shipping office would turn out to be a wasted exercise. A postcard from one of his English girl friends in Brighton says it all: 'Don't tell me you are <u>working</u>!' she had teased. It was not that he balked at accepting responsibility, but more the fact that, while in Bordeaux, other business had occupied his time. A piece of landed property he had inherited had needed a number of improvements and he had to engage in some tricky negotiations with workmen employed to sink a new well – with an eye to getting good value for the job – and several other matters connected to the management of the estate at Maillebois to be attended to. As to making decisions on a future career, clearly that would have to wait until there were far fewer distractions.

As anticipated, the proposed Latham-Parmentier expedition to Abyssinia received official approval from the appropriate French Ministry without any difficulty. They planned to take a route along the banks of the White Nile as far as Khartoum, then onwards as far as the capital city, Addis Ababa. If time permitted they would conduct an additional survey of the unknown mountainous area of the kingdom known as Galla Land, which lay further to the south.[10] On completion of the journey, they would prepare a report on the condition of the land, its population and any commercial opportunities identified. Even as these plans were unfolding, however, an ambitious concept was already taking shape in the back of Latham's mind. For as long as he could remember, a delicate water-colour picture of an elephant had hung in a corner of his little bedroom in Maillebois. In it, a small figure wearing a pith helmet was depicted perched high in the howdah on the elephant's back. Underneath, his father had penned an anticipatory message addressed to his infant son: 'Hubert, when he makes his tour of the world'. Perhaps it was now the time for his dead father's wishes to be fulfilled? After all, a precedent had been set. The ambition to follow in the footsteps of his travel-loving father was the perfect excuse to make an escape and this forthcoming expedition might be the start of an ideal solution for his restlessness. When finished in Abyssinia he could continue southwards by sea in the direction of the true land of elephants, Indochina. Now, here was a goal to aim for! But it might be sensible to bide his time for a while yet before making any announcement on this score.

# THREE

# Into Africa: Land of the Queen of Sheba, 1906-07

To see the Abyssinian expedition of 1906–07 as merely an interlude in Latham's life would be to ignore its later significance. Viewed in the context of the final period of his life, the experiences encountered during this journey may be seen as having laid the steely courage which showed itself when he gained fame as a pioneer aviator.

Like many before him, Latham's early introduction to the seductive pleasures of desert lands had left him primed for what was about to blossom into an enduring love affair with Africa. No later experience ever quite came to completely replace it. What did he find there that held most appeal? Was it the simplicity of life, the closeness to nature, the necessity to hone skills for survival? Did new sights, sounds, tastes and rituals act like a magnet to seduce a keen, enquiring mind? Or was it the intoxicating sense of being totally in control of one's destiny? Not until he discovered another outlet for this need, alone and high in the air at the controls of his Antoinette monoplane, would he find anything to match the sensation.

Latham's own personal reflections on Africa in the meticulous notes he set down in private journals or in letters home to his mother reveal only an occasional glimpse of the inner self and it is indeed fortunate that further insight on the first stage of his Abyssinian journey may be drawn from diary notes and photographs taken by Léon Parmentier.[1] A reflective comment made by one of the Gastambide cousins when writing an account of this time some twenty years later helps to reveal a tantalising sliver of understanding in its evocation of Latham's private fears and we get the sense that a corner of the veil of reluctance to speak frankly about his travels had been lifted, albeit briefly. 'It was Latham's considered opinion', Robert Gastambide wrote, 'that when two white men are alone in the bush for a great length of time, they are in danger of getting too close, too intimate. Arguments can arise and the situation can become explosive, especially when guns and hunting knives are lying around'.[2] The quotation prompts the question: had something disturbingly dramatic happened in the course of the Latham-Parmentier expedition through the Sudan and Abyssinia? Only the briefest of comments in a diary kept by Léon Parmentier gives any hint of this possibility, although there are indications that not all went smoothly during the four-month-long trip. The party endured many setbacks and frustrations which caused disappointment and delays and there were several times when tempers must certainly have flared, which is not altogether unexpected when consideration is given to the three companions' mixture of conflicting personalities. The eldest Parmentier, Léon, comes across as a warm-natured, fussy and precise organiser. He was to later serve with distinction as a combatant in France in the early days of the First World War, which was followed by a posting as an agricultural advisor to General Hubert Lyautey, one of France's great military heroes who was the Resident-General of Morocco at that time. The enterprising Léon was put in charge of the colony's agricultural output and sent off to Algeria to bring back cereal seeds used in making couscous and a form of bread, in a successful effort to keep French armies well supplied with basic foodstuffs during hostilities.

By contrast to his brother Léon, Jean Parmentier was the possessor of an outstandingly brilliant and ice-sharp mind. Distinctly more calculated and detached from deep emotion he, too, saw distinguished campaign action in 1914 and, when recovered from wounds received on the battlefield, he was also posted to Morocco, arriving there in 1915 to supervise the financial affairs of the colony. This excellent career move brought him swift promotion. By the end of the war he had become one of the elite corps of back-row advisors to the French Diplomatic Service during the rounds of negotiations being conducted between the Allies and the other World Leaders of Russia and the United States.

Then there is Latham himself.

In many respects, the characteristics of his personality are markedly out of tune with both of the brothers. Although well able to keep pace with them intellectually, he had struggled for years to gain mastery over his health problems, and this had given him an outer shell of toughness, but it was one that concealed an inner compassion for weakness in himself and in others. Outwardly suave and composed, his letters home reveal how deeply his affection could run and how philosophically he could approach problems. The existence of sympathetic affinity to his brother-in-law Dr Paul Armand-Delille's decidedly left-of-centre political sentiments – which were perhaps strangely at odds with that of Latham's elder sister Edmée, who reputedly disapproved of her husband's friends and associates to the extent of refusing to 'receive' them – had developed in him a sense of social justice and an unconscious respect of others from less privileged backgrounds. Latham's easy acceptance of alternative mores was an attribute which would stand him in good stead during his later aviation career. Endowed with a naturally friendly nature, he accepted all people at face value and despite having a temper that could be quickly sparked, fits of bad humour were a short-lived process for him. Perhaps this is why he and the Parmentiers remained such staunch and supportive friends long after all the ups and downs of their African adventure.

The trio's expedition to the Sudan and Abyssinia had begun in the most conventional and mundane manner with departure from Paris on 7 November 1906. A week earlier Latham had received the official sanction from the *Ministre de l'Instruction Publique des Beaux-Arts et de la Culture* giving authorisation to him as leader of the expedition and, in naming the others as *collaborateurs*, granted them 'a 30 per cent reduction on all packet-boat fares between Marseilles and Alexandria and freedom of passage during their travels in Egypt, Abyssinia and Indochina in pursuit of zoological, botanical and geological

The inveterate chain smoker:
Latham in a cheery mood.
(HLPP)

research for the National Natural History Museums'. On the day of their departure, Léon Parmentier records how the three young men had visited the Ministry of Agriculture in the company of a senior *Administrateur* of the Paris-Lyon-Marseilles (PLM) Railway Company – an uncle of the Parmentiers by marriage – who had turned up to wish them *bon voyage*. They then dined with Latham's brother-in-law, Dr Paul Armand-Delille before taking the night train to Marseilles to embark for Egypt the following day.

Although their long association as friends since childhood had created close bonding, it is probable that Latham found his friends' conservatism and inexperience of desert and bush-land travelling trying his patience to its limits on many occasions. A picture of Jean being carried from one of the Nile ferry boats perched upon the shoulders of a rag-tag bunch of turbaned Arab porters in his tailored Paris suit, collar and tie, socks and polished shoes speaks volumes. A week or so later, aboard the first of their camels, the Parmentiers' suits, collars and ties and tidy boots remain while Latham has already donned a more relaxed military-style bush jacket, jodhpurs and riding boots. Not until they had left Khartoum do the brothers reveal signs of more relaxed open-necked shirts and rolled up sleeves.

Disembarking from a Nile steamer, November 1906. (Parmentier Collection)

On arrival in Egypt nothing had gone quite as smoothly as expected. There had been several small upsets to their careful plans. Léon notes in his diary – with a growing air of exasperation – that a crate containing their saddles had gone missing somewhere in transit between Marseilles and Port Said. At first thought only to have been delayed, several days of waiting and a plethora of ingenuous excuses proffered by their shipping agents, ends with him putting finality to the saga on 18 November: 'The saddles are definitely lost'. This setback meant the trio were reliant on camels rather then horses for the transportation of men and equipment. A camel train had to be ordered up but it soon became clear that the animals and their handlers could not be picked up in Khartoum until the end of the month. More delay.

That was not the only snag: the French consul in Cairo had washed his hands over their difficulties in importing the party's hunting guns because they were of a heavier calibre than the usual rifles used by such expeditions. When exported over the border to Sudan they could be construed as 'weapons of war' – which was not a wholly desirable first impression for travellers to make in a country that was still racked by violent tribal skirmishes. The consul, who was accustomed to how things worked behind the scenes in Middle East border diplomacy, had cannily claimed such problems were 'none of his business' but advised them to 'purchase' the requisite permits from the British Authorities with the aid of a compliant local official.

Having despatched his friends on a sight-seeing tour of Luxor and Thebes, Latham set about pulling the necessary strings to get clearance for their guns from the British Department of Ordinance. Time dragged on. It was 22 November before the permit was obtained and signed:

> An authorisation has been sent to the director of customs in Alexandria to allow the importation of: six smooth-bore sporting guns, eight carbines (2500) cartridges for your personal use and party. These arms and any unexpended cartridges must be re-exported from Egypt and the Sudan on your leaving the country after the completion of your tour, otherwise they will be liable for confiscation by the police.[3]

At last, they could make a start for Khartoum. The party took a leisurely meander along the Nile and negotiated their luggage through the mean shacks that constituted the border post without difficulty. The desert was all around them now. Making the most of this extended time in the Sudanese capital with good grace, the friends absorbed the atmosphere of the crowded streets and Arab Souk which had changed little over the centuries. Each day Léon's diary records discoveries and strange encounters in the bazaar, sometimes provoking exclamation marks of outrage or amusement; the strange food and drink; the dancing of bare-breasted Sudanese women wearing impressively huge amber and silver bead necklets; a marketplace full of men who had congregated in a group as if segregated, while women on the other side of the market languorously displayed their bodily charms for sale to clients. But the novelty of these sights and experiences soon wore off; they were growing impatient of hanging around while their agents haggled over the arrangements for the camel train.

By the end of the first week in December all seemed ready. Their supplies had been packed up and camels, camel handlers, hunters, armed gun bearers and porters acquired.

By the standards of the day it was a small enough caravan, perhaps only twenty-five men in all, with ten loaded baggage camels and another five to provide transport for themselves, for the guide and for a French-speaking interpreter, Joseph (Youssef), who would double up as a cook. Yet another week was to drag by before the caravan set off. A four-month journey to Addis Ababa lay ahead.

This disorganised start should not be read as any lack of coordinating skills on their part, rather it was the culmination of several adverse factors, not least of which was the fact they were a party of Frenchmen passing through a joint Egyptian-British-mandated territory. It is reasonable to believe that intelligence would have already been gathered by the authorities to note these travellers' politically influential family backgrounds in banking, railway and commercial enterprises, and it may be taken that a certain amount of British diplomatic concern could have been provoked in view of the rivalry that continued to exist – despite *entente cordiale* – between the two nations in this part of

The camel train is loaded in Khartoum, Sudan, December 1906. (Parmentier Collection)

Departure for Addis Ababa, Abyssinia, December 1906; a four-month journey lies ahead. (Parmentier Collection)

the world. This party would be watched. Abyssinia had already looked to France for the construction of its first railway line to link into French-held Somaliland and, although this contract turned out to be a financial disaster which had been rescued by an injection of capital from British shareholders, it was one of the moves that had been seen by London as calculated to further the ambition of France to exercise greater political and economic control of resources in this region.

The expedition had commenced by taking a route along the left bank of the Blue Nile until Ouda-Meani, after which they would follow the bed of the Rahad river, which ran along the foothills of the Abyssinian mountains. Once across the frontier they would present themselves to local tribesmen as emissaries of the Emperor Menilek II. Latham had arranged with the French consul to provide them in advance with a series of letters of introduction from the Emperor for each of the powerful local chiefs in the remote hinterlands they intended to traverse.

All went well until they reached the town of Gondar, on the Sudanese border with Abyssinia, at which point they discovered that none of their camels, handlers or porters would be allowed across the frontier. The whole region was rife with ancient territorial rivalries and it would be necessary to negotiate the hire of mules and mule handlers and a completely new platoon of Abyssinian porters and bearer before being allowed to proceed. A simple enough task, one would think, but it had held them up for three more weeks while Latham chivvied the French consul into finding another amenable English inspector willing to help smooth things out.

The unscheduled switch to a mule train, although bringing further delay, actually proved to be blessing in disguise. Unused to camel-riding, they had all found the experience of trekking through Sudanese territory decidedly uncomfortable. Even the well-experienced Latham, writing home, wryly describes their steeds as veritable 'instruments of torture'. Léon, in particular, was truly glad to see the end of the camels. Not for nothing have these animals earned the sobriquet 'ships of the desert' and, having suffered woefully with seasickness on the boat trip across the Mediterranean, his endurance of the equal discomfort of nausea when on board his mount's undulating motion had been almost too much for Léon to bear.

Writing later of their trek southwards through the Sudan, the picture Jean Parmentier paints is a classic description of what an explorer might expect to find in uninhabited and uncharted territory. 'Everything is controlled by the desert,' he writes, 'and, of course, tracks are non-existent. In a number of [other] places, particularly in the areas where we come to a river bank, we are obliged to open up a path with our axes.'[4] As they press on, the landscape changes to vistas of dramatic heights and lush valleys and by the time they are within three days of the frontier with Abyssinia, having 'travelled forty kilometres through the monotonous bush without water', they come to a village which is 'surrounded by apparently prosperous cotton plantations'.

Today, a jaundiced perception of treks like the Latham-Parmentier expedition dismiss these journeys as being a wasteful indulgence for the privileged, but it should not be forgotten that sportsmen who went to Africa in the first decade of the twentieth century still had a role to play in expanding and refining knowledge of areas that had not been

Latham checks the day's bag, December 1906. (Parmentier Collection)

adequately covered by earlier forays into the interior. Often charged with surveying uncharted regions more thoroughly, these travellers brought back answers to archaeological and ethnological puzzles, re-assessed population levels, land and mineral resources – often with the a view to setting up communication links. Specimens of animal life, birds, fish, insects, shells and botanical finds opened up a world of knowledge and also provided new vistas for beneficial medical research. With no roads to traverse, trekking on foot required expeditions to bring teams of up to one hundred porters and, to keep an entourage of this size well supplied with food while out in the bush, it was essential to hunt and shoot game of every description en route. But nothing was ever wasted. Having measured and taken detailed notes of each individual specimen, any fresh meat not consumed by their men was given away to the indigenous population, or dried into strips for sustenance when game was scarce. Then the animal skins were tanned and the bones cleaned and packed carefully for despatch to European museum collections.

In the light of the unremitting tragedy still being played out in this part of East Africa a hundred years later, it is poignant to read how their reports repeatedly highlight problems of conflict between the Islamic and Christian traditions in this region and it may be recognised that their awareness of the delicate political situation was never far away from their minds. Jean Parmentier's notes take pain to observe that centuries of history had

Ownership of a horse bestows status to this local chief, February 1907. (Parmentier Collection)

seen the northern regions of Abyssinia 'inhabited by Muslims from Yemen, Sudan and the lands on the banks of the Red Sea' and that large areas, which had not yet recovered from the ravaging attacks of Dervishes, had been left depopulated. 'There is no longer any significant Christian influence in these regions and no one strong enough with intellectual moral to take it on', he writes. Yet he believed the neglected and once-fertile land in the interior could be recovered and returned to productivity. Less optimistic was the expedition's discovery of 'scattered pockets of population which do not appreciate [the value of] agricultural work'. Having squandered natural resources in exchange for guns and ammunition, the travellers found that the ambition of most of the male inhabitants in remote village settlements was not to cultivate their land or rear cattle but to 'gain employment as soldiers for a powerful local chief'. Parmentier's wry comment on the recurring scenario says it all: 'Bands of brigands leave the place wrecked and it is not restored or repaired'. The observation strikes a familiar chord today in relation to conditions in that part of the world.

Since his accession to the throne, the Emperor Menilek had been pushing hard to encourage improvement to the commercial life of his kingdom but, by 1907, only mixed results had been gained. The detailed briefings Latham gave in private to the French consul in Addis Ababa, for despatch to the Ministry of Colonies in Paris, clearly point out how a serious imbalance of import and export movement existed within the commercial life of the capital – the centre for international trading.[5] Commerce was dominated by European firms and Indian traders who concentrated on importing goods and services. Trading opportunities which might originate from the interior were ignored by the European firms who, for the most part, followed their own agendas and these did not always serve the best interest of Abyssinia or its people.

As they proceeded slowly southward, the expedition assiduously surveyed the terrain through which they passed. Soil fertility, population, climate, and commercial possibilities for growing crops such as cotton and coffee were assessed. To give them due credit, their approach would seem to have contained a sincere desire to offer sensible assessment of the drawbacks as well as the improvements that might be needed to benefit this impoverished and backward nation. Léon Parmentier was busy with his camera while Latham had the task of collecting specimens for the Natural History Museum in Paris. Personal gain was not a consideration. They discovered evidence of useful mineral resources such as salt, bitumen, and petroleum but found the greatest disadvantage to be the lack of reliable and secure communication links for traders. No roads or rail lines linking to the coast ran through these mountainous regions. The terrain was spectacular in its beauty – and remains so to this day – but it was difficult to traverse and, as they came to experience for themselves, it was necessary to travel with men who were armed with rifles and ammunition because active bands of looters continued to attack caravans passing through these territories.

The ferocity of these fearsome tribesmen was legendary. Like others before them, Latham's party did not escape violent attack. When ambushed by brigands, however, the ensuing battle turned out to be a low-key affair and shrugged off with laconic dismissal, 'Thanks to the intelligence and courage of our men, we were able to disarm them without anyone getting shot'. Nonetheless, their account carries a distinct air of miffed disapproval which surfaces when two Egyptian officers in charge of the garrison at the frontier tell them that such skirmishes with local banditry are merely 'amusing' little incidents and not to be taken too seriously.

Despite all these distractions, the party ploughed on southward, doggedly honing their diplomatic skills by accepting the hospitality of a succession of trigger-happy tribal chiefs who treated them with great deference and fed them spiced delicacies in native huts furnished with Arabian divans and the skins of exotic animals. Warned that the Emperor expected them to inform these local chiefs of any finds of 'black stones' (coal) or other valuable mineral resources, they kept a tactful silence over any signs encountered of clandestine slave trading, well known to operate from the region.

As the travellers penetrated deeper into unknown territories, one must wonder what did these three sophisticated young Frenchmen make of a land whose people continued to be controlled by deeply held beliefs in magic and superstitious practices? Parmentier describes how they explored some of the most ancient Christian churches in Africa – now abandoned – and the crumbling ghost-ridden ruins of royal palaces where, if local inhabitants were to be believed, the voices of the old kings, the descendants of Solomon and the Queen of Sheba, came back to life as soon as darkness fell. Had the spirits of old kings stirred uneasily at the coming of these strangers? In African folklore, all magicians

On Lake Tana,
February 1907.
(Parmentier
Collection)

have the power to fly. Perhaps the spirits would look kindly on the visitors – especially
the one called Latham for he, too, was to be touched by a magic that was to bring him
mastery of the air. If later guarded from all harm by juju – might these ghostly spirits
bring him troubled dreams?

When the party reached the shores of beautiful Lake Tana, a place first discovered by
the ancient Greeks, the vegetation was lush and full of exotic and colourful birdlife. Game
abounded and their guns were kept busy collecting specimens that were carefully packed
to be sent back to Paris; oryx, kudu, water buck, antelope and buffalo-horned heads, many
of which still hang today in the hallways of their families' châteaux. Lake Tana was also
home to a native tribe who still navigated its waters on *tanqua* or papyrus-reed boats of a
design unchanged since the time of the pharaohs. The baggage could be now transported
southward by raft.

We should not be deceived into thinking that the serious nature of this expedition
was never enlivened by lighter moments. But it is only Latham who leaves a tiny clue
of what may have been a shared joke. Unlike Léon's notebooks which were crammed
full of meticulous record-keeping, the mainly blank pages of Latham's small, personal
diary remained bereft of personal comment – except for one scrawled entry to record
two bawdy limericks - written in English and displaying the low, quirky vulgarity much
favoured by Oxford undergraduates. The first line of each verse begins with the innocent
enough traditional opening: 'There was a young man of...' but what followed in one of

Emperor Menilek II holds court, April 1907. (Parmentier Collection)

these verses was certainly not intended for repeating later in his mother's drawing room at home.[6] What better evidence to bring us up short – to remind that these three young men were not world-weary sophisticates but still callow enough to enjoy the silliness of suggestive double entendres.

Addis Ababa, capital city of Abyssinia, was reached by 5 April 1907. Built by Menilek II only twenty years earlier on a highland plateau that stood almost 8,000ft above sea level, the city bore the distinction of being the highest capital in Africa. Having been made welcome by the French consul and the small community of resident French nationals, they found an invitation awaited them to attend a formal dinner hosted by the Emperor. The ruler's reception of their party was warm – he was always keen to entertain European visitors to his kingdom with displays of lavish hospitality – and Latham later wrote home to comment that he had found him 'charming'. They had presented their host with a Swiss clock and, with a mind to the illustrated lectures he was to give to the Geographical Society in Paris, Léon gained the rare permission to take photographs of the Emperor's entourage of gun-touting hill tribesmen. On the face of things, everything seemed very satisfactory. Behind the scenes, changes lay ahead.

The trio's arrival in Addis Ababa was soon to mark the parting of their ways. Léon and

The café at Gallebat, January 1907. Left to right: Hubert Latham, Léon Parmentier and Jean Parmentier. (Parmentier Collection)

Jean Parmentier had decided to go home. In his correspondence to his mother at the time of his companions' departure, Latham does not comment further on the split, apart from saying he was 'sorry to have to abandon his friends' at this stage of the expedition and it is tempting to suppose that the decision to break up the partnership may have come about as a result of increased tensions developed en route. A revealing note in Léon's diary records how he had been obliged to 'come between' Jean and Hubert on at least one occasion during the journey, charitably attributing their violent disputes as the result of the boys getting 'too much sun'. But if Latham did indeed come to blows with Jean at some time or other, the brothers were later never anything but loyal to their old friend and would never proffer any alternative explanation for their sudden return to France. Indeed, it is entirely feasible to suppose that Jean Parmentier must have been entertaining an increasing anxiety to return to Paris before the end of April, at which time a six months' leave of absence from the Ministry of Finance may have been due to end. Léon, with the instincts of a homing pigeon, may just have been homesick.

At the same time, it might be considered that some more subtly disturbing factor had come between the three young men. Photographs taken by Léon around this time often show Latham with a small native-made pouch hanging by a string around his neck. Was it a native fetish or talisman? A stash of gold dust? Or maybe some strange substance for survival in the less than kind conditions to be endured in the bush. His innate curiosity for the unconventional and exotic – the driving force behind his need to explore new places and experience new sensations – would surely not have ignored the chance to investigate elements within Abyssinian culture and tradition which offered interesting experiments to stimulate his mind and body? To experiment with narcotic substances was very much the rage at that time and the dangers were unknown, or at least ignored. There was no official legislation proscribing their use and young men of Latham's class, especially if plagued by health problems, were very prone to indulge in all types of inquisitive dabbling with mind-bending opiates – usually with little thought of adverse consequences. If this was so in his case, it might explain the mood swings, the bursts of anger and the occasional reckless optimism he displayed. It may be assumed he encountered nothing fundamentally damaging, perhaps even the contrary, for his letters home throughout his Abyssinian adventure had all stressed the continued excellent state of his health. At the same time, his need to observe an almost obsessive assiduousness in controlling his albuminuria does crop up now and then in his correspondence and he had many ingenious ways of keeping up his intake of sugar from fruits and vegetables – which indicates he was never far from the worry of signs which might show the complaint was deteriorating into diabetes. It was a tedious task for an otherwise healthy and vigorous young man.

On taking their leave of their friend in April, the Parmentiers took a route home eastward by train to the coast and the port of Djibouti, from whence they immediately embarked for Marseilles. In the meantime, having been left to complete the trip in charge of a small party of native mule handlers and porters, Latham had set off alone to explore an uncharted region of the kingdom lying due south, the homeland of the Galla People – a Christian race of great antiquity, reputedly descendants of King David.

For the next four months Latham trekked a series of circular routes through the Galla lands and environs of Sidamo. The going was extremely tough. Terrain varied from scrubby desert, with hardly any sustenance for their mules, to open plains covered with the distinctive vegetation called 'white grass' which is still found in the Nechisar National Park. In his report, which later appeared in the *Journal of the French Geographical Society*, he describes how '… the Abyssinians pretend that a certain white grass gives the mules and horses a mortal illness but does not affect donkeys,' adding a typically laid-back aside that '… we didn't investigate whether or not our mules would be affected'.[7] Caution had prevailed. Unlike the earlier stage of the travels with the Parmentiers, during which they had headed southward in an almost unbroken straight line, the mapped trail of Latham's later explorations branched out in many directions. Out of communication with the outside world for weeks on end, he continued travelling even when beset by the difficulties of the rainy season, writing later of coaxing his mule train up slippery mountain tracks through deep mud and of camping in sub-zero temperatures in the high alps. This is spectacularly rugged country of dramatic mountain ranges intersected by deep rift valleys. High in the mountains, he recalls occasions 'when reaching the altitude of 2,300 metres, I myself have seen frost in the mornings in July'. Descent into valley floors plunged his team back into tropical forests which blossomed with exotic flowers and he

Trekking through the bush, 1907. (Parmentier Collection)

writes that he has collected some beautiful specimens of butterflies which he will send home to his brother-in-law, Paul. Even today, Ethiopia still provides some of the most breathtaking scenery to be found anywhere in the horn of Africa and is often likened to the more spectacular sections of the European Alps – something Latham certainly noticed, for he describes the shores of Lake Marguerite (today's Lake Abaya) to his mother as reminding him of the beauty of the Italian lakes.

With no other company except that of his 'boys', the porters, mule handlers and gun bearers, there was one consolation for Latham on these treks. On departure from Addis Ababa he had received two prized permits to hunt down a total of six elephants; three in Sidamo and three in Aroussi. Had he promised the Parmentiers before they left that he would bring home a pair of trophy tusks for each family? Perhaps. To hunt an elephant was an ambition he was determined to fulfil before leaving Abyssinia and, as he struggled though inhospitable countryside to stalk his prey, would he have recalled how his father had pictured his little boy out hunting elephants, riding high in the comparative comfort of a howdah? That dainty scene was nothing like this hard and physically demanding battle to out-manoeuvre several of these enormous but elusive creatures. In a letter home, Latham described how one group kept moving ahead up through the steep, fissured canyons to reach regions where, 'high in the clouds', brief sightings would melt away into the mists which came to wreath the mountain peaks with dramatic effect.

In the end, however, Latham finally cornered his elephants. By August 1907, his wanderings had came to a temporary standstill and he writes home from the town of Alata with the news that he has made plans to leave Abyssinia very shortly, adding that he is carrying two very fine pairs of ivory elephant tusks with him. Significantly, this letter plays down the fact that his planned timetable for leaving had probably fallen apart and, for the first time ever, he allows his guard to slip with the admission that he is 'sick of Abyssinia and the Abyssinians'. As well he might. A really serious problem had arisen.

He had returned to Addis Ababa only week or so earlier with the intention of packing-up his gear for departure, only to find that a huge row had erupted during his absence. The French consul was in a state. Somehow, Latham had incurred the wrath of Emperor Menilek by committing a heinous and insulting offence and it was now doubtful whether he would be given permission to leave the country until things were sorted out. Even more disturbing were rumours which carried mutterings about a possible prison sentence. What appalling crime could have caused such a furore?

It soon came out that the charge of insulting the Emperor had resulted from his successful hunting down of those elusive mountain elephants. Had no one thought to warn him? He had stalked and shot two immense creatures of a size which the palace now claimed had been reserved specifically for the Emperor's sole use and benefit. One suspects, however, the crux of the problem rested on Latham's consequent entitlement to ownership of the two pairs of large and valuable tusks of ivory. His licences to hunt had been issued by a couple of different districts – a situation which may have fermented the already simmering rivalry of local warlords bent on causing trouble over their territorial hunting rights. Embroiled in this controversy, he writes home discreetly of a misunderstanding without revealing the seriousness of the situation and hinting that these difficulties may have been concocted by elements which were trying to make excuses to challenge the Emperor's authority. Although ostensibly 'ruled' by Menilek, such inter-tribal disputes had long thrived on the creation of difficult and sometimes violent clashes over similar issues. The unwitting involvement of a hapless European hunter had only served to spice up the makings of a fresh spate of contentious issues.

As the result of this row, several long months of tedious hanging about in the environs of Addis Ababa had to be endured while Latham waited for news of the Emperor's gracious pardon and permission to leave the kingdom. Perhaps it was as well he had not known how many more weeks and months were to pass before a settlement was reached. He went off to visit an Ostrich farm run by a German and discovers a remote lake-island tribe which '… no other European has ever seen…' while a series of long, drawn out and delicate negotiations took place between the relevant resident diplomatic missions in Addis Ababa and the French Ministry for Foreign Affairs in Paris. Never one to miss a trick, the canny Emperor had grasped the opportunity to mightily impress his recalcitrant warlords by turning the dispute into the makings of an international incident.

According to accounts of the *contretemps* via family oral evidence, it was probably late November by the time the dust finally settled. What terms were finally hammered out remains unrecorded, but it may be assumed these were generous enough to smooth the

Emperor's ruffled feathers of pride in addition to providing adequate compensation for disgruntled local chiefs. It must have been with considerable relief that Latham finally received word that he was free to leave the kingdom. One of his last tasks to attend to before he left Addis Ababa was to arrange for the immense tusks to be crated, carefully wrapped in their basket-work straw cocoons, and shipped off to France, where they remain on display to this day.

It was almost mid-December when Latham reached the French-held Somaliland capital, Djibouti. On arrival at the seaport's best hotel, The Grand, he was swiftly – and one may assume enjoyably – ensconced back into the white tie and tails of the French Colonial social scene. The diversion of a new face was always welcomed in small outposts of Empire and the doors of all the most distinguished had opened effortlessly. A gilt-edged dinner invitation card from the Governor of Somaliland and his wife, Mme Pascal, dating from this time, has survived among Latham's papers. Using curiously worded language, it requests him to honour them with his presence at a formal dinner with 'the government'. One may assume his recent experiences in the neighbouring kingdom will have provided plenty of entertaining anecdotes.

A long letter despatched to his mother from here – the first he had sent her for months – is profuse with apologies and disingenuous explanations for his long silence; the reliability of mail services in Abyssinia's more remote regions is non-existent, he complains. Probably not wanting to cause unnecessary worry, this letter refrains from saying much about the incident with the tusks and the real reason he had been forced to linger so long in Abyssinia. But elephants are clearly still on his mind for he tells her that he has decided to continue his journey eastward to visit the French Colonies in Indochina. He is looking forward to this 'land of elephants' but, more than anything else, perhaps again triggered by the recollection of that little boy shown setting off on his 'tour of the world', and his father's passion for the Orient, he is anticipating the joy of renewing acquaintance with the mysteries of the Eastern art world with which he had been surrounded in childhood in Maillebois. '*C'est l'art, l'art des hommes, cette seule preuve de leur supériorité sur les animaux*' (it is art, the art of men, that can alone prove their superiority over animals), he tells her, adding that this was what he had missed most of all – there was no beautiful art to be found in Abyssinia. Had those final weeks of frustration in the land of the Queen of Sheba left a something of a sour taste in his mouth? The edgy and dangerous wilderness of the unknown had presented nothing of the purity and truth he had anticipated from living a simpler life close to the natural world and it may have been with relief that he could now allow the sensitive inner core of his psyche to search out a new trail. Within days he is writing a second letter home, having just received the news that his sister Léonie was making firm arrangements for her wedding. In this despatch he speaks of cutting short his 'tour of the world' when he had finished his visit to Indochina, in order to attend his duties at the forthcoming nuptials.

On 21 December, Latham embarked from the port of Aden on a P&O vessel bound for the Indies via Bombay and thence to Calcutta from where he could continue on to Singapore. He knew that shipping lines from Calcutta also offered an alternative and more direct route to Saigon via Colombo, capital of Ceylon, and it was this route which ended up as his preferred choice. By 1 February 1908 he had reached the Hotel Continental, in Saigon, the chief city of Cochinchina (now Southern Vietnam), from where he writes conveying his intention to travel north to Tonkin. Two weeks later he is sending word home that he has arrived in Nhatrang, the major city of Annam, the central region of Cochinchina.

Very few of Latham's letters to his mother have survived from this period and notwith-standing his aspirations to increase his knowledge of Oriental art during his sojourn in Indochina, there is no further mention of any cultural topic in any of these. The surviving letters from Latham speak of meeting up with Prince de Broglie and his son in Saigon and, perhaps influenced by their enthusiasm for shooting tigers, he writes about a plan to fulfil a new ambition, which is to shoot a tiger for himself. But these creatures are even more elusive than the Abyssinian elephants and despite waiting up for several nights in hope of sighting one, he has no luck at all. By March, having arrived in the northern protectorate's bustling city of Hanoi, he writes with the promise to be home in time for Léonie's marriage.

What had Latham gained from his extended travels? Leaving aside the satisfactory outcome of the expedition in terms of the reports submitted by him and the Parmentier brothers to the French consul for transmission to the Colonial Office and other Ministerial Departments, the past months may have left him to some extent disillusioned and dissatisfied. Yet, he had learned to live successfully in wild places, which had given him the practical skills of surveying and mapping uncharted territory, and he had gained an understanding of diplomatic negotiation with often hostile indigenous peoples. He had been able to fine tune his knowledge of art in its most primitive forms and develop an appreciation of the ancient rituals and superstitions of bush lands and lost civilisations in addition to the more sophisticated creative traditions of the Orient. While giving credence to these alternative cultures and beliefs, he remained very much his own man. He may have come to accept danger with unconcerned fatalism but his sense of a real affinity with the natural world never left him. Several years later during the 1910 Reims Air Show, amid all the tension and bustle created by competitive flying, Latham once displayed sudden annoyance with his engineer, when Levavasseur tried to brush a ladybird off his sleeve with an impatient gesture just before the aviator was ready for a take-off.[8] Latham had stopped him disturbing the tiny creature from where it had landed on his arm with words to the effect that the ladybird, too, was poised to take wing any moment and who were they to cause her difficulty? She might be angry. It would bring bad luck – a traditional superstition. One is left wondering if he had he always nurtured such a concern or shown himself to be so vulnerable to outside forces over which he had no control?

# FOUR

# Excitement in the Air: Artists and Engineers Provide a Potent Mix

An entirely different twist to his career awaited Latham on his return to France for the marriage of his sister Léonie to Emmanuel Gaston de Witt on 8 May 1908. Swept right back into the swing of the social scene he found that in his absence many acquaintances – especially those interested in motor racing – had become gripped with enthusiasm for the latest signs of progress in the civilised world: flying machines. A new and exciting adventure beckoned.

During his years away travelling there had been an acceleration of the great debates which raged as to whether gas filled 'lighter-than-air' methods such as balloons would provide more success than 'heavier-than-air' machines or contraptions built to make use of some form of powered propulsion. Acknowledged experts, on the whole, tended to favour the use of the more successful hot air balloon or motor-driven dirigibles such as had been developed by Count Zeppelin in Germany. Balloons and huge airships were now able to fly non-stop from Paris to Germany, across Hungary and past the borders of Russia itself, and it seemed very unlikely that rival man-carrying kites or gliders would ever catch up on such inventiveness despite a spate of imaginative experiments.

Technically minded aeronautical engineers had continued to battle with the problem of keeping the 'heavier-than-air' machines airborne by using engines that were light enough to provide sufficient motor propulsion, and the success of these early experiments had attracted some of the world's wealthiest and most daring sportsmen. In France, more than in any other country, the skills required to pilot these new flying machines became a much sought after and *chic* accomplishment. Soon after the turn of the century, hardly a weekend passed that did not see little groups gathering to watch excitedly as trials with strange-looking flying machine contraptions were conducted by enthusiasts in open spaces and parks. Louis Blériot had been one of the first to conduct a number of unsuccessful trials with a monoplane fitted with water skis on the river Seine, while in the sand dunes of Berck-sur-Mer, a French Army captain, Ferdinand Ferber, and his friend, Gabriel Voisin, patiently tested their colleague Ernest Archdeacon's design for a glider biplane. Despite tumbles and bruises, some reward was finally achieved when the pair managed to remain continuously airborne for just short of half a minute.

The Bagatelle Gardens in Paris became a favourite and easily accessible venue for spectators. All shapes and sizes of flying contraptions were to be seen and curious visitors

The first aeroplane flight in Europe: Santos-Dumont flies in the Bagatelle Gardens, Paris, 23 October 1906. (Royal Aeronautical Society Library)

could be entertained by the sight of canvas and wire hopping and flopping with varying outcomes of success and it was to be of enormous advantage that the authorities took it all in their stride. In 1905, the old army parade grounds at Issy-les-Moulineaux, on the left bank of the Seine in the south-west of the city, was made available for the more serious experimentation carried out by members of the French Aero Club. It was here, also in 1905, that a glider made by Archdeacon, cunningly towed by an automobile, finally took-off splendidly and thrilled spectators by rising all of 33ft into the air. The following year saw the rich, Brazilian-born playboy and darling of society, Alberto Santos-Dumont, flying over the heads of Parisians gathered to watch in the Bagatelle and making even more of a name for himself by covering a length of over 700ft in twenty seconds.

The watching crowd of spectators were mightily impressed and until the summer of 1908 it was still assumed that all these French-based aeronautical developments were the most advanced in design and performance. Nobody had taken seriously the rumours that two young American brothers, small-town owners of a bicycle shop, Orville and Wilbur Wright, had already perfected techniques for staying airborne as long ago as the dying days of 1903, at least four years earlier, and had been perfecting their methods ever since. The reliability of the Wright brothers' creative efforts had tended to be dismissed as pure speculation or, at the most, an exaggerated claim, and it had come as quite a shock when the news broke that brothers were going to allow the true capabilities of their flying machines to be demonstrated for the first time in Europe. The event took place at a flying field at Le Mans, in France, during August 1908. It was said that the Wrights had been carefully guarding their secrets for fear of commercial predators – but now they were looking for orders and to everyone's horror, once they took to the air, their machines showed themselves to be obviously superior to anything being produced in France at that time. The blow to the esteem of all French aeronautical enthusiasts and, indeed, to the whole of the country's national pride had been quite palpable. In Le Mans, a gathering of the most experienced French aviators were dumbfounded at what they saw. Finally, one voice summed up their thoughts: '*Eh, bien. Nous n'existons pas! Nous sommes battus!*' (We just don't exist any more. We are beaten!).[1] To think that such an indignity could occur! How could the traditional inventiveness and entrepreneurial skills of French aviators have been so clearly overtaken! And by a pair of American bicycle-makers! It was too much.

It was not only the French who were taken aback by the Wright brothers' display. The Wright's public demonstration had attracted a significant crowd of international observers. Among the businessmen, politicians and other rich and powerful personages who had flocked to the flying field was the former journalist Alfred Harmsworth, now elevated to the peerage as Lord Northcliffe and the owner of leading English daily newspapers, the *Daily Mail* and, more recently purchased, *The Times*. To say the Press Baron had been deeply impressed by what he had seen would be an understatement. A powerful political lobbyist, his was a voice which had held strong views for years on the threat foreign aircraft might present to a traditional defence policy in England if war – especially war with Germany – ever came. The topic had become one of his driving obsessions, which was why he had made it his business to be present in Le Mans to witness the Wrights' demonstration for himself. What he saw there made him intensify his message on the pages of his newspapers. 'England is no longer an Island' would shortly become one of the most well-known *Daily Mail* slogans.[2] The government and people had to be warned of the dangers to national security in the future if they did not wake up to the fact that Admiralty naval vessels would no longer be able to safeguard the protection of their coastlines from enemy aircraft. It could be argued, naturally, that flying machines were not yet developed enough to travel long distances across the sea. He knew this would come, given time. Seizing every opportunity, he continued to hammer out warnings of the threat in his newspaper columns. To his great annoyance, however, the English public imagination still failed to be gripped by excitement over the possibilities and potential offered by aeronautical experiments and Northcliffe became even more impatient. England would almost certainly be left far behind if this attitude continued. Something had to be done.

The newspaper proprietor was well aware that, back in 1906, there had already been one attempt to stimulate interest in an aeroplane flight across the Channel – instigated by a publicity-seeking firm of champagne makers from the Loire valley, the Ruinarts. They had offered a prize of 12,500 francs – about £500 – but there had been no machine capable of flying that distance in those days and, consequently, no takers. Now, two years later, the Press Baron decided it was high time to resurrect the idea and introduce it as an inspirational *Daily Mail* project. He would equal the offer of a £500 prize to tempt an undertaking of a Channel flight and announce it in his newspaper. Not one to do things by half measure, he

A fur-coated Lord Northcliffe eagerly lends a hand to haul a Wright plane during a flying demonstration at Pau, February 1908. (Royal Aeronautical Society Library)

saw to it that the *Daily Mail* competition was subsequently given maximum publicity – and when no immediate response was forthcoming, Northcliffe doubled the prize money to £1,000. Sooner or later, there would be an intrepid aviator ready to accept the challenge and the English nation would be forced to sit up and take notice.

In the meantime, in contrast to British lethargy and stung by the performance of Americans on French soil, the rest of Europe had becamc flying-machine mad. Any new feat in these new machines was guaranteed to catch public imagination as a newsworthy event and a spate of newly fledged aeronauts vied with each other to beat world records for height, speed and length of flights. French aeronautics was once more in ascendancy and young international sporting gentlemen were gravitating to Paris in their droves to gain notoriety for their increasingly daring exploits in the air. It seemed that not a week passed without some new record being broken by one of these popular heroes. The world's first purpose-built aerodrome was planned to be opened in Juvisy, about twelve miles from the city, by late spring of the following year. Clearly, the Wright brothers were not going to be allowed to have it all their own way.

Before turning to how Latham came to be drawn into a closer association with pioneer aviation, it may be useful to pause for a moment to consider some significant twists and turns experienced by the Antoinette Motor Company with which his name came to be inexorably linked, for they would have bearing on the outcome of later events.

The triumph of the company with the Levavasseur engine at the 1905 Monaco Motor Yacht Regatta had brought great business benefit to Latham's cousin, Jules Gastambide and his engineer. Their improved financial situation had allowed them to return their attention to earlier ambitions of designing an experimental flying machine which could take advantage of the lightness of this engine. All around there was evidence of progress being made in the development of air flight and they were confident that they could produce a machine that would match, if not outdo, the performance of any current models.

In 1906 the rekindling of this dream had received a boost when Gastambide was approached by a successful manufacturing businessman with an offer of an investment package. The timing was extremely fortunate. The Antoinette Motor Company was poised to go ahead with the idea and this would–be partner was known to be someone with an uncanny eye for a good business venture. He had also been dabbling in aeronautics for quite some while. His name was Louis Blériot.

Blériot had done well as a manufacturer of head lamps for motor cars and by all accounts he was a man whom lady luck had favoured kindly; a man with an penchant for opportunity. By then in his mid-thirties, Blériot had trained at the prestigious *L'École Centrale des Arts et Manufactures* and had set-up his firm just as the boom in motorcar sales hit Paris. He had made a lot of money – but was destined to spend a lot of it, too, most of it on an obsession to design and build the perfect aeroplane. His biographer, Brian Elliott, traces Blériot's earliest efforts to build a flying machine back to 1900, and cites the report of a finished model – an ornithopter, or flapping wing type emerging from his workshop by 1902.[3] There was only one serious problem. It did not work.

By 1905, Blériot had been doggedly pursuing different concepts of design. He had formed a partnership with Gabriel Voisin, a young man who, while training to become an architect, had had started experimenting with gliders. It was to be an uneasy working relationship, doomed to failure, for each had their own ideas how progress should be made and Voisin and Blériot soon found it increasingly difficult to agree on any important decision. Almost imperceptibly, each began the process of going their own way; Voisin recruited his brother Charles and they set up their own manufacturing firm, while Blériot cast around for a new business associate. What he needed for his concept was a much lighter motor and he had come to the conclusion that Levavasseur's Antoinette engine would be perfect.

Blériot's initial approach to Gastambide and Levavasseur in 1906 had been welcomed with open arms. Not realising that his ambitions were at odds with their own aspirations to build aeroplanes they agreed to re-group their company as the *Société Anonyme Antoinette*, accepted a substantial injection of funds from him, which, as a major shareholder, guaranteed Blériot not only a place on their board, but appointment to the powerful position of deputy chairman.[4]

The promising new partnership was not destined to last. A serious conflict of interest arose when Henri Farman came along soon afterwards seeking Gastambide's help with his new design for an aeroplane. Up to then, Farman, a former racing cyclist and

60. **SPORTS · *Aviation* — L'Appareil ' Blériot-&-Voisin ' (1906)**

The partnership of Blériot and Voisin achieved no success with their Blériot III in 1906. (HLPP)

another of the participants chasing prizes on the water at the Monaco Regatta, had been working with the Voisin brothers on the construction of his proposed machine. Disputes had arisen and he, like Blériot before him, had fallen out with this pair. Now he was looking for a new firm who could undertake the production of chassis and wings and, thinking on exactly the same lines as Blériot had done, was also considering making use of Levavasseur's Antoinette engine.

Farman's approach to Gastambide and Levavasseur was tempting and they immediately expressed enthusiasm to take up on his offer. This was just what they needed to expand the company into the total manufacturing end of the business. With the Antoinette motor and the Farman design, it was a logical marriage to create a successful new product. But they had forgotten the power that could now be wielded by their new shareholder.

To their dismay, the proposal met with Blériot's instant disapproval and it became clear that their new partner had bought into the *Société Anonyme Antoinette* solely to gain access to their engine and not to engage in any expansion of their company's activities into shop-floor construction techniques. The new deputy chairman was firmly against any move towards a contract with Farman for the manufacture of a completely finished machine and he let it be known that he fully intended to keep that side of things for himself, under the control of his own firm.

What was to be done? For a while a stalemate existed. Neither side would budge an inch. Leaving uncertainties hanging in the air was no recipe for the future of any flourishing enterprise and eventually, business being business, a compromise was reached. Following negotiations which must have been to some extent acrimonious, the deputy chairman agreed to resign from the board around January 1909. In retrospect, the deal that was done might be seen as a strangely calculated move on someone's part; one of the former managers of Blériot's Headlamp Company, Pierre Chalmard, was allowed take his place on the board.[5]

From this time on, an element of suspicion and circumspect revenge rumbled under the surface of the *Société Anonyme Antoinette's* future relationship with Blériot. It finally grew into full-scale rivalry. Following the contretemps, Blériot refused point-blank to purchase any more Antoinette engines. Instead, he invited the assistance of an Italian engineer, Anzani, who had developed a tiny three-cylinder motor capable of 22–25hp which only weighed about 132lb. While it was undoubtedly very light in weight, it was considered by many to be too flimsy for the machine Blériot was building. Blériot was a stubborn man, however, and the decision had been made. Anzani engines would in future power all the Blériot monoplanes.

As to the operation of the *Société Anonyme Antoinette*, it appears – surprisingly – that there must have been extraordinarily levels of *naiveté* to be found within the management of the Gastambide and Levavasseur firm and it has to be said that such lack of guilelessness was not often reflected in the ethical conduct of rival companies. The world of aeroplane sales was thick with schemers, charlatans and outright crooks, but the directors of the Antoinette Company were slow to learn that nobody should be trusted. Even the straight-laced and God-fearing American Wright brothers were not beyond condoning devious behaviour when it suited their cause, as can be illustrated.

Nothing is truer than the old adage that to sup with the devil one needs a long spoon. By 1907, the Wrights had started to employ the talents of a shady international arms dealer, Charles R. Flint, even though they deeply distrusted his methods.[6] Known in certain circles as the 'merchant of death', in Flint they had a gentleman well connected to the Houses of Rothschild and Morgan, a friend of Theodore Roosevelt and someone capable of persuading certain top people to whisper the right words into the ears of many foreign government agencies.[7] Exactly how Flint had pressurised Lady Jane Taylor in London is not known but, at his bidding – and a reputed 2 per cent on sales – she used her influence to create a favourable view of the Wright machines not only in the minds of the British Secretary of State for War, Lord Haldane, and the First Lord of the Admiralty, Lord Tweedmouth, but also in that of that all-powerful manipulator of public opinion, Press Baron Lord Northcliffe. The delicacy of these negotiations is clearly apparent; Taylor and Flint 'wrote to each other in code when discussing her assignment'.[8]

For their European sales and publicity, the Wright brothers had appointed a brash, fast-talking, spats-wearing, go-getting American salesman called Hart O. Berg. There was nothing Berg would balk at on their behalf. For instance, quite serious ructions were created within the management of the *Société Anonyme Antoinette* when Berg pulled a fast one on the unsuspecting Levavasseur by calling one day to introduce a fellow countryman whom he described as an 'engineer acting in an advisory capacity for a keen American buyer' who was interested in purchasing their engine.[9] Levavasseur, easily flattered by the attention and thinking a lucrative order might be in the offing, had immediately arranged for Berg and his companion to be given a tour of their workshops. Sheets of detailed drawings and calculations were rolled out and the visiting engineer shown all the latest design innovations, refinements and specifications. The stranger was even allowed to run a few tests for himself in order to demonstrate the intricacies of the Antoinette engine. Only when the visitors had left – without placing an order for the engine – did Levavasseur discover to his fury that this 'advisor' for the spurious 'buyer' was none other than Wilbur Wright himself. He had been totally duped into handing out sensitive information and innovative design solutions to one of their major competitors. It did no good that Levavasseur threw a tantrum. The damage was done and the incident only served to prove to his fellow directors that Léon Levavasseur was assuredly lacking in survival skills when let loose in a jungle stalked by commercial predators.

In the wake of Blériot's departure from their board, the *Société Anonyme Antoinette*'s directors came under pressure to seek out a new investor they could trust. It would have to be someone reliable and committed; someone prepared to accept a hands-on involvement that carried no hidden agenda; someone capable of being trained as a pilot. Is it any surprise their thoughts returned to Latham and the skills he had displayed when promoting the Antoinette engine on their behalf at the Monaco Regatta three years earlier? He was just the person to fit the bill.

The approach to Latham was made by Jules Gastambide's son Robert in the early weeks of 1909.[10] Having spent the previous two years coping with the tropical heat and humidity of Africa and Indochina, the traveller's homecoming return to the climate of Northern Europe that summer must not have been easy. Moreover, the winter of 1908–09 that followed had been harsh and more than unusually cold. Slushy snow lay on the pavements and rooftops of Paris for weeks on end, well into springtime. Latham must have found the transition trying in the extreme, but there was no more talk of him resuming his 'world tour'. His mother had insisted that his presence was needed at Maillebois and he seemed to have accepted the responsibilities now being thrust upon him without too much complaint.

In Robert Gastambide's later account of their meeting he describes how he found Latham 'fishing in the river *La Blaise*' which runs through the grounds of château de Maillebois. The scenario strikes as a romanticised setting for a cold January. The house would have been normally closed up for most of the winter months and only opened up for the family gatherings marking the Christmas and New Year festivities. Latham must have been bemused when his cousin Robert arrived out of the blue to suggest an exciting business venture. Robert had pressed the point that flying machines were the coming thing and Gastambide and Levavasseur were willing to offer Latham a place on the board of the *Société Anonyme Antoinette* in return for an investment in the company. Moreover, they were looking for a suitable pilot to enter their Antoinette monoplane in competitions. Would Latham care to learn how to fly their machine?

Latham's initial response was guarded. He told Robert that his only plans for the moment were to take some time off to rest and live quietly while attending to the estate in Maillebois. His mother had made it quite clear it was high time he settled down to his responsibilities. It was expected of him. He agreed to give Robert's proposal some careful thought and would speak to his mother over dinner, indicating that her opinion

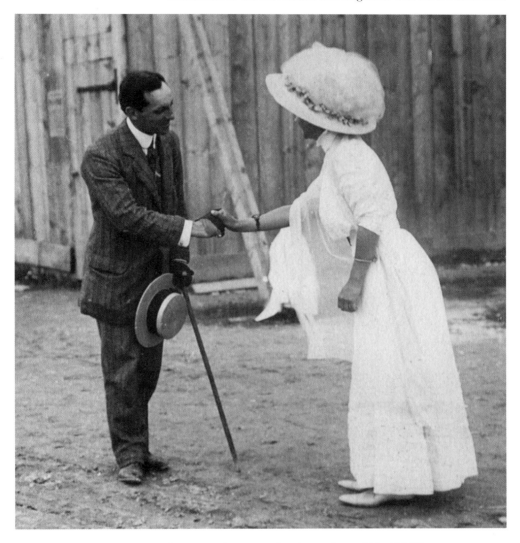

Posing for a publicity shot – Latham greets his cousin Antoinette Gastambide. (HLPP)

was worth having, while reminding Robert he did not wish to risk family capital on anything foolhardy.[11] Privately, he was probably remembering his past experiences in Monaco, where he had been too often caught in a trap between the elder Gastambide's hesitant caution and the impatient genius of fiery-tempered Levavasseur. There had been plenty of difficult and near-explosive situations during the preparations for events which, but for the formidable presence of Jacques Faure to act as a diplomatic peacemaker, might have turned very nasty and unresolvable.

Never one to turn away from a challenge and more possibly already bored by the trying to live up to his mother's wish for him to adopt the quiet life of a 'gentleman', Latham, in fact, wasted little time in accepting Gastambide's offer. By the end of the month he was spending many days at a military flying field at Châlons-sur-Marne in the Champagne-Ardennes region of north-east France and had begun to take lessons from one of the four Welferinger brothers, the skilled family of aeronautical mechanics who had been associated with the company since its inauguration.

Latham found that learning to pilot this fourth version of the monoplane, the Antoinette IV, was not easy. To his embarrassment, there were crashes and mis-judgements causing extensive, and expensive, damage to struts, wings, fuselage and undercarriage and all this before he had even managed to get the machine off the ground! His initial clumsiness has been explained by Elliott as being part due to Latham's 'great physical strength'.[12] The would-be-aeronaut's previous experience of controlling a motor-driven machine had been acquired through speedboat and road racing conditions both of which required a great deal of stamina – and neither provided an ideal apprenticeship. Brains and not brawn were the techniques needed now. He had to learn that aeronautical pilots must acquire a light and sensitive touch for the successful manipulation of complicated control systems. It was to his advantage that this young man was already accustomed to adopting different techniques for a variety of sporting skills; he was a crack shot, competent horseman, a successful hunter of wild animals, and expert driver of sports cars. There was nothing new in having to persist with a quiet and determined patience until a targeted level of expertise was gained through much practice, trial and error. He was not easily beaten. Once the skills had been mastered, then there would be no stopping him.

Latham soon began to attract the attention of the aeronautical press. Shortly after making his maiden flight at the airfield in Châlons he had beaten the world record by flying to the height of almost 330ft (100m). He had also kept his machine continuously airborne, albeit it at a mere 130ft (40m) high, for well over sixty minutes, thereby creating a new French record for continuous, motorised flight. It was also a world record for a monoplane-type machine. Commentators agreed that this achievement was truly amazing. It meant that French cross-country aviators could now travel across country for twenty-five miles non-stop. It also meant that French confidence of their superiority in the air could be reclaimed with honour.

It was also reported that Latham had thrilled a watching crowd on one occasion by nonchalantly taking his hands off the steering rudder in order to light a cigarette with a great show of sangfroid. Another first! Known to be a voracious chain-smoker, it was said he ordered ashtrays to be installed in the cockpit of all his planes after this incident. Here was some character! Quite the showman!

All agreed that Latham's achievements were magnificent and aficionados of the sport told each other it was splendid to see French superiority once more in the ascendancy. The creation of new records were undoubtedly breeding renewed confidence all round.

As yet, however, no aviator had yet attempted a sustained flight over an unbroken stretch of water and the offer of a prize to be given by the British Lord Northcliffe suddenly began to attract greater attention. Was another pioneering record about to be broken? The world's press held its breath. If a Frenchman could conquer the English Channel by winning the English *Daily Mail*'s prize of £1,000 then what a splendid way to restore that nation's confidence! By the start of the summer of 1909 excitement had heightened. The

Latham flies at Châlons. (Harman Collection)

mid-season's traditional doldrum days for newspaper readership was being tweaked by an increasing number of aeronautical reports and lengthening column inches of coverage. The question being asked now was not if there would be a Channel flight – but rather when would it take place? And who would be the first aviator to take the risk? Just one name sprang to everyone's lips: Hubert Latham, the latest young hero of the air.

British readers of the *Daily Mail* and *The Times* were soon to be, if anything, rather better informed than their French counterparts who sought news of Latham in the Paris newspaper *Le Matin*. Who was he? What was his background? The Northcliffe group of newspapers speedily made sure to emphasise that the young sportsman was by birth Anglo-French and enjoyed an impeccable pedigree which included several generations of Londoners and a father who had nurtured a distinct pride in the family's English roots. Moreover, the aviator spoke English with an ease of someone born to it and had completed his education at Oxford.

Puffing up such stories allowed their aeronautical correspondents to appeal to their readers' partisanship and public opinion was soon swayed into taking this young man into their hearts. Here was a stalwart son of Anglo-Saxon descent, his blood only slightly diluted on his mother's side, whom the British could claim to be as good as their very own. Meanwhile, journalists writing for *Le Matin* and other French publications, equally anxious to garner loyalty and to forestall a possible annexation of a forthcoming hero, were not slow to remind themselves of the great importance of the prestigious families which featured on the Mallet side of his family. Between them, Latham was thus presented to the public on both sides of the Channel as the most splendidly perfect candidate to

Latham and the name Antoinette were to become inexorably linked. (Harman Collection)

epitomise the tenor of *entente cordiale* that had reigned in London and Paris since 1904. Only those with rather more private knowledge experienced a tinge of uneasiness over some of the lesser-known facets of this young man's family background. His much publicised ease and fluency in speaking French and English was matched, for instance, by impeccable High German. A minor point, perhaps, and one that had not merited any attention in the excitement. It could be of no possible importance, could it?

Latham's return to France and instant success as one of the newest 'aviation personalities' most certainly opened up several more interesting doors within society for him. It is intriguing to discover the timing of Latham's renewal of friendship with the artist Eileen Gray coincides with the publication of the Italian writer Marinetti's *Futuristic Manifesto*, which had made its first appearance in the Paris newspaper *Le Figaro* on 20 February 1909.[13] This thought-provoking Italian writer's work propounded theories which were dangerously attractive to a generation which had become obsessed with the wonders of technical advances. Marinetti's message pushed the analogy of machines in the modern world to the extreme, making them appear like wild beasts. The violence of speed was celebrated – but was he aiming to shock, outrage or merely tease a complacent world? He was predicting that machines would eventually dominate all their lives and destroy the freedom and the inter-dependence of man and nature. It was a seductive debate.

On rekindling his acquaintanceship with Eileen Gray, Latham would have found her to have become a much smarter and more confident woman than the one he had met some four years earlier following his record-breaking ballooning exploit. In the intervening years, Latham and Gray had each developed personalities which shared similar traits of individualism and it might be argued that both would have found the initial Futurists' principles of intuition, personal freedom and abstraction immensely appealing.[14] The future, Marinetti claimed, would open up unimaginable scenarios: 'We are going to be present at the birth of the centaur and we shall soon see the first angels fly! We must break down the gates of life to test the bolts and padlocks! ... We hunted death like young lions...'[15]

Gray's biographer, Peter Adam, believes her immediate reaction to the Futurist movement's focus on the glorification of violence, war and machines within literature and the arts was enthusiastic – she had immediately gone out and bought a copy of his Manifesto – but it did not last.[16] From Latham's point of view, however, one could speculate that there was a distinctly uncomfortable affinity to be traced between the daring life-threatening challenges faced by aviators in progressing development of airborne machines and the dramatic prose which built up an uneasy glimpse of the coming century that was both threatening and dangerously stimulating. Were they truly 'standing on the world's summit to launch an insolent challenge to the stars!' and did this message carry an exhortation to court death itself on the altar of flight? 'We went up to the three snorting machines to caress their breasts. I lay along mine like a corpse on its bier...'[17] One may well ask how seriously Marinetti's readers took all of this to their hearts. Much later, Futurism came to be regarded with grave suspicion because of its drift towards Fascism and its author's growing affinity to Mussolini but, in 1909, this murky future could not have been foreseen. The young avant-garde artists, designers, technocrats, aviators and enthusiasts of speed would have found a common bond in this breaking of boundaries offering release from the stultifying constraints of their parents' generation.

Gray was seeking out innovative art forms for her creativity and Latham would have understood only too well the truth in the Futurist celebration of wild beasts' natural ability to protect themselves: 'Smell is enough for them'.[18] Years of experience in Africa had taught him to deeply respect a beast's reaction to danger and regret how much of man's in-born self-preservation instinct had been lost in a modern society.

In retrospect, Latham's ballooning adventures with Faure and the excitement of his first encounter with Abyssinia with the Parmentier brothers now strike as having taken place in a far more innocent world. Even his friendship with Gray had moved into another dimension for they had both moved on apace since then. She was firmly established as a designer sought by astute investors; Latham was about to make a name for himself once more in the world of aeronautics. Not so much an accident of fate, as a predictable possibility, their friendship had blossomed because they both moved within the same privileged and overlapping social circles where many mutual friends were linked through business, the arts, politics or family. Eileen was an attractive woman and throughout her life she developed romantic relationships with lovers of both sexes which were all, for the most part, conducted with discretion in accordance with the mores of the times.[19] Although often drawn to much younger men, she was never short of interesting male suitors and companions who fell for her easy charm with an affection deep enough to remain for the rest of their lives. When she met Latham for the first time, she had been wooed already by Everard Colthrope, the Orientalist, and the renowned explorer, Henry Landor.[20]

Like many of her associates in the Parisian art world, Eileen Gray was fascinated by all the new technical inventions being made available for popular use. In 1905, during a visit to England, her first, thrilling taste of aerial sport had been to take an ascent in a balloon with one of her mother's young high-society friends, The Honourable Charles S. Rolls, third son of Lord Llangattock of Hendre – now more famously remembered as one of the founders of the most prestigious motor companies in the world, Rolls-Royce. The balloon ascent with him had been her first introduction to 'the world of aviators'.[21]

Often described by commentators as having been good friends, Rolls and Latham were the product of not dissimilar privileged backgrounds. In this respect they had much in common and most certainly came to know one another quite well through a shared an interest in many sporting activities long before either young man took up flying aeroplanes. Charlie Rolls had been one of the founder members of the Aero Club of the United Kingdom and, with an additional mutual interest in motor racing, was already acquainted with Jacques Faure, Latham's cousin, through ballooning. In due course, Rolls's closeness to Latham developed from their competitive rivalry as pilots. In this respect, Rolls is something of a dark horse. As his biographer, Gordon Bruce, takes pains to point out, the intensity of his focus on the potential of British aviation has been overshadowed by his more famous association with the motor company that bore his name.[22]

Socially, Gray, Latham and Rolls all fitted easily into the more fluid dilution of class boundaries which marked *fin de siècle* Europe. Rolls's parents, Lord and Lady Llangattock, had a distant but mutual Scottish connection to the lineage of Eileen's mother, Baroness Gray. They were among the privileged social set which had grown up around the Prince of Wales, now King Edward VII, whose lives were mainly spent in a series of pleasurable activities dictated by the season. Country estates offered hunting, shooting and fishing in the autumn and winter, which were replaced by Mediterranean yachting trips in the spring, followed by the annual launching of debutantes in London. The summer then ushered in house parties for boating, tennis and ballooning, for by 1908 this sport had 'arrived', as Bruce says, 'as a socially acceptable activity, equivalent to Ascot, Goodwood or Henley'.[23]

In Paris, rather more than in London, a heady mixture of balloonists, aviators, inventors of combustion engines and former practitioners of arts and design had been sharing experimental concepts for years in order to perfect the skills of keeping the new 'heavier-than-air' machines successfully airborne and, while her balloon ascent with Charlie Rolls in 1905 had given Eileen Gray her first taste of what was to become an intense interest in flying, it should be noted that she already knew – from her art schools days – many of the people who would be Latham's colleagues, friends or rivals. Foremost among these was the aviator Henri Farman who, like Latham, had an Anglo-French background: his father was the English-born Paris correspondent for the *Daily Telegraph* newspaper. This art student had been rather more keen on his hobby as a racing cyclist, however, and when he abandoned his endeavours to embrace a career as an artist he had joined his brothers in the motor trade. It was a move that brought Farman into contact with the world of racing drivers and the advancement of the internal combustion engine on land, sea and, inevitably, in the air. He soon found his true creative *métier* when he started to dabble in aircraft design. From there it was but a short step to flying the machines.

A similar successful transition had been made by Léon Delagrange, an up-and-coming sculptor and art college tutor, who had trained in *L'École des Beaux Arts*. He was already

The Hon. Charles
S. Rolls. (From the
collections of the
Nelson Museum and
Local History Centre,
Monmouth)

exhibiting his work at the prestigious Paris Salon when a growing fascination with aerodynamic-design concepts drew him into becoming a leading aeronaut. It was exactly this same juxtaposition of creativity within arts and engineering that had encouraged Léon Levavasseur to turn techniques learned during his days as a student into innovative experiments with a light-weight motor – the invention that was to later change Latham's life.

Latham's friends, René Raoul-Duval and his English wife, the former Jessie Gavin, or Jackie, as she liked to call herself, were life-long close companions of Eileen Gray. Eileen and Jackie had come to Paris in 1902 to study art, first at the *École Colarossi* and then at the *Académie Julian* together with a third girlfriend, the Scottish-born Kathleen Bruce, who went on to become a Rodin-trained sculptor of some note before marrying Captain Robert Falcon Scott, of Antarctic fame, in 1908. In their art school days, the girls were known in Paris as the three '*jolies anglaises.*'[24] All keen followers of early motor sports and aviation development, their upper-class backgrounds had ensured all the right introductions gained them easy acceptance within French '*Bonne Société Protestante*' which encompassed many of the circles of friendship wherein the Latham and Mallet families and their associates socialised.

In such gatherings, it is easy to recognise the usual quota of eccentrics found hovering on the fringes, but the outcome of Eileen Gray's relationship with Aleister Crowley, the notorious self-styled magician of the black arts is curiously oblique. Many of her mutual friends, who were also acquainted with Latham, had encounters with this self-styled 'wickedest man in the world' and his seductive message of a new age in which the only rule being preached was that of self-indulgence: 'Do what thou wilt is the whole of the law'.[25] This concept of self-fulfilment was fuelled by 'the idea that every man and woman was a star; every individual unique [with] the divine right to develop as it sees fit.'[26] In the half-light of speculation, it is possible to ponder whether their links with Crowley's long-fingered ill will had some way later touched many of these lives with disaster.

During her days as an art student, Eileen had been vigorously pursued by Crowley with offers of marriage, all of which she refused, having noted with wry amusement how he had chased every one of her closest friends in turn with equal enthusiasm.[27] She was not alone in her wariness of him. Her friend, Kathleen Bruce, who, quite coincidently, was to be drawn into the aviation world surrounding Latham, had been also subjected to the predatory magician's romantic advances, but forewarned by Eileen, the canny Kathleen would have none of it and sent him packing.[28] Nonetheless, it may be considered that some residue of Crowley-inspired dabbling in experimental mysticism remained with Eileen, nurtured by her continued fascination with the paranormal – something she may have shared with Latham when they met up again following his experiences of other cultures in Africa and Indochina. In the *outré* circles within which Gray and many of her more intense friends moved, the magician's disturbing, if dubious, claims to otherworld powers and his exhortation to indulge oneself in personal fulfilment to the exclusion of all else bore mighty appeal for adventurous minds. For the unwary, however, many strange and dangerous paths lay in wait within its labyrinth.

However, with assurance gained already as a seasoned practitioner in the art of self-fulfilment – perhaps we make take it that Latham had no need of further encouragement from a guru to believe in himself?

# FIVE

# Rising to the Challenge: The *Daily Mail*'s Channel Flight Prize, 1909

It is impossible to ignore the really big question which continues to hang over the account of Latham's attempt to be the first man to fly a powered aeroplane across the English Channel in response to the *Daily Mail*'s challenge. Had it been merely bad luck that brought about his failure or had he been unfairly cheated of success as a result of outside forces interfering in the outcome of events for their own ends? It may be argued either way, for the unfolding of this intriguing episode in Latham's life offers plenty of speculation.

In the small seaside village of Sangatte which lay close to the port of Calais in northern France, the rumour of forthcoming excitement was quickly doing the rounds by word of mouth, '*Les aviateurs arriveron! Bientôt!*' (The aviators will be arriving – soon!) It was the first day of July 1909, and this small section of the French coastline was poised to become famous. All the talk for some time had been about the £1,000 prize for a flight across the English Channel, offered by Lord Northcliffe's *Daily Mail*. Now, at last, a serious attempt to win this prize was imminent. Significantly, it was said this particular stretch of coast west of Calais was considered the most favourable point of departure because of the high ground afforded by nearby Cap Blanc Nez and the relative short distance to Dover, just over twenty-or-so miles away across the straits. The inhabitants of Sangatte had waited and wondered. Maybe the novelty of the event would bring a spate of curious spectators to the area? If so, that would be good for everyone. It had been a bad summer so far, with not many visitors. The weather had been unseasonable and hotels, shops and bars had been quite unusually empty for the last few weeks. If nothing else, locals told each other, the arrival of *les aéronautic* would generate some much needed free advertisement for business.

Back in London, the *Daily Mail*'s aerial correspondent and former theatre critic, Harry Harper, had been given instructions to install himself and his wife in the Terminus Hotel in Calais for the duration of the competition. The newsworthiness of this newspaper's Channel Flight Prize was building up nicely and promised to be the very stuff of an excellent 'splash' story. Harper had to be on the spot to milk it for all it was worth. Not for nothing had Lord Northcliffe coined the paper's advertising slogan many years ago as the 'The Busy Man's Daily Newspaper'.[1] The policy of the *Daily Mail*'s style was to unashamedly target human interest stories that would appeal to a readership the more supercilious of its editors like to call the '*hoi polloi*', and while a publicity stunt like this was undoubtedly a great boost to circulation figures for all Northcliffe newspapers, in reality the emphasis behind this particular story was not just about increasing sales. No, the real impetus of the Channel Flight Prize was a political one – designed to convey a not too subtly disguised message to British newspaper readers. Northcliffe, the former journalist turned newspaper mogul, whom his staff referred to behind his back as the 'Chief', was once more dipping meddling fingers into the political lobbying pot and was determined to publicise the startling fact that continuous airborne flights could now be measured by hours and not by minutes. He wanted it widely known that new aeroplane designs allowed greater manoeuvrability, speed and achievable heights for machines. Moreover, the real importance of drawing attention to a powered flight by man across the straits of Dover lurked deeper than that. He was worried over the competence of the British Parliament and their war department to realise the fragility of the safety barrier of high seas that lay between them and Europe. For too long, public representatives had assumed that British invulnerability could never be shattered by an airborne attack from a foreign power, particularly Germany, and it was high time their complacency was shattered. In truth, once the first aviator conquered the straits, Northcliffe's favourite slogan: 'England is no longer an island' would be proven without doubt.

By late June 1909, Northcliffe began to accelerate matters. News reporters and aeronautical correspondents soon recognised that in his championing of Hubert Latham, the 'Chief' had cleverly identified an attractive contestant guaranteed to generate plenty of romantic appeal to readers. By early July, the *Daily Mail* columns were featuring personal profiles and pen-pictures of their chosen candidate for success, describing Latham in flattering terms as '… having light-brown hair and a fair skin showing a golden tan. He speaks gently and precisely … giving the impression that he has read well and is fastidious in his taste'. They write how he is to be found working beside his team, '… dressed in brown canvas overalls giving his brief orders in caressing tones to the workmen in blue jeans.' The portrait being drawn of the young aviator, with his slim good looks and charming manner, was an exemplary model for the new age. Latham was already an intrepid white hunter and explorer of foreign lands. He was brave and adventurous and ready to risk unknown perils; he was every boy's dream hero and every girl's romantic ideal. In addition, because he could be claimed to enjoy a mixed Anglo-French parentage this factor could only indicate the very essence of what the *entente cordiale* was all about. He was perfect for the part. It would remain to be seen whether such a ploy to grab the popular imagination would work as well as expected.

Naturally, this calculated priming of the public to feed and nurture a hidden world of political lobbying was all far from the minds of those who gathered to witness the adventure that was about to take place in Sangatte. Practical matters had to be decided. A week earlier, Latham had already conducted a survey of the English coastline with his friend, René Raoul-Duval, a mining engineer with expert knowledge of the geological coastal terrain on both sides of the straits. They sought a suitable landing place on the English side of the Channel. Writing to his mother on 27 June from the ferry on the return journey Latham comments on the intense curiosity of English people in the *Daily*

Latham's sister, Edmée, visits the camp at Sangatte, July 1909. (HLPP)

*Mail's* prize for a Channel flight. He was being asked lots of questions about aeroplanes and especially from young people. Their keen interest in aeronautics quite amazed him.

Within a couple of days his mother sent him a guarded reply from the fashionable Spa resort of Vichy, which she was visiting to 'take the waters'. Mme Latham is clearly not over-enthusiastic about her son's latest spree. She urges him to be prudent but does not suggest she should return from her *vacances* in order to witness his historic venture. One can almost hear her impatient tut-tut of annoyance over such foolishness. Perhaps fearing the worst, she is deliberately turning her back on the forthcoming exploit in the hope it all might safely fade away. By contrast, the other members of his family would seem to have been wholeheartedly behind him. His sister Edmée is captured in several casual camera snaps taken at the time, cheerfully inspecting all the preparations. It was all going to be a great thrill.

If the proposed flight was to go ahead from Sangatte, Latham required a piece of ground that would allow him to attain the good launch or 'take-off' crucial to sustaining his machine in the air. He would need to rise to about 250ft for the traverse of the straits and, if the craft was to clear the Shakespeare cliffs at Dover for a safe landing, it was important that there be no significant lessening of height during the journey.

One of first despatches to be filed by *The Times* announced that Latham 'had chosen a point on Cap Blanc Nez for his trial and starting place'. The site selected for his team's camp was beside the abandoned ruins of an ambitious but abortive project for a Channel tunnel to provide a railway link beneath the sea from Calais to Dover. The scheme had failed more than twenty years earlier when the English investors pulled out for political reasons. Both Latham and Raoul-Duval had personal connections to the railway companies which owned what was left of the old buildings. Gaining permission to access this site proved no problem. Some of the ruins were still usable and there was a tower that would provide a structure on which a wireless apparatus could be erected to send messages to Dover. It also provided basic shelter for the tents and temporary sheds that would be needed for the reassembly and preparation of the monoplane, following its journey from the Antoinette workshops in Puteaux, near Paris. The technicalities of reassembling and testing all the machines' components were not to be the greatest problem facing the Latham camp in the weeks that followed, however. One of the most serious and continuous setbacks was to be the inclement vagaries of wind and rain that summer. An early comment by an aeronautical correspondent that Latham was 'unable to fix upon any date for his attempt in advance, as he will await favourable weather',[2] was to be the forerunner of many similar and increasingly frustrated reports.

Yet, hopes were high and it may be seen that the aviator's access to an excellent network of support systems on both sides of the Channel was to prove of immense assistance. Not only was M. Depasse, chairman of the Parliamentary aviation group in Paris, receiving regular reports on progress from Latham's good friends in the French Aero Club, but the social standing and reputation of family connections – the Mallet and Latham directorships in ports, shipping and transport facilities and the conglomerate of mercantile business conducted from the port of Le Havre – would have very much eased the nod made in the direction of the Calais Harbour Board in seeking support of the venture. Add to all this Latham's other closely inter-related and politically well-connected cousins, the de la Roches, the Gastambides and their friends, and it can be seen that it would have been no trouble at all in arranging for a quiet word be sent to gain assurances from the Minister for the Marine so that provision of officially sanctioned shipping assistance for the flight attempt – tugs, escort vessels, look-outs and so on – could be put in hand without any difficulty. Such arrangements lessened much of the concern in regard to safety factors. But it would still be a dangerous undertaking.

Logistical arrangements in the organising of assistance in the port of Dover had been equally smooth to set up. As the *Daily Mail* was quick to note, Latham was already friendly with one of the sons of the powerful chairman of the Dover Harbour Board, Sir William Crundall – they had been companions on a motoring trip with friends during Latham's Oxford days. It was now very much to Latham's advantage that his friend's mother – the wife of Sir William – was a member of a local family called Iron who had been Harbour Masters of Dover since the 1700s. Sir William's influential position on the Board would certainly ensure Latham was to find all the help he needed here. In due course, having witnessed the first Channel flights as young boys, several of Sir William's nephews would be destined to add their own names to aviation history.[3]

When interviewed by a *Daily Mail* reporter on 9 July, Sir William's praise of his son's friend, Latham, was effusive: 'I know him well. He is a dear, good fellow, modest and unassuming, as plucky as possible and one of the best motor drivers in the world. If I was a betting man, I would put my money on him...' This might sound all very splendid but, to some, such an endorsement carried a whiff of sulphur. Sir William was a controversial political figure in Dover. The owner of a successful timber merchant firm, he had been the Conservative Mayor of the town since 1886 but had lately lost out to the challenge of the Liberals. Here was a man who was both heartily disliked and highly revered for having run the town on 'mafia' lines for decades. Re-elected to office in unbroken tenure twelve times, he had brought the town electricity, trams, street-widening, house building programmes and, more recently, an upgrading of the port's commercial status, having persuaded the Kaiser Wilhelm to use Dover as a port of call for German Atlantic liners. Not everyone in the town had looked on the latter achievement in a favourable light, for even the most tenuous display of sympathy with Germany was becoming increasingly suspect. Yet Sir William's control as chairman of the Harbour Board had continued unchallenged. He had no trouble at all in providing a guarantee that Latham got everything he might need at Dover.

The efficient backup provided by the *Daily Mail* newspaper included the provision of a special telegraph apparatus – another innovation being tested out, courtesy of the Marconi Company – which would link Calais and Dover. It was to be set up on the roof of the town's Lord Warden Hotel. Across on the other side of the Channel, in Sangatte, the relay equipment to receive and send transmissions was being erected on the ruined buildings which marked the site of the abandoned Channel tunnel project, close by the Latham camp. A flotilla of small boats would be on standby in Dover Harbour for any rescue attempt needed, and every other facility would be laid on with full civil approval. It was all very gratifying. Everyone was being splendidly helpful.

Meanwhile, on the French coast, the services of a French naval torpedo boat, *Harpoon*, had been assigned to the project as an escort vessel and the tug *Calaisien* – chartered by Latham – would be standing by in the port of Calais. According to the newspapers, on receiving a signal from his camp, this vessel would steam ahead to a position some four or five miles in advance of Latham's planned flight path. As soon as his plane was seen to leave the shore it would then steer for Dover at full speed. The tug had been fitted with a derrick and every facility for picking up the machine should it drop into the water. With all contingencies catered for all that was needed now was some decent weather.

The fragility of aeroplane construction, which relied on the lightest of fabric, wood, and wire in those early days of flying, meant that a craft was very much at the mercy of rising wind currents and adverse weather conditions. Havoc could be caused in strong or gusty breezes, unexpected rain flurries, fog, or failing light. The *Daily Mail* competition rules specified that the Channel flight must be made between sunrise and sunset. This was with good reason, because coping with the offshore and onshore winds along the coastline were just some of the hazards that presented themselves in this location. The most settled and calm conditions were normally experienced immediately after dawn before the heat of the sun precipitated a rising breeze, or late in the evening, as winds dropped back under a creeping dusk.

Latham gives the gathered pressmen a briefing. (HLPP)

Days dragged by. After over a week of waiting, with nothing much left to write about, the reports of even the most stoic newsmen begin to hint of desperation as they tried to keep the story alive by resorting to meteorological topics:

*The Times* (From our special correspondent) Calais, 9 July 1909.

It seems very improbable that M. Latham will be able to attempt his cross-Channel monoplane flight tomorrow. The weather is fine today but the barometer is now falling and there is a very high wind. M. Latham's monoplane was taken from the machine shop at Sangatte today and placed in a tent. Mechanics from Paris will probably be kept working all night affixing the wings. Interest in the approaching flight is intense.

In the meantime, there were developments. Two more contenders for the prize, the Comte de Lambert and a newcomer named as Arthur Seymour, emerged to declare their intention to enter the competition. *The Times* newspaper reported that the former was to set up his headquarters at Wissant and was 'keeping his plans more or less secret'. Described as being 'well known as one of the pupils of Mr. Wilbur Wright', the report added that Comte de Lambert 'has modified a Wright aeroplane with which he will make the attempt. Mr Seymour is said to have purchased a Voisin aeroplane but it is regarded as doubtful if he will make an attempt to cross the Channel'.

For the air correspondents to give the impression that there were now three competitors was pushing it a bit. In reality, Seymour was a complete novice and still taking flying lessons, but the Comte de Lambert was indeed someone worth watching. He had been one of the first students at Wilbur Wright's flying school set up at Pau earlier that year and was recently reported as having made several demonstration sales flights of the Wright brothers flying machine in Holland. Those in the know reckoned it was not altogether surprising that he and Latham were now setting themselves up as sporting rivals for the *Daily Mail* prize. They both belonged to the same elite crowd of socialites which had competed for motor yacht prizes in the 1905 Monaco Regatta at the time Latham first put the Antoinette engine through her paces so successfully.

Usually described as a Russian Aristocrat, the Comte was a member of an exiled French family which had been forced to flee their homeland during the Revolution. Such minor disadvantage had presented no bar to their continued reception within the best society circles in Europe and, quite recently, de Lambert had married the granddaughter of a minor English Lord. Her family were landowners; well-connected and wealthy enough to divide their time between their stately home in North Yorkshire and a château in Normandy.[4] Nothing of this was ever revealed to the reading public. The British press in those days abided by strict rules of what and what was not considered suitable to include in a despatch. Delving into the background and private life of notables would be deemed impolite and intrusive. In any case, the press was wholeheartedly behind Latham.

Charles de Lambert in his Wright machine. (Harman Collection)

As the preparations for the forthcoming flight across the straits continued to make progress in Sangatte it might seem strange now that there was no mention in the extensive press coverage of another up-and-coming French aviator who might mount a challenge: Louis Blériot. The general British reading public might be excused of having no interest in this flyer – but the French aeronautical correspondents would have known that here must be a formidable contender, if he so chose to take part.

Looking back on the unfolding of events of this time, it would seem that Blériot had at first treated the *Daily Mail* competition with considerable disdain, possibly looking upon it as a dubious publicity stunt – which, indeed, it was. Someone must have asked him about the possibility of attempting the Channel flight because he made an announcement that he was too busy concentrating on preparations to enter the French Aero Club's competition, the *Prix de Voyage*, which was due to take place on 13 July. This was a prestigious contest and he more or less inferred that it carried rather more value as a boost to the business of selling his Blériot monoplanes and was, therefore, more worthy of his concentration. It was also less risky. French aeronautical journalists knew that, in contrast to Latham, Blériot was not one of those sporting personalities eager to rise to a challenge for the fun of it. The fact was that he did not much like flying and as one fellow aviator dryly remarked, 'Blériot wasn't an instinctive pilot'.[5] He was far more comfortable tinkering with a machine on the ground than being up in the air. But what the French commentators did not know, perhaps, was the history of Blériot's past commercial difficulties with Gastambide and Levavasseur, or that there may have been a legacy of unfinished business.

From the start Latham had entertained a convinced belief that the Channel prize would be his. When beset by the many difficulties that came to upset his plans, his unshakeable confidence in Levavasseur's Antoinette never wavered. Two weeks following the team's arrival in Sangatte, he confided to a journalist from *The Times* that six months earlier, long before he had even mastered the piloting of the monoplane, he had laid a wager that he could win Northcliffe's prize by 15 July. Was serious money involved? The laying of substantial odds on sporting events was part and parcel of the lifestyle which attached itself to most wealthy young gentlemen in his circle. If things did not go right, one had to take reverses with stoic acceptance. Latham's patience was to be well-tested.

Once more, *The Times* aeronautical column reporting on the Channel flight had to rely on gloomy discussion of adverse weather conditions. From Dover on 12 July 1909 the correspondent wrote: '… little likelihood of a change this morning … appearances most unfavourable … blowing fresher than yesterday … a rising barometer points to more to higher winds … the outlook on the French side equally unpromising …'

And yet, despite all the uncertainty, the size of the crowds congregated at Sangatte to watch the flight were judged by contemporary commentators to have been quite phenomenal – perhaps even as high as 10,000 people, drawn from all walks of life.[6] Enthusiasts had motored down from Paris or Rouen to mingle with curious locals, farmers, fishermen and trades people. They lined the roads and waited patiently. Some congregated at the perimeter of Latham's camp. On the Dover side of the Channel spectators gathered, waiting anxiously for weather reports, fearful of missing this historic event.

Levavasseur poses beside the monoplane as Latham is ready for take-off, Sangatte, July 1909. (HLPP)

For everyone who waited, there was nothing more frustrating than the changeable weather that belied the expectation of sunny July summer days. Reports of falling barometers, high winds and squally showers persisted. Finally, a glimmer of hope helped to lift wearied spirits. *The Times* special correspondent on 13 July 1909 in the late edition dared to predict better conditions for the morning:

> The weather had undergone a sudden and complete change for the better, the clouds are dispersing and the wind is veering towards north-north-east. Local weather experts, fishermen and sailors declare that a splendidly fine day is certain tomorrow… I have received advice from Calais that M. Latham intends to make a trial at 4 o'clock this morning, if the weather is suitable. This will be followed by an attempt to cross the Channel at 6 o'clock. The weather conditions are much improved.

During the night, hoards of sightseers began to congregate once more in Sangatte to witness the departure of the flight. Preparations had begun at the first glimmer of light. By 7 a.m., the mechanics could be seen moving fussily in and out of the shed where the flying machine stood. Then, after what seemed an age, the aeroplane was being wheeled very carefully into the open. It was then slowly manoeuvred up the hill, from where the first trial flight was to be launched. And all this time, more and more people had been arriving; on foot, on bicycle, or by motor. Everyone was tremendously excited. The anticipation of a truly momentous occasion electrified the chilly salt-filled damp air. Latham and the chief engineer, Levavasseur, then made their appearance. Intent on checking the machine, they took no notice of the hush that fell across the waiting spectators. The *Daily Mail's* reporter at the scene writes how Levavasseur the 'inventor' was bustling around while the head mechanic looked 'white and anxious'. In his description of Latham 'the flying man' who was wearing a 'brown overall jacket' over his ordinary clothes, the commentator noted how the aviator, 'was exactly the same quiet undemonstrative figure as always. His hand was as steady as a statue's and the usual sleepy, far-away look was in his eye'.

By 8 a.m., Latham had swung himself up into the machine and took his seat at the controls. The engine was started. There was a movement forward, a gaining of momentum. Then the moment! The craft rose splendidly into the air and, as it circled the area over their heads, the gasps of the watchers rose with it like a sigh. The machine flew several full circuits and then, caught by a sudden rising breeze, swooped around again to descend rapidly over a field of clover on the far crest of the hill. The apparatus came down and shuddered to a tip-tilted stop. When Latham stepped out unhurt, following this apparently awkward landing, the crowd's sigh turned to a cheer. 'Bravo! Bravo!' But the unorthodox landing had broken a strut in the undercarriage and one of the propeller blades had been damaged when it had hit the ground. There would be no Channel attempt that day but, if everything could be fixed quickly, all augured well for a successful flight the following morning.

But hopes were to be dashed. Fickle as always that summer, the weather once more turned wicked. There were reports of wind and fog in the Channel. Another day's wait had to be endured. Still the crowds continued to arrive and among them were some rather more intriguing, if not entirely un-anticipated, visitors spotted by journalists eager for interesting copy.

*The Times* special correspondent reported on 14 July 1909 in Calais:

> Owing to the coincidence of the *Fête Nationale* an immense crowd had collected at Sangatte at daybreak, and the disappointment was great when it became known that there would not even be a trial trip. Many people had come down from the surrounding district. Among the visitors who had come from Paris was Mr Hart O. Berg, Messrs Wright's European manager … who was accompanied by M. Clemenceau, the Premier's son…

Aeronautical correspondents were well aware that the Comte de Lambert was currently the pilot engaged to demonstrate the capabilities of the Wright brothers' planes in Europe. De Lambert's aspirations to compete in the Channel flight would have been high on the priority list of the Wright's top salesman, Hart O. Berg, who now came rushing down to Sangatte in a move to ingratiate himself with French Premier Clemenceau's family – with an eye, maybe, on smoothing out the path for potential lucrative army contracts. Aiming to gain as much publicity for the Wright's machine as possible, he may have found the Comte, despite his excellent charm, was not sufficiently the hard-nosed salesman with the necessary fire in his belly to recognise the urgency required in a promotional campaign such as this. The Comte was fussy. He wanted everything checked and double checked and progress was leisurely. He wanted his wife and children be brought down here to be at his side. Berg would need to chivvy him along and gave waiting pressmen an interview:

… Today, [Mr. Hart, on behalf of Comte de Lambert] said to a correspondent of the *New York Herald* : 'We are not trying to win the *Daily Mail* prize. Even if we cross the Straits tomorrow, we shall proceed with our programme. In order to meet with every emergency, we have two Wright machines. We shall take advantage of the fine weather at the first opportunity.'

Berg went on to say that the Comte was not only 'ambitious to make the journey to England in the air, but also to return in the same way'. A double crossing! That, indeed, was a challenge! But it has to be said nobody took it very seriously. Now all eyes were on Latham. A *Daily Mail* despatch is down beat, reporting how: 'Mr. Latham looks tired and depressed. We are all haggard and hollow-eyed'. The flight would take place tomorrow for certain.

For many years, a story that was current currency carried the notion that Eileen Gray had flown across the Channel in an aeroplane with Hubert Latham. Despite it being a tale that regularly did the rounds whenever her name was mentioned, the rumour was not true. Certainly, she had come to Sangatte during the preparations for Latham's flight, as her own account for her biographer, Adams, can attest:

Her friend, René Raoul-Duval called Eileen early one morning and invited her to come and watch him [Latham] take off. They drove to Sangatte, near Calais. 'It was a vile summer's day' she had recalled. By the time they reached the coast, a number of newspapermen had gathered and also quite a few elegant men and women from Paris society. Latham's engineer/inventor, the burly red-bearded Léon Levavasseur, tried to keep the curious crowds at bay. The terrible weather persisted, and at night they finally gave up.'[7]

As with other watchers, her first attempt to witness this historic event had been thwarted. However, she would be drawn back to the coastal resort to be at Latham's side when conditions for flying eventually improved.

Sangatte was not the only place where minds were concentrated on what lay ahead in terms of the potential use of aeroplanes. Conscious that the topic of defence in times of the threat of war was one guaranteed to garner popular interest, members of His Majesty's British Government had been solemnly debating the need for further investment in the Naval Fleet. On such occasions, Richard Haldane, the secretary of State for War and Cabinet spokesman on such matters, would rise to his feet in the Houses of Parliament and, although knowing the majority in the chamber traditionally placed their faith in battleships to defend the nation, had many times pleaded passionately for greater resources and support for the British Army. While conceding that resources for the navy were important, he argued that the French military people were planning to engage in a series of experimental initiatives. He pointed out that, for instance, the French army top brass were investigating the possibility of using a fleet of army aircraft instead of balloons for many practical and tactical uses. But, his words, as a rule, fell on deaf ears. The chamber listened dutifully, but sceptically. Earlier that year – on 28 January – an official military report had been issued which had seen no trustworthy evidence that aeroplanes had a future.[8] Up to recently, Haldane had been inclined to believe these findings. As recently as May of that year he had been writing to Northcliffe echoing his Defence Committee's conviction that 'aeroplanes are a very long way off indeed being the slightest practical use in war'.[9] Now, he was not so sure. Backbench wits liked to suggest that, naturally, the army's cavalrymen would claim the sight of machines in the air on a battlefield would frighten the horses. There was much laughter and quips parried from each side of the House. But the serious conclusion was always almost unanimous. It was clear to the honourable members that flying machines were just fanciful novelties for sportsmen which presented little or no advantage to a nation's defences. Even Winston Churchill, who was never short of some pithy comment, was still uncertain of their usefulness. He privately expressed doubts but was ready to concede that if flying machines were to be developed at all, it should be done scientifically and professionally. But Churchill had not made up his mind either and, in fact, was sitting in his usual position on the fence, carefully biding his time before making a decision. For his own part, Haldane favoured taking a careful and unhurried scientific approach to the idea of aircraft as war machines. He was inclined to think that amateurish enthusiasts and sporty types should not be left to their own devices on a project like this. These sort of people were probably less than reliable and the novelty and excitement of a flying competition was all very well to increase the sales of newspapers but hardly worthy of serious government consideration as a positive step to progress.

Outside of Parliament, however, there were those who knew otherwise; who were more far-seeing; who had plans in hand; and who were not averse to engaging in a little manipulation if necessary. This lobby was pleased with Northcliffe's widely publicised newspaper prize for a Channel flight, for it had created an excellent climate for a revision of opinion. People were beginning to realise how vulnerable the defences of England stood if the War Office continued to ignore aeroplanes – and the Press Baron was about to whip up more support when, without warning, some news broke which threatened the whole of his carefully orchestrated campaign by casting a slur on his hero of the *entente cordiale*. It made no difference that reports from Sangatte for the *Daily Mail* and *The Times* were reaching their peak, with daily, almost hourly, despatches to build up the excitement of the forthcoming challenge, now all was about to be lost because some sharp-nosed newspaper journalists in Germany had begun to claim that Northcliffe's favoured aviator was seriously flawed as a champion. They were saying that Latham had a family relationship to recently appointed German High Chancellor, Theobald von Bethmann Hollweg.[10] It was akin to having blood ties to the Devil himself.

This terrible news could not have been worse. The more imaginative commentators immediately offered panic-filled speculations that Latham had the makings of a cunning spy. Was not the whole British Naval Fleet to be shortly mustered in Portsmouth for a Royal Review? Had not the chairman of the Dover Harbour Board – known to be friendly with Latham – engaged with the Kaiser to encourage regular visits of German liners to the port? A flying machine with a pilot carrying a camera – as Latham was known to have demonstrated – could take photographs from the air and produce a clear ordinance record of their strength and number. The outcome was unthinkable. Little credence was given to the fact that this reported family relationship carried a dubious level of importance, for the link had been forged many years ago when Latham's maternal grand-aunt married the German politician's father. Such arguments carried little weight.

In the scurry in high places that followed, someone remembered Latham was indeed as fluent in the German language as he was in English and another source discovered that an aunt on his father's side of the family was rumoured to have married a man of German extraction. As a potential hero to boost the image of a strong English-French *entente*, Latham had become an impossible choice.

It may be seen that these complaints must have been difficult enough for Northcliffe to handle for he was acutely aware that, while his own aunts, Grace and Caroline, had each also married into German families, it did not automatically follow that it made them in any way disloyal to the land of their birth. Nonetheless, he would have been aware that the Latham family enjoyed a reputation for pragmatic ruthlessness; they had fingers in a lot of pies and, possibly, had not been above a bit of dodgy trading in the past. But spying, no. He probably realised this hysteria was not credible – but, at the same time, this German Chancellor was as much feared as the Kaiser – and any mention of von Bethmann-Hollweg was enough to sound alarm bells ringing as far as the British public was concerned. It was clear that if he did not think up a rescue package for this whole Channel Flight Prize scheme, the moment would be lost – and a great deal of money wasted to no avail.

Northcliffe knew his readers were the most malleable of audiences and it was a relatively easy task to get them all steamed up about an alternative flyer instead of Latham. But who? It would have be a Frenchman, for they were the only ones capable of success. Was it possible to put a spin on events so that, if an suitable unequivocally French winner of the *Daily Mail* prize could be found, then that nation could depicted as a glorious and worthy ally to counterpoint their own brave men of adventure – Baden-Powell, Shackleton, and now Captain Scott, of whom there was again high hopes for new Antarctic exploration? To allow a Frenchman to take the prize instead of his Oxford-educated hero would serve his purposes just as well – and was probably a risk worth taking. He could safely guarantee a change in allegiances was possible, even at this late hour. Public opinion was putty in his hands. Who could be approached? The ineffectual Comte de Lambert would be useless. There had been another successful aviator recently in the news – a man called Blériot. Was his little plane capable of flying the Channel? It was worth a shot.

In the meantime something would have to be done about Latham. His candidature was now found to be fatally flawed, no matter what anyone said. The way to do it would be nothing as crude bringing up as all this nonsense about spying – but Latham's attempt must be somehow delayed or stopped until an alternative aviator was sought out and prepared. One way or another, it could be done. With the confidence of a skilled strategist, Northcliffe knew it was possible. There was never any problem in finding suitable ways and means to get one's way, when it was felt necessary. But would there be enough time?

On 15 July, the patience of the waiting crowds in Sangatte and Dover was finally rewarded. The dawn broke to reveal an unbelievably beautiful and calm morning. Conditions were excellent; almost too good to be true. The Latham team had risen early to prepare his machine for the famous flight. There was nothing else now that could go astray. How wrong they were!

When the chief mechanic went to collect the spare accumulators needed for the engine he found them missing – gone, mislaid – how could this have happened? Nobody knew.

One rumour had it that they were not missing but just unexpectedly left un-charged and useless. Another rumour, published in *The Times*, darkly hinted they had been stolen.

Stolen by whom? And why? The press latched into the story not without some glee and relief for having something tangible to write about at last. The first really fine weather they had seen for ages and now this. What a disastrous and uncanny strange twist of fate. Fans on both sides of the Channel were seething with frustration. On 16 July, Latham's elderly English cousin, Morton, writes gloomily from Farnham to advise him to 'have a £5 in your pocket – otherwise if stopped by the police you will be sent back as an alien', hinting he should watch out for the activities of people like the 'friend' who had stolen the accumulators. Morton Latham, who had married a Belgian lady more than thirty years earlier, was well aware of the British distrust of everyone and everything deemed 'foreign'.

Latham was now grounded for hours, perhaps the whole day. In addition, this further delay would cause one of the careful logistics to unravel. It was the last day his team would have the assistance of officially deployed naval escort vessels, for they were due back on regular duties in the morning. This meant a trip up to Paris to re-negotiate for further support. It would be too risky to fly until adequate sea-borne rescue services were back in place. Poised on the brink of success this latest setback was heartbreaking. Not insurmountable, however.

Four days later and everything was once more quite perfect for flying: the weather, the machine, the preparations.

At 4.30 a.m. on Monday, 19 July, the clear dawn was surely the harbinger of good fortune. Hundreds of eager spectators once more gathered in their droves outside the Latham camp at Sangatte as the tug *Calaisien* left the port of Calais to stand by for the signal to proceed across the Channel. The navel vessel, the *Harpoon*, by now re-assigned to its duty to attend the Channel flight, was already in position and ready to steam ahead as soon as the flying machine took to the air. Another early start. Would this be the time for success, at last?

A small tricolour had been attached to Latham's machine just before it was wheeled out of its shed at first light. It had been lashed to one of the forward struts in such a way as to make it a simple job for him to release its folds at the moment of take-off. One might speculate and wonder had he, by chance, heard adverse whispers concerning these endorsements by the English newspaper and the over-fanciful claims being made about his Anglo-Saxon blood and loyalties. He had many times disputed such nonsense, insisting he was but one quarter British and in his heart a true and total Frenchman. Had he not completed his military service in St Cloud like every other Parisian? He had not been famously toasted with whisky and soda in Maxim's for having only one quarter English blood?[11] Flying the flag of his country on his epic flight would perhaps go some way to remind people of these facts and dispel any notions otherwise.

Soon, the machine was being carefully guided through the narrow country lanes which led onto the slope behind the camp where the take-off point had been designated on Mont d'Escailles. It was a slow business. Levavasseur was not in attendance for the final supervision but had joined a party of Latham's friends and relations who had earlier embarked on the

A crowd of sightseers watch as the Antoinette monoplane is brought to the take-off point, Sangatte, July 1909. (HLPP)

*Harpoon*, to watch the flight from the sea. A series of shots from the port would signal they were underway and this would alert Latham's team to be ready. Latham, wearing a knitted blue jersey, with cap to match, had climbed up into the machine and waited patiently for his team to align the aircraft in readiness for swinging the propeller into action.

The *Daily Mail* journalist wrote later of the moment that: 'He is a youth of marvellous self-control ... he was to all appearances as calm as if he were starting for a bicycle ride...'

At last! At last! Latham made an adjustment to his goggles. Made sure he could reach the string of the tricolour to release it just before he left the French coast and headed for England. Ready? His hand was on the throttle. The senior mechanic's hand was held high. When it dropped, two assistants would activate the propeller. This was it. In a matter of seconds he would be up and away. At last!

'*Alors – alors! Attend!*' But what was this? A faint cry was rising from the bottom of the hill. A figure running, waving wildly. Agitated. Shouting, panting ... the words choked back by the effort of charging up the hill towards them. 'Stop! Stop!' The senior mechanic turned sharply, annoyed. Already nervous at being inexplicably left in charge by Levavasseur at this crucial moment, he bristled with anger at the interruption. The men standing by the propeller hesitated. Latham craned his neck to turn and see what was happening. It was a disaster to come – averted at the very last minute.

A despatch to *The Times* on the following day related the drama: someone had just realised that the aircraft's tanks had been only partly filled; there was barely enough fuel left in them to clear the headland. If Latham had taken off at that moment, the machine would have stayed aloft for only a few minutes. How could such a mistake have come about? It was appalling; a mystery. Significantly, Levavasseur had been missing – he had left earlier to sail out on the escort vessel. If he had been there as normal this could never have happened. He was usually so fussy when preparations were in hand. He would be here there and everywhere, bellowing orders, checking and re-checking and arguing points to a maddening degree that only served to get in everyone's way most of the time. Surely he had left instruction for someone to check on the re-fuelling of the petrol tanks? A posse of helpers was sent scurrying downhill to the fuel store, where the cans of petrol were kept in readiness. Luckily, several motor cars had been parked nearby by visitors and the cans were swiftly loaded into one of these which was then driven up to the launch point at breakneck speed. No time for delay or the moment would be lost!

The senior mechanic was beginning to panic, blaming everyone around him for the *debacle*. Even the youngster who had saved the day was getting the rough side of his tongue, instead of being thanked for averting a calamity. Strange. But this was no time for asking questions or debate. It was almost 6.30. It would take another ten minutes or so to complete filling the tanks. And then, with luck, the Antoinette would get safely away.

At 6.42 a.m., Latham's machine, the monoplane Antoinette IV, rose gracefully into the air. The little French tricolour was unfurled as planned and the watching crowd whooped and cheered as he circled the immediate area. The plane swept over the chimney of the Old Channel Tunnel works and then headed straight out across the sea. Soon he was just a speck in the sky. In a few minutes he was out of sight. The first flight of an aeroplane across the English Channel was underway.

Out at sea, anxious eyes were watching out for the appearance of the tiny monoplane. This was the second time Latham's family and friends had taken to the water on board the designated escort vessels. There had been the frustration of an abandoned flight in the early hours of the previous day – cancelled at the last minute when the wind had risen too quickly and unexpectedly. With the flight aborted, the boats had put about and returned to port with a contingent of passengers who tried to hide their disappointment with as good grace as could be mustered. Now, almost exactly twenty-four hours later, hopes were once more raised. The morning was clear and calm. On board the *Harpoon*, Léon Levavasseur and the inevitable posse of journalist had been joined by Latham's elder sister, Edmée, her husband, Dr Paul Armand-Delille, and a party of other close friends. Eileen Gray was among the invited guests.[12] Everyone hoped for better things. So far it was looking good.

Latham's Antoinette was travelling steadily, gaining height – perhaps to 900ft – and everything looked splendid as it overtook the positions of the escort vessels and continued its way towards the horizon. He was going to make it! His machine was almost out of sight of the watchers and already nearly halfway to Dover. However, something was wrong! The plane was dipping lower.

It was true. The Antoinette was descending with a slow and gentle gliding movement. What skill! With relief, the spectators saw Latham bringing his machine down like a seabird – gently, smoothly and unhurriedly.

The watchers from the shore, 19 July 1909. (HLPP)

Someone shouted, 'He is down! The craft is floating on the surface!' And so it was.

Those with the strongest binoculars could see Latham clearly. He was climbing out of his seat and was balancing himself on one of the wings. Thank goodness he was safe! His arm came up with a salute, a wave to signal he was unhurt. The *Harpoon*, not too far away, was steaming towards him at full speed. A cheer rose up. Latham had now re-seated himself on the wing, waiting for his rescuers with his feet propped up on one of the wing struts. Another cheer went up. Latham had taken out his cigarette case and elegant holder and was lighting up a fag with a flourish. There was sangfroid for you! What a character, or what a fool? What if the petrol tanks had been damaged? A lighted cigarette – fuel fumes – fire at sea. Latham was taking an unthinkable risk. But those that knew him well remembered his tense cigarette chain-smoking habit, especially when under stress. Latham's cool handling of his descent – like a smooth parachute landing – would have taken its toll. Still, what a story! One of *The Times* newsmen accurately caught the moment:

> The intrepid aviator, safely sitting on the wing plucked out of the sea while quietly smoking a cigarette. He had escaped possible disaster with nothing worse than a pair of wet boots... Far from being a failure, this safe drop to the sea from a height of some 150ft marks one of the most brilliant achievements in the history of aviation!

Latham is down in the sea, 19 July 1909. (HLPP)

But how had it happened? The plane's magnificent take-off and smooth flight had held no hint of impending disaster. The weather had been perfect. The air currents of no obvious concern. A mystery indeed. There would be no questions until later. The atmosphere on the *Harpoon* was one of joyous relief and celebration. Lines were being thrown seaward to secure the wreckage of the monoplane until the tug *Calaisien* arrived to undertake the salvage of the aircraft. The damaged Antoinette machine was then lashed to the tug for towing back to port for repair. A cry went up. Three cheers for M. Latham. A truly heroic first attempt to fly the English Channel! Three more cheers for his near-success!

From the special correspondent of *The Times* Calais, 19 July 1909:

M. Latham has been kind enough to tell me his own views of the flight briefly as follows: 'I was about 600ft above sea level when leaving land, and gradually attained an altitude of 1,000ft, my speed being from 40–45 miles an hour. I had travelled about 7 miles out to sea when the engine stopped and I was obliged to glide down, which I did in one straight line without undulations. I struck the water so gently that only a tiny splash was caused and I merely felt some spray in my face. The machine floated splendidly, as I expected, and I kept my feet dry by raising them on to the framework. After a few minutes the Harpoon's boat

Safely rescued – Latham on board the escort vessel with René and Jackie Raoul-Duval and Paul Armand-Delille, 19 July 1909. (HLPP)

came to me bringing ropes which I fastened above and below the centre of gravity and then we towed the aeroplane alongside the destroyer. She is considerably damaged from rocking about in the water all this time, and will be sent back to Puteaux to be repaired but I hope to have another similar machine at Sangatte in a few days and to make another attempt to cross the Channel as soon as possible.' M. Latham considered the cause of the engine stopping was probably that the salt air had a bad effect upon the carburation, but of this he cannot of course be absolutely certain.

The rapturous reception Latham received on his return to Calais might have been one for visiting royalty. Dignitaries scurried forward, eager to be the first to offer congratulations. There were cheers and handshakes; hats went flying in the air and children lifted onto shoulders to get a glimpse of the heroic man. The port's Festival Queen – a buxom beauty, crowned during the *Fête Nationale* – was pushed forward to offer a welcoming kiss. Indeed, the scale of excitement was such one would think the Channel flight had been completely successful and the prize won. It was the most amazing recognition of a failure ever seen.

Next day, every newspaper headline declared Latham's flight to have been a splendid triumph. And this was not just the London papers; the news stands in Paris were full

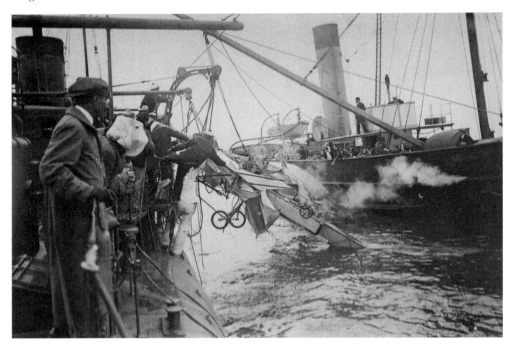

Lifting the wreckage from the sea, 19 July 1909. (HLPP)

The monoplane's mangled structure is hoisted high in the air, 19 July 1909. (HLPP)

What remains of *Antoinette* is brought back into the port of Calais, lashed to the side of an escort vessel, 19 July 1909. (HLPP)

Latham receives an enthusiastic welcome on the quayside, 19 July 1909. (HLPP)

of ecstatic accounts of Latham's brave enterprise. Word went out that as soon as repairs to his aeroplane were completed, he would make a second attempt. But before then, it must be discovered what went wrong. The first question would be to ask why the fuel tanks had been almost empty; the second would be what had caused the engine to die so dramatically?

The aeronautical correspondent for the *New York Herald* suggested that the reason for the Antoinette's empty fuel tanks was because the journey up to the top of Cap Blanc Nez had used up too much fuel. It was an ingenious explanation which in some other journalists' opinion did not wash because, as far as they understood, the machine had been man-hauled by technicians aided by a local farmer's plough horse for a greater part of the journey.

A greater mystery surrounded the reason for engine failure – and an explanation would soon be offered which only partly solved this question. In the meantime, there would be yet another delay while the necessary repairs to Latham's Antoinette were undertaken. For the aeronautical correspondents covering the story, the only element without speculation was Latham's firm determination to have another go. Readers of the *New York Herald* were told that:

> M. Latham left by motor car for Paris at 3.30 p.m. after stating that he intended to return here about Friday next. M. Levavasseur is staying tonight at Sangatte but future plans seem rather uncertain. Both gentlemen, however, wish to renew the attempt at the earliest opportunity.

It was with some grim satisfaction, however, that those who kept a careful watch over the unfolding of events noted Latham's own admission of his intention to take photographs with a small camera from the cockpit during the flight. Perhaps some of the scare-mongering rumours that this man was a spy in the pay of the German Chancellor might not have been entirely unfounded, after all?

# SIX
# Betrayal or Political Expediency?

With Latham attending to business matters in Paris, the engineer Levavasseur had set about tackling the repairs to the damaged monoplane. It was more daunting than expected. The task of hauling the ditched machine back to Calais and the eager descent of many overnight souvenir hunters who had stripped away bits and pieces of the structure had actually caused more substantial damage than the crash itself. Following an inspection in the morning, it was decided that it would be useless to send the aeroplane all the way back to the manufacturing plant in Puteaux and although Levavasseur confidently announced that his team could tackle the repairs here in Sangatte with no difficulty, it was soon looking doubtful how quickly the work could be done even if they began work immediately. So many new parts would have to be sent down from Paris. How long would all this take? It was very worrying.

For some reason, perhaps to allay other rumours floating around, an accredited journalist from *The Times* had been invited up to the Latham camp to be shown an interesting discovery made during the dismantling of the engine. When he arrived, the aircraft tent was empty except for the machine itself. Work had already begun on the monoplane's damaged wing struts. The V8 motor had been removed and lay on the ground beside the undamaged front section of the craft. The process of stripping it down had also begun and various engine parts had been laid out in a neat formation in preparation for reassembly.

Under the eyes of the journalist, Levavasseur had lifted up a small piece of bent metal wire which had been laid out amid the other machine parts. This piece of wire had been the culprit. Such a thing should not have been in the engine. In due course, under the headline: 'Channel Flight: The Mishap Explained', the reporter dutifully reported this discovery of the rogue piece of wire in his despatch: 'Levavasseur declared it must undoubtedly have been the cause of the motor's having stopped'. However, it is quite significant to note how the journalist was careful to add a level of scepticism, clearly dissatisfied with the engineer's lack of clarity: 'Where it came from I did not gather, but had to be satisfied with the explanation that it had found its way into the delicate mechanism and was [in Levavasseur's words] "the wicked cause of the catastrophe".'[1]

There were other versions of the incident put forward. The *Daily Mail* correspondent believed a piece of insulation had broken off and had damaged one of the brass moving parts in the distributor.[2] The writer for the *Westminster Gazette* attributed the failure to the engine's lack of having two systems of ignition. Other opinions included the notion that vibration of the engine had shaken something loose while it was taxiing up to the take-off point. None of these explanations made a lot of sense. The unanswered question left hanging was: had it been a deliberate piece of sabotage – or not? And, if so, who had been responsible? In journalistic circles there were rumours that Latham had asked to be given the rogue piece of wire so he could have it fashioned into a scarf pin. That was the story. Or, perhaps, he wanted it for another reason. It was a useful piece of evidence to have.

It became soon apparent that Levavasseur was wasting valuable time trying to reassemble the damaged monoplane for another flight. Too many crucial parts had been stripped away by the night-time looters. In retrospect, it is curious that nobody thought it odd that the machine had been left unguarded and so vulnerable, or asked what kind of people would want to carry off wheels and pieces of wing. But it seems as if no one had taken the trouble to ponder too deeply on these matters at the time. They were far too busy.

A change of plan had to be made. They could not afford the luxury of an extended delay. Luckily, their next and slightly improved model, the Antoinette VII was almost ready. Latham's next flight could be made in this machine just as soon as it could be delivered from Puteaux. On arrival, the machine would need only a few hours' final assembly. However, while the motor of the new monoplane and the general construction were precisely similar to Antoinette IV, some extra refinements which included a technique called wing warping – a variation intended to offer greater control – would need some practice before Latham took it out over the Channel. But this could be done. No further setbacks would be tolerated.

In Paris, Hubert Latham had many people to see. First of all, he visited the Chamber of Deputies in order to thank M. Depasse, the chairman of the Parliamentary aviation group for his message of congratulation. In the meantime, as reported in *The Times*, the escort vessel assigned to his flight, the *Harpoon*, had been ordered to rejoin her station at Cherbourg and it was necessary to seek a further favour from M. Depasse.[3] Could he once more request the Minister of Marine to place another destroyer at his disposal? He was assured there would be no difficulty at all. But as Latham relaxed with friends in Paris, well satisfied that the project was back on track and all would be well, a new twist to the turn of events was about to accelerate matters in a most unexpected way.

The next morning, all the leading newspapers carried a bombshell announcement. Out of the blue, Louis Blériot had declared an intention to compete for the *Daily Mail* Channel Flight Prize, after all. He had spoken to the representative of *Le Matin*. He would fly on Thursday or Friday next and would make his attempt with his small monoplane No. 11. *The Times* correspondent explains to its readers that if the wind blew from the west he would start from the English coast; if from the east he would set off from near Calais. So now Latham had a serious rival. He would need to return to Sangatte almost immediately, much earlier than planned. His next flight must take place without any further delay.

Louis Blériot was to set up his rival camp at a place called Les Baraques almost halfway between Sangatte and Calais. He had received permission to use land owned by the

LAT.HAM IN HIS MONOPLANE

Latham in his Antoinette Monoplane. (HLPP)

military authorities, close to the shore and separated from the sea by high sand dunes. It was an ideal position for his lighter, smaller machine. How he had managed to drum up enough influential backing to wangle this official co-operation at such short notice remains something of a puzzle, but there he was. It would not take long to prepare for his first test flight.

By Wednesday afternoon Latham had returned posthaste from Paris. The swift arrival of Blériot had created a new sense of urgency, which was now further heightened by the formal politeness extended by the two flyers to each other. Latham had issued a courteous invitation to Blériot to visit the Antoinette camp; his rival had returned the compliment. Watched by the invited Press Corps, they admired each other's machines and praised the work of all the mechanics. Had Latham noticed how Blériot, in his exchanges with journalists, was extremely cautious in his conversation? The older man was being very wary of being drawn on the subject of his immediate plans.

The way things stood, it looked like the challenge for the Channel flight was turning into a race. Much depended on who would be ready first, Latham or Blériot. And would the weather hold? That was the question on everybody's lips. It was still unseasonable for this time of year. The winds blew in an unpredictable fashion. The delightful sunrises seen earlier in the week were slipping away and stable conditions looked like breaking up. The tension was unbearable.

For once, the presence of high winds was an element working to Latham's advantage. It was now he who needed one or two days' grace to prepare his new machine for a fresh attempt. It would be galling if the weather improved unexpectedly, allowing Blériot to steal a march.

Latham and Levavasseur
keep the press informed
on developments.
(HLPP)

The forecast for Friday morning had held little hope of any flying and they could do nothing but wait. By late on Saturday, however, both aviators were advised that the next day augured well. A calm dawn was expected. There was only one further snag – taking to the air on a Sunday might court disapproval on the far side of the Channel.

Latham had received a letter from Harry Harper, the *Daily Mail* correspondent. It warned him that Northcliffe had telegraphed to say the British public, known to be fervent guardians of the traditional joyless Sabbath, would not take too kindly to a flight on a Sunday.[4] In truth, the 'Chief' may have been less worried over offending religious scruples than by the thought of losing an additional weekday evening edition of the *Mail* and the extra cost of making-up a fresh front page for Monday morning. However, in the heel of the hunt, even Northcliffe's God-like power counted for little when faced with an obvious total reliance on suitable weather conditions. If the weather was right, the machines would fly.

On Saturday night, 24 July 1909, the Latham and Blériot teams hastily convened a meeting to organise the arrangements for their individual escort vessels. With both pilots poised to make the crossing of the straits in the early hours, too many naval vessels were now standing by in Calais. It would be nigh impossible for them all to leave the harbour at the same time. The discussions grew tense and difficult. Latham had had to run the course of a stiff argument with an intransigent Blériot, who insisted on telegraphing the French Minister of the Marine in Paris for a ruling to give precedent to his assigned naval destroyer, the *Escopette*.[5] It made no matter that Latham had made all the running in the contest up to then and had had his experienced flotilla waiting for a longer period. It was argued that Blériot's destroyer was clearly the faster vessel. Just before midnight, with the knowledge that they would need to be airborne within hours, a compromise was finally hammered out. The Commander of the *Escopette* was to be prepared at 2 a.m. The vessel would be ready to steam ahead into the Channel following a signal from the coast when a take-off was about to commence. The destroyer would then follow the flight of whichever of the two aviators started first.[6] All was now ready. Would tomorrow be the day?

The unfolding of what was to follow, if created in a novel, could not be more amazing than the actual sequence of events. As has been shown, the series of small mishaps and delays which successfully held up Latham's first attempt to fly the Channel leave a distinct impression that covert scheming was taking place. Some of the incidents may have been pure misfortune or genuine accident – the broken strut on the undercarriage and an early problem with a leaking radiator. Naturally, the part played by the adverse weather conditions was something no one had any control over. But other subsequent delays were less easy to explain away. Who or what had brought about the problem with those stolen or mislaid accumulators, the empty petrol tanks just before take-off and the mysterious piece of wire which had caused engine failure? Then there was the scale of the destructive overnight looting of 'souvenirs' which had spirited away so many crucial parts from the unguarded and damaged monoplane which had been left in temporary storage on the quay at Calais, following its dip into the sea. It looked very much as if these foraging raids had been calculated to ensure the machine would be, to all intents and purposes, grounded for good. It was all very strange and more than fortunate that the Antoinette's works in Puteaux had an improved new model on their production line, which was ready enough to be finished in a hurry.

It is possible to argue that subtle pressures were brought to bear on Latham's team. There could have been promises of army aircraft contracts or substantial financing for further experimental development of the Antoinette. Perhaps not for nothing, an unfounded and possibly scurrilous rumour had been going around that, true to form, that unflaggingly unscrupulous operator, Hart O. Berg, was inveigled in some mischief in order to give de Lambert's Wright machine extra time to prepare a challenge. Naturally, Levavasseur had been quick to dismiss any such suspicion of sabotage. But one should consider that wagers were being laid on the outcome of the flight; it was an odds-on chance that a relative outsider like Blériot might just pip Latham at the post. In the end, perhaps it was all more a matter of politics. The role of the *Daily Mail* and other Northcliffe newspapers had been clear; they had whipped up public enthusiasm for the competition in Britain, but the true *raison d'être* behind the prize was being driven hard by the 'Chief's' obsessive political lobbying for air power to be taken seriously by the War

Office. His newspaper's slogan 'England is no longer an Island' was about to be proven in the most effective way possible. Just how deep was his finger in the pie? Whatever or whoever held the answer, it remains certain that an element of stage-management of this historic occasion was swinging into action to ensure a successful and acceptable outcome. Time had been gained. In the space of a few days, the formerly disdainful Blériot had revised his opinion as to the worth of entering this competition. It was now a race to see who could get airborne first: Latham or Blériot. Intriguingly, the most uncanny incident of all was yet to come.

A report in the *Lancaster Guardian* later makes it clear that in order to get an early start, Latham had agreed to sleep in the team's Hôtel de la Plage in Sangatte that night, instead of his rather more luxurious accommodation in the Grand Hôtel in Calais, where he usually stayed.[7] In *The Times*, their despatch adds how:

> M. Latham, at the express desire of M. Levavasseur, agreed to get as much sleep as possible between 1 a.m.– when he returned to Sangatte – and the time he should get up and mount his machine. To ensure this, M. Levavasseur possessed himself of M. Latham's alarm clock, and it was settled that he should call the aviator at 3 a.m. if the wind seemed light enough for a trial. In any case he was to arouse him at 4.[8]

This crucial fact – if it is true – that Léon Levavasseur took away Latham's alarm clock is a startling revelation and an important point that was overlooked by many aeronautical correspondents. There is similar version of this story which claims Latham had given a written note to his engineer at midnight reminding him to 'waken him at 3.30 a.m. and to send the team to the shed'.[9] Either way, the evidence is there that Latham fully intended his engineer to wake him in the early hours, whatever the weather. It is not too speculative to believe that the tussle just endured down at the port over whose escort vessels were to be used would have convinced him that Blériot intended to fly within a few hours. His rival's threat was not a tentative aspiration, but a certainty. Latham would have been determined to be up at first light, ready to be the first away.

Aeronautical history has ignored, and rightly so, another fanciful anecdotal account passed down as family history by the descendents of one branch of Latham's English cousins. This version hinted that the aviator could not be roused in time on the fateful night because he was 'in the arms of a beautiful woman'.[10] It can only be assumed that Latham's reputation with the ladies, when combined with implications drawn from of Eileen Gray's presence in Sangatte, quite possibly stirred up quite a bit of gossip at the time. Whether this story can be taken seriously as the deterring factor is highly debatable in the absence of evidence.

The agreed account put out by most press reports which came to be generally believed puts the blame fairly and squarely on Levavasseur for not waking Latham in time, but allows his excuse that he had looked out at the weather several times during the night and had decided the wind too strong, each time. However, it is important to draw attention to the fact that this information does not quite tally with how *The Times*' correspondent recorded the events of that night, afterwards writing that:

Incredible as it may sound, though, there was virtually a flat calm at 3 o'clock, M. Levavasseur did not apparently realise the fact, and allowed M. Latham to sleep on. At 4 o'clock he again completely misjudged the weather conditions.

And so it was that the occupants of l'Hôtel de la Plage were allowed sleep on undisturbed while Blériot's crew had been very wide awake and very busy. Just after 4 a.m. they had their man and machine in the air.

The reporter for *The Times* who, apparently, had been more assiduous than Latham's engineer in waiting up all night to watch the weather, subsequently gives a graphic account of the scene he witnessed soon after dawn broke. He had spotted the lone figure of Levavasseur up and about in the empty Latham camp at 5 a.m. and had witnessed the sight of him looking up skywards as Blériot passed overhead:

> From 4 a.m. until the departure of M. Blériot I had frequently turned my glass on M.Latham's aeroplane tent adjoining the old works, clearly visible about three miles away and was astounded at the absence of any life or movement in the vicinity. I was well aware that Antoinette VII was practically ready for a flight, and that M.Latham … had [made] all final arrangements for starting from 3.30 a.m. onwards; and I realized the splendid opportunity for an attempt afforded by the virtually calm weather. On arrival there about 5.15 a.m. I saw no sign of M. Latham, though M. Levavasseur was wandering about, and had just previously been gazing at M. Blériot's monoplane vanishing like a big bird in the dim distance.

In vain, *The Times* wrote later:

> While all homage is rightly being paid to M. Blériot in tribute of his epoch-making success, every one will deeply sympathise with M. Latham when the… facts, of which I and only a few others were fully cognisant, are realised.

In the light of these reports, it cannot go unasked why Levavasseur had waited until he was certain Blériot was well on his way before he made a move to rouse his own team? Had a deal been done? In *The Times*, a leading article later scathingly pointed an accusing finger at the 'supineness or excessive caution of his [Latham's] friends'. And that was not the end to it.

Throughout every one of his despatches, *The Times* aeronautical correspondent repeatedly gave indications of deep unease in his assessment of the whole affair. The tenor of these reports should not be ignored. The journalist was careful to point out that, following the shock of finding Blériot had stolen a march on that fateful morning, the Antoinette machine had been brought out of its shed 'rather tardily' by the mechanics who worked under the supervision of Levavasseur and Gastambide. Then, despite the machine being 'ready' it was still some three hours later before Latham was up in the pilot's seat, revving the engine and impatiently poised for take-off. In the meantime, his pair of co-directors kept him waiting, standing with their backs to him immersed in a long-drawn out discussion. The longer they hesitate, the stronger the rising breeze is blowing. It must be wondered what brought about this further delay? Was it fear that Latham would do damage to their latest pristine, just-out-of-the-workshop model VII Antoinette? Was it their concern for his safety? Or was it, perhaps, that they did not wish him to follow immediately in the wake of Blériot with a faster crossing time, which he undoubtedly would do with a more powerful engine, as would be later proved, for this would steal much of the thunder from the Blériot triumph. Whatever their reason, the blow eventually fell with devastating effect on the young pilot. They had waited so long that the wind was now too strong. They would not allow Latham to fly. As *The Times* put it: 'The man who had undoubtedly led the van in the attempt to fly across the Channel was thus robbed of a splendid chance to carry out this project.'

As Latham climbed down from the cockpit of his machine, several less than loyal newsmen noted the tears in Latham's eyes and wrote gleefully that the young man had 'cried like a child'. It was a cheap and facile comment. The emotion demonstrated was not evidence of immature disappointment but rather more the signal of a dark emotional and bitter anger that his wrath could not hold back. He had been let down and let down badly by people he thought he could trust.

Stoically, Latham had immediately sent a telegraph in French to M. Blériot: 'Cordial congratulations,' he wrote, adding the message 'I hope to follow you soon'. He had then walked back to his hotel, seen by most of the watching newsmen as a lonely figure, although the *New York Herald* adds a sympathetically piquant touch by telling readers how he was 'leaning on the arm of his friend Rolls'. Only *The Times* correspondent seems to have been allowed a true glimpse of Latham's ice-cold anger and frustration: 'At 8.30 I left him locked in his room, orders being given that he was not to be disturbed. "Why won't they let me start? It is cruel," he kept saying to me, "… I have often flown in as strong a wind as this"'.

Maybe so. But, clearly, he had not yet realised that his flying skills were not as important as other elements on the agenda of those who wished to make a strong political point out of the historic first flight of the English Channel. Northcliffe's scheming had worked. The dread of impending danger from hostile foreign aircraft flying into England from Europe was no longer an unfounded fear. The message had been hammered home. The reaction can be summed up by a despatch that appeared in the often critical rival journal, the *Daily News*: 'A rather sinister significance will, no doubt, be found in the presence of our great fleet at Dover just at the very moment when, for the first time, a flying man passed over that sacred silver streak and flitted far above the masts of the greatest battleship.'

As might be expected, press coverage all over Europe for the first-ever Channel flight was extensive and not just a godsend for newsmen struggling to find something to write about in the dog days of a mid-summer languor. The *Daily Mail* swiftly set about portraying the previously almost unheard of winner of the prize as a simple family man with five children. It puffed the apparent *naïveté* of Blériot's question asking onlookers 'which way is it?' as worthy of some innocent bumbling amateur prepared to take-off without compass or clear directions. It drew attention to his bravely disregarded injured foot that was burned in a previous accident which, despite the pain, had not put him off flying. The clear intention was to present him as unspoiled and unpolished; quite the antithesis of his erstwhile rival Latham, the cool and sophisticated international sportsman and daredevil record-breaker.

Blériot has landed at Dover, 25 July 1909. (Royal Aeronautical Society Library)

The account of Blériot's landing on the cliffs above Dover, as his friend, the aeronautical correspondent for *Le Matin*, Charles Fontaine, guided him down by waving a huge French tricolour, has been well documented in print and graphic illustration and needs no repetition here. Whoever had hit on the idea of providing the enormous tricolour had concocted a masterstroke of stage management for the occasion. The ploy is clearly identified by Wohl, who writes how: 'Fontaine's flag became an important constituent of the ensuing celebrations… constantly at Blériot's side'.[11] With its appearance in almost every photo opportunity in London and Paris, the symbolism of the French tricolour was milked for all it was worth.

The editor of *Le Matin* unashamedly climbed on the bandwagon by declaring his newspaper had been working 'behind the scenes' at all times, and as if to provide further proof of their close association with Blériot and the demonstrable power and influence of the French press, *Le Matin* arranged for his aeroplane to be placed on display outside the windows of their offices in Paris for several days.[12] One has but to wonder if Northcliffe's pride was not a mite dented by all this rival publicity?

All in all, it is not an exaggeration to say that the reaction throughout the whole of the French press was ecstatic. Each of their reports endeavoured to outdo the next with undisguised partisan glee, moving *The Times* to comment dryly that:

> Paris has been attacked by a violent attack of Blériot fever, and for the moment, everything else, including the new Cabinet and its programme is forgotten… Leading articles in all the newspapers hail M. Blériot's flight as a great French victory.

Every French journalist worth his salt scrambled to include a mention of notable heroes of the past who could illustrate similar achievements to boost national pride. *Le Temps* cited Blanchard, the pioneer of cross-Channel flight in 1785, Zedée the inventor of the submarine, Lavoisier, Lamarck, Cuvier, Claude Bernard, Pasteur, Berthelot and Curie, claiming how: 'In serving science these great minds have done a service to their country…'

Much was made of the fact that the winner was 'a Frenchman born and bred' and M. Quinron, the president of the French Aerial League, taking his cue from the *Daily Mail*'s mantra, was quoted in *The Times* as saying: 'The sea is no longer a barrier. Relations between nations will undergo a change. The strategic and political situation of certain peoples will be transformed'.

It was all gripping stuff. Aviation in France was once more in ascendancy and in Britain, the Northcliffe bandwagon was launched.

When viewed in the cold and analytical light of retrospect, Blériot's reception in London was a triumph for Northcliffe's cause. The publicity triggered Parliamentary debate and the air defence lobby once more moved into action with much belligerent argument and agitation as to whether practical experience was preferable to the setting up of government-sponsored and science-based research.[13]

Aéroplane BLÉRIOT

Monoplan, type XI *(traversée de la Manche, 25 Juillet 1909)*. Envergure des ailes: 8=60; longueur: 7=50; surface portante: 14 m. carrés. Moteur **Anzani** 25 H P; Hélice de 2=10 à 1250 tours. Poids total avec pilote et essence pour 2 heures: 300 kilos.
A. M. L.

*Opposite:* Fontaine and his French tricolour accompanied Blériot on every possible occasion, 1909. (Royal Aeronautical Society Library)

*Right:* Blériot's aeroplane hanging on display outside the windows of the offices of *Le Matin*, in Paris, 1909. (Harman Collection)

It is interesting to reflect at this point on the attitude of editorial staff at *The Times* newspaper in their reportage of the Blériot triumph, and it cannot be ignored that there lay a distinct undercurrent of support for the leading part Latham had played in the episode. To what extent this demonstrates a subtle determination on the part of *The Times*' editors and leader writers not to ape the *Daily Mail*'s slant on the story is worth considering. These were difficult and disturbing times for the people who worked for the paper. Northcliffe's purchase of their august journal, some sixteen months earlier, had been a long-drawn-out process, much of it conducted behind the scenes and, despite assurances to the managing director, Moberly Bell, that editorial freedom in *The Times* would be maintained, the change of ownership had not gone down well with the paper's old guard. Northcliffe's methods were looked upon as dubious and deep concerns easily voiced. It was believed by the staff that *The Times*, as an institution, had a reputation to maintain a certain style and, in their view, the 'Chief' did not understand how things should be done. He had no background of elite public school and university and their opinion was that: 'He is not a man educated to English standards. His mind is not akin to the class of people to whom it [the paper] is designed to appeal.'[14] Such criticism carried a distinct whiff of class distinction, but the fact remained: The 'Chief' was not one of them. And never would be. '*The Times* was a caste newspaper, and Lord Northcliffe did not belong to that caste'.[15] Already, signs of storms to come were ruffling the waters. A deep-set suspicion was festering between the editor-in-chief, George E. Buckle and the new owner, and while Northcliffe may have dropped his official championing of Latham in favour of Blériot, *The Times'* editorials fixedly continued to remind readers of the importance and sterling worth of the young Anglo-French aviator's contribution to the historic episode. How Latham had made the running; how Latham conducted the first, albeit failed attempt: 'the world will surely not forget to honour this man's pluck, ability, and pioneer attempt at flying the Channel'. It seems obvious that some people near the top were keen to remember that this urbane and experienced sportsman had been an Oxford and Balliol College man. There is the faint sound of ranks closing. As for the triumphant Blériot? In the eyes of *The Times'* editorial staff, he was probably just a jumped-up little tradesman from the backwoods of Cambrai who spoke no English and looked as furtively foreign as a string of garlic sausages.

In the meantime, a well-satisfied Lord Northcliffe had arranged a celebration lunch at the Savoy Hotel and planned to be at Victoria Station to meet the train bearing Blériot and his wife from Dover in order to greet them in person. Among the notables he had assembled at the station were Comte de Lastours, who represented the French Ambassador, Paul Cambon, who would join them later; Lady Augusta Fane, Lady Letchworth, Colonel Bonham, and, not surprisingly, the directors of the London branch of M. Blériot's motor headlamp business. Interestingly, the welcoming party also included Latham's friend the Hon. C.S. Rolls. A motorcade had been arranged to bring the VIP party to the Savoy Hotel, where even bigger guns were waiting to offer greetings and congratulations.

Foremost among the guests at the luncheon was the Liberal Government's Secretary of State in the War Office, Richard Haldane. It was a tremendous coup for Northcliffe to have persuaded this prominent politician to drag himself away from Cabinet and other pressing Parliamentary duties, even if only for the length of time it took for him to make the welcoming speech. Had Latham been invited to the gathering? Perhaps. But he was not there.

The luncheon guest list reveals that Northcliffe had not hesitated to call upon as many influential people as he could find. Despite the short notice, he had managed to garner the support of an impressive number of the great and the good; and a fair complement of the not so great, nor so good, to boot. Apart from the most prominent members of the French Diplomatic service, the distinguished invitees included the renowned Sir Thomas Lipton, the sporting yachtsman of Lipton Teas fame, while British aeronautical interests were represented by one of the founders of the British Aero Club, the wealthy wine-merchant and balloonist, Frank Hedges Butler, who had been joined by Colonel Capper, an army man and one of the best-known experts on ballooning and aviation. Major Baden-Powell of the Scots Guards, brother of the famous Mafeking hero had been also wheeled out to acknowledge his role as the author of Northcliffe's famous phrase 'we should no longer be an island' and there were several of Northcliffe's old cronies and business and legal advisors who had rallied round. Another current popular idol of the public's imagination was also in attendance; the arctic explorer, Mr Shackleton, never a one to miss a free lunch and the chance of some publicity.

Perhaps striking a more sinister note was the presence of a certain Dr Glazebrook, who was rumoured to have had close ties to Sir Basil Zaharoff, the notorious arms dealer about whom there were always guarded whispers whenever men lingered over their port and cigars. If the Press Baron was intent on making his point that the flight across the Channel was a graphic warning of the possibility of dangerous air attacks during wartime, maybe Glazebrook had a role to play.

Hoards of press people had been roped in to provide a decent audience for the speeches. Moberly Bell, managing director of *The Times*, was there, as were the editors of both the British and Continental editions of the *Daily Mail* together with the sub-editor of the *Evening News* and, crucially, the *Daily Mail*'s advertising manager. Northcliffe had insisted that invitations be sent to the most loyal of the paper's advertising revenue customers: 'Must have them. They will be impressed no end,' he is quoted as saying.[16] Moreover, guests like the American retail giant, H. Gordon Selfridge, were important to have present: not only were they the key to the survival of his newspapers – they were wealthy, innovative and extremely astute in marketing a message. When the Blériot aeroplane was subsequently brought to London to be put on display to the public, Selfridge arranged for it to be viewed in his magnificent newly opened department store in Oxford Street. It was the largest retail store in Europe, if not in the world. The little flying machine was installed beside the Department of Sports, Motor Requisites and Motor Clothing, so that curious shoppers could gawk in awe at the machine of the future. The response generated from the general public was amazing. At least 120,000 people filed past it in the four days it remained on view here.

As might be expected, Northcliffe's speech at the luncheon had been carefully crafted to link Blériot with the names of France's most glorious heroes and, the following day, *The Times* dutifully published his oration in full. The 'Chief' had declared M. Blériot to be:

… one who the whole world today knew most truly represented the old blood of Gaul…[who had] created a record which would rank for all time with the best of the deeds of the best Frenchmen (cheers), with the first flight of Montgolfier, with the first photograph taken by a Frenchman, Niepce, with the first colour photograph taken by Lumière, with the discovery of radium by M. & Mme Curie, with the invention of iron-plated ships, indeed, one tired in naming all the ideas which had come out of France.

Naturally he wove in a skilful reference to the *entente cordiale*:

… we who call ourselves Anglo-Saxons … always in the van of progress … must reflect sometimes that ideas, like M. Blériot, come out of France. (Laughter and cheers.) He was one of those who held that every man had two countries, his own and France, (cheers) who greatly rejoiced in the good feeling which existed between the two countries, who believed and knew that the peace of the world largely depended on the relations of those two countries.

It was a clever speech and one that would please patriots on both sides of the Channel. M. Blériot's splendid French *élan* was duly admired and his business given a mention. Northcliffe 'supposed there were many present who had travelled thousands of miles at night by his lamps'. The Press Baron had then drawn attention to the presence of their own Mr Shackleton, sitting there beside the honoured guests, thereby raising more cheers from the assembly. Was he ignoring the fact that, like himself, Shackleton had been born in Ireland into an Anglo-Irish family?[17] This Irishness was a distinction which they were equally shy of revealing and certainly, it would not have been useful in putting forward the point that followed, for he went on to declare:

> '... if they searched the two countries over they could not find a more typical Frenchman and a more typical Englishman. In Shackleton, they had careful preparation, immense determination, the hardihood amid sufferings, the patience, the plodding, the never-turning back determinations that enabled him to do a deed of which Englishmen were as proud today as the French were of M. Blériot.

And he went on to speak of:

> ... the contrast of having here the genius of the two peoples who had done more for civilisation in the world that any other peoples. He felt proud that his newspaper was in a most humble and unexpected way associated with M. Blériot.

It is tempting to speculate how he might have couched this speech if Latham's earlier attempt had been successful. With Latham as the winner of the *Daily Mail* prize could Northcliffe have alluded to the two heroes as Anglo-French and Anglo-Irish gentlemen with quite the same dramatic effect? Probably not.

Latham, in any case, would have most likely protested loudly and in public at being labelled as anything but French. His quarter English blood had been always a sensitive point, despite the closeness of his English cousins and ease with which he moved in English society. Some measure of how bitterly he later resented the way these claims had been puffed up by the Northcliffe newspapers for their own ends before he was dropped so hastily in favour of the unambiguously Gallic Blériot may be read into his reaction, some two years later, when the aeronautical magazine *Flight* mistakenly included his name among the invited guests at a Northcliffe garden party. The following week they published a recant, almost an apology, having received a trenchant letter from Latham strenuously denying that he had attended such a gathering.[18] It was as if the idea of his presence as an invited guest to a Northcliffe soirée was – for him – utterly inconceivable.

The public fêting of Blériot also suited the mood in Europe as much as in England. Soon after the event, it was tartly observed by *La Revue Aérienne* that 'Blériot, a family man with five children was no *angliche* dandy' and it is clear that the cartoonists of the day made much of what Fortier describes as Blériot's 'drooping moustache *à la gauloise* which gave the French masses a hero'.[19] For *Daily Mail* readers everywhere, Blériot had fitted the bill almost too perfectly as the image of a perfidious foreign invader from the skies.

On the day of the Blériot celebratory luncheon, another item tucked away discreetly in a different column of *The Times* is worthy of mention. This is a report that the outgoing French government had been pleased to announce the conferring of *Legion*

BLÉRIOT          ET SA FAMILLE

Le célèbre Aviateur Français qui a passé le premier sur son Monoplan,
le Détroit du Pas-de-Calais, le 25 Juillet 1909

Blériot – the family man – was no '*angliche* dandy'. (Harman Collection)

*d'honneur* decorations on a number of French aviators. These included M. Blériot, Gabriel Voisin, Delagrange, Levavasseur, and Archdeacon. The despatch added that the Minister for Foreign Affairs was arranging for the bestowal of similar honours on various foreign aviators. These names were made public a day or two later. The recipients were Wilbur and Orville Wright, and Henri Farman. The Officer's Cross of the same Order was conferred upon the Brazilian pioneer, Santos-Dumont and the Wright brothers' American salesman, Hart O. Berg. There was no mention of Hubert Latham. His day to be decorated as *Chevalier de la Légion d'honneur* was yet to come.

In the meantime, back in Sangatte, Latham had not given up on meeting the challenge. The waiting had ended in the damp morning chill just before 6 a.m. the following morning, Tuesday 27 July. Loyal spectators once more gathered, everyone was eager to see if Latham could now make a successful attempt. The atmosphere was low key but anticipatory and some who witness the occasion may have reflected how swiftly such a historic achievement could become almost *passé* in people's minds. Latham had been a popular hero and his charm had generated widespread empathy, but still, the fact remained that the feat was no longer a novelty. The ultimate honour had been snatched by a rival. All his most dedicated fans could hope for now was that he might match the challenge.

It was not a pleasant morning. The weather had again deteriorated and, although the air was calm, rain showers intermittently swept across the camp. The watchers muttered incantations, half prayer, half mantra, as they watched Latham's monoplane take off and head seaward. The crowd cheered dutifully and the aviator waved an acknowledgement. Then he was gone.

Everyone agreed it had been a splendid take-off. The speed of the Antoinette aircraft appeared far superior to Blériot's machine, too. Within a few minutes he was already almost out of sight. Latham was flying higher and faster and within fifteen minutes the aeroplane had passed completely out of view. It was going to be a total vindication. The Antoinette engine was more powerful that the little Gnome that drove the Blériot machine and while Latham's monoplane was a much larger and heavier craft, it was capable of far higher speeds. What chances he would complete the crossing in less time and create a new record? The waiting was unbearable.

Some twenty minutes later there came a shout from the wireless room. There was news. He had been sighted approaching Dover! But the report was not clear. Could he be there already; was it possible? Those who had confidently predicted his superior engine power would see this crossing logging up a record time, far less than Blériot's thirty-six minutes and thirty seconds, were already clapping each other on the back excitedly. Then someone ran out of the wireless room, waving a message. It was true! The straits had been crossed in a much faster time, but the Antoinette and its pilot were down in the sea just two minutes short of Dover harbour. There was nothing for it but to make haste into the station to hear the confirmation for themselves. Quickly the word went round, Latham was jinxed again!

This second failed attempt provoked no shortage of newsworthy despatches which echoed the bitter disappointment of Latham's loyal aeronautical correspondent in *The Times*: '… A brilliant failure is the only description that can be applied to M. Latham's second attempt, yesterday.'

The sturdy Antoinette engine had let him down once more – but this time it was within moments of landing – just as he made his approach to the cliffs above Dover's harbour and within earshot of all the welcoming ships' horns and sirens. Although shocked by yet another mishap, Latham had remained cool and had set his machine to glide down onto to the surface of the water. But the conditions were not as benign as had been on his previous ditching into the sea. The wind was stronger and the waves more choppy. The plane landed heavily and he was thrown forward against the struts on impact, breaking his goggles. Shards of glass cut deeply into his forehead and nose, his face was covered in blood and he had the beginnings of a swollen black eye. Later, after his rescue and return to dry land, the house surgeon from Dover Hospital, a doctor called Ridgway, was called into the Lord Warden Hotel to stitch his face. The *Daily Mail* reports how five stitches were needed, adding that the medic said he was not very much hurt. Even so, he was lucky not to have lost the eye. Curiously, this same Dr J.C. Ridgway was to recall that encounter with Latham not without a certain unease some three years later when in Africa.[20]

When interviewed by *The Times*, Latham had spoken of his reaction to the mishap:

> … in another couple of minutes, if the motor had held out, I should have been able to land near Shakespeare Cliff… I wasn't too anxious after the aeroplane struck the water. From my previous experience I knew that it would float for some time, and I had seen the quantity of shipping that there was in Dover harbour and knew that some vessels would get out to me soon… As soon as I saw the warship's pinnaces and tugs coming out to me I stood up

in the monoplane and waved my hand to let them know that there was nothing seriously the matter with me.

Finding out what had caused engine failure had the rumours once more circulating among the aeronautical correspondents, although, this time, the main culprit would seem to have been the weather. In the *Daily Mail*, Latham was quoted as blaming 'excessive moisture in the air' or on rain getting into the sparking plugs. *The Times* correspondent had little to add to this theory: 'I had a few words with M. Latham before his departure from Dover last night, when he merely reiterated his intention of making further attempts to cross the Channel, but was disinclined to say much about his unlucky flight…'

Writing in *Motor News*, the following week, its Irish editor R.J. Mecredy sagely comments on Latham's second experience of engine failure: 'More, often, can be learned by failures than by successes.' This expert goes on to wonder if – unlike Latham – perhaps Blériot's over-cautious habit of not flying at full throttle had put less strain on his little engine?[21] Yet the outcome clearly was the cause of some worrying concern:

> It might have been the good luck of one, bad luck of the other. As sportsmen, we like to think so in Latham's case. As enthusiasts, we do not like to think so in that of Blériot. As the Americans say in their advertisements, 'There's a reason.'

He was not the only expert left scratching his head.

In the meantime, various gatherings had been arranged to honour Louis Blériot. The English Aero Club was to present him with a gold medal and the roll-call of invited guests to attend a ceremonial dinner at the Ritz Hotel read like a *Who's Who* of recent aeronautical achievements. Charlie Rolls and René Raoul-Duval both turned up, as did many of Latham's other loyal friends. During the evening, they generously toasted his absence and put another spin on the story of his plucky failed attempt by blaming tricky down winds on the Cliffs of Dover, which had obviously precluded any attempt he may have made to successfully glide his stalled machine for the last remaining minutes far enough to make a safe landing place on the headland.

Apart from his friends in the British Aero Club, other London supporters of Latham were also not for letting the French have it all their own way in bestowing honour on just one hero of the hour. A short item in *The Times* on 30 July gave notice that one of the City's most prestigious and ancient livery companies – The Clothworkers' Company – was to confer the distinction of honorary freedom of the company to Hubert Latham in recognition of his great courage and achievement in aviation. The despatch reminded its readers that Latham's great-grandfather, Thomas Latham, had been master of the company in 1810–11. As it turned out, this decision to honour him, which marked their members' purposeful acknowledgement of Latham's English blood, had been a mite hasty in view of his French nationality – which was thought to disqualify him – but this disadvantage was subsequently overcome by a committee aptly, and usefully, chaired by one of his English kinsmen, William Latham.[22] The ceremony of honorary admission to the brotherhood took place four months later, he having received their approval: 'so far as regards its social amenities and advantages, *quantum valeat*'.

The *Daily Mail*, too, perhaps stung into action by the continued popularity of Blériot's rival in the public mind, had announced it would award a consolation prize of a £100 (2,500 francs) silver cup which they said was '… a tribute to Mr. Latham's pluck, which rises superior to repeated misfortunes'. So despite everything, Latham was still in the news. Everyone wanted to know his plans.

*The Times* declared that: 'Tonight, M. Latham leaves for a few days rest in the country, and M. Levavasseur attends a meeting of the Antoinette Company in Paris tomorrow to decide upon the renewal of their cross-Channel attempts…'
and the despatch goes on to add: 'M. Latham arrived at Calais at 10 o'clock yesterday morning and had a most enthusiastic reception. Notwithstanding the injuries to his face, he expects to be able to make his next attempt within a few days when his new aeroplane is ready.' But it was not to be.

The directors of the Antoinette Company had made a decision. They now ruled that Latham should abandon another attempt to cross the Channel for the time being. The news must have made Latham seethe with frustration and annoyance. Yet, when interviewed by a journalist he is clearly seeking reassurance: 'Will not everyone say I am giving it up like a coward?' he asks. Although being told 'emphatically' this would not be the case, his next observation still carries a poignant note, 'Very well, I will agree to their wishes and will do my best to prove at Reims [a forthcoming air show] that I and my machine are not *always* failures!'[23]

Latham's optimism and confidence were close to breaking point. The injuries he had sustained on coming down into the sea at Dover, although superficial, had brought on an attack of fever, thankfully short-lived, but he would need to be careful; the legacy of the long battle to control his albuminuria had left him vulnerable to any extra strain on his health. All he could do for the time being was rest, recuperate from his injuries, and try to keep up his spirits in the hope that his two co-directors would keep their promise to have two Antoinette monoplanes ready by 22 August for him to fly in what should be a noteworthy event: the world's first Air Show, in Reims.

Meanwhile, it was a comfort that at least one aeronautical correspondent had remained so supportive. A cheery postcard from *The Times* man, Harry Delacombe, bearing the message: '*Au Revoir*. Get well soon!' had been followed by a personal letter addressed to him from this journalist's West Kensington home to say that he was going to cover the show at Reims and would see him there.[24] A despatch dated 2 August had merely informed readers of the aeronautical column that: 'M. Latham left here for Paris this afternoon with his mother. The injuries which he sustained on the occasion of the last attempt to fly across the Channel have not yet healed, and his head is still bandaged.'

Once back in Paris, the trickle of sympathetic letters received from close family and friends was turning into a deluge of supportive messages. Each post brought a new batch: many from well-wishers who were perfect strangers, some merely addressed to M. Latham, Aviator, Paris. One enclosed a four-leaf clover for luck. The letters and postcards arrived from his French and English fans alike; from the hands of young children to long and detailed commentary which offered analytical theories on aerodynamics. His friend from Dover, Eric Crundall, writes to 'congratulate you on what everyone admits

Poster for the World's First Aviation
Show at Reims, August 1909.
(HLPP)

to be a splendid example of pluck and enterprise', declaring that: 'No one was more sorry
than I that Blériot forestalled you – but it was the machine and not the man and, as far
as you personally are concerned, your achievement is far greater than his.'[25] Crundall's
only gripe is reserved for the Antoinette's dubious engineering innovations. 'It may seem
rather rash of me to criticise a man like Levavasseur,' he went on, '[but] I would not go
up in the machine for an extended flight unless it had a magneto ignition and a proper
carburettor. They would add very few pounds to the weight…'

And then, among the letters, one that was rather more special. Written from the Carlton
Hotel in Pall Mall on the day following Blériot's flight, twenty-four hours too late for him
to have received it before his last attempt, the bold and exuberant hand writes in English
of witnessing the Blériot flight and tells him of plans to pass through Calais the following
Thursday. She writes:

> I don't know whether I shall be able to stop … perhaps you might come to the train – I
> sent you a wire from Dover. I was there at the time of Blériot's arrival … saw everything. I
> wanted you to come to London but I know it is quite impossible. I know also that you will

have been terribly hurt and disappointed … I want to see you, to comfort you. Please be prudent: you are so young, dear, only go slowly. You will make your name. I love you, dearest and quite confident you will do something soon. Write, my dear…[26]

The flamboyantly distinctive penmanship is signed Edith – and while her identity remains a mystery, it is a name which can be attributed to at least two of Latham's known acquaintances. One was Edith Latham, an English cousin about his own age with whose family he had a close and affectionate association, while the second 'Edith', also possibly close to him since his days at Oxford, was related by her marriage to one of his cousins in the City – which raises a question over the use of one phrase in the letter: 'you are so young, dear', suggesting this writer may have been a person somewhat older than him. Curious and tantalising, because the true identity of this ardent correspondent remains unsolved to this day.

As for the upcoming Air Meeting in Reims, had Latham known that his luck was about to take a hugely improved turn for the better, his heart and spirits would have been given an even higher lift to boost confidence. Good times lay ahead.

# SEVEN
# Idol of the Crowds

The world's first international air show, the *Grande Semaine d'Aviation de la Champagne,* was an historic occasion for the French nation. Planned as a festival designed to display France's renewed leadership status in aviation, it was held on the Bétheny Plains, just north of Reims, for one week, commencing 22 August 1909.

With the intention of making it a noteworthy event on the social calendar, the president of the organising committee, Melchior, Marquis de Polignac, the well-connected head of the leading champagne-making firm, *Pommery,* and one of Latham's sports-loving acquaintances, had seen to it that all the other principal champagne producers in the area had been roped in to provide sponsorship prizes. This guaranteed a copious supply of free bubbly for aeronautical correspondents and invited guests. The firms of *Moët et Chandon* offered the prize for height; *Pommery* for the fastest daily lap; *Veuve Clicquot* for the longest passenger flight; *Heidseick, Monopole et Roederer* combined for the prize given for the fastest three laps of the course. The *Grand Prix de la Champagne* for the flight of the longest duration was to be shared by all the sponsors, and in addition, the American entrepreneur and owner of the *New York Herald*, Gordon Bennett, was to offer an annual trophy and a purse of £1,000 for the highest speed over two laps. It would be a veritable glimpse into the future – for no one could be sure what might be the outcome of all this aeronautical experimentation. Those with vision plotted an astute mixture of business and pleasure. As spectators watched the aeronauts performing in the skies above their heads, there would be plenty of opportunity for relaxation in the splendid dining facilities at the venue, provided by the proprietor of the Paris Hôtel Castiglione, M. Borgo. Cannily, the aviators themselves were not paid to fly. The reason for this decision, as the *New York Herald* later carefully explained to its readers at the time of the second Reims Air Show, was to foster a truly altruistic spirit. The aeronauts 'will have to win the prize-money by sheer effort and skill and the sporting interest is thus accentuated.'[1] The organisers of the 1909 show hoped it might prove to be an invigorating social event to liven up the dull days of August. They were not to be disappointed. Despite prevailing wet and windy conditions the public had responded to its novelty value with enthusiasm. Crowds flocked to the venue, undeterred by either rain squalls or mud underfoot. The grandstand alone could hold 10,000 people and it was reckoned that by the end of the week the attendance had reached almost 500,000 spectators.

Latham's Antoinette attracts plenty of attention from spectators at the Reims Air Show, August 1909. (HLPP)

The people came for thrills and excitement and a glimpse of famous faces. Apart from well-publicised names among those participating in the events there was a gathering of world-class notables among the distinguished visitors. And what a coterie of notables! Their presence in itself attracted a larger than usual amount of press correspondents. Pressure to find decent accommodation in the area became impossible. Although top journalists like the *Daily Mail*'s Harry Harper could earn at least eight guineas a week, there were complaints that:

> ... all the hotels are full, also furnished houses hired for the occasion or spare rooms placed at their disposal by tradespeople. A single-bedded room in an ordinary hotel £1 12s (40 francs). For a double – not less than 75 francs (£3). The best hotel rooms cost 100 francs (£4) a night.[2]

Northcliffe's newspapers were punctilious in reminding their readers that the famous pilots who were to demonstrate their skills in the competitions were almost all French: Blériot, Delagrange, Farman, Ferber, de Lambert, Latham, Lefebvre, Paulhan. There was one Briton, George Cockburn, and one American, Glenn Curtiss. Some of the other press correspondents in attendance questioned why the Wright brothers had declined to make an appearance and it was put about that they were otherwise engaged. Orville Wright had pre-arranged to demonstrate their machine in Germany, hoping for some firm orders and his brother Wilbur was not in Europe at all, but busy holding the fort at home. Perhaps on the advice of their agent Hart O. Berg – whose Channel hopeful, the Comte de Lambert, had pulled out of the *Daily Mail* contest without much of a fight – the fashionable sporting occasion at Reims may have seemed to them to promise just another frivolous distraction from the serious reality of selling aeroplanes to various European war departments. The honour of winning prizes and competitions was all very well, but did such prizes garner sales in the end? When it came to the crunch the Wright brothers' dedication to flying was not so much to gather sporting accolades as to gain business deals.

In writing about the Reims meeting, the *Daily Mail* journalists had not made much in their despatches of the 'Chief's' own attendance at the show. Northcliffe, the expert publicist, knew when a discreet level of privacy was more politic. Nonetheless, a selection of his senior news correspondents such as Hamilton Fyfe, the leader writer for the *Daily Mail* and the author, Edgar Wallace, had been invited to join him in his private box. Official observers despatched by the British Government included Generals Henderson and Grierson and the top cavalry man, General Sir Robert French; the Admiralty sent Captain Robert Falcon Scott, who was already preparing for his Antarctic expedition. It was rumoured that Secretary of State for the Army, Richard Haldane, had also quietly slipped across to Bétheny to see the potential performance of the latest aircraft designs for himself.

Quite a frisson of excitement was generated when a *Daily Mail* despatch mentioned that the Liberal Chancellor of the Exchequer, David Lloyd George, was also visiting the show at Reims. A story had been circulating among the Press Corps all week that a quietly arranged meeting had taken place between Lloyd George and Northcliffe.

Latham's 'lucky 13', the Antoinette IV in which he did so well at Reims, August 1909. (Royal Aeronautical Society Library)

Known to be vociferous opponents in their politics and public statements, rumour had it that these gentlemen had found themselves, on this occasion, in complete agreement in their views on the future importance of aviation. Conscious that there was only one Englishman competing for awards at Reims, the *Daily Mail* took the risk of publishing an interview with Lloyd George, in which he frankly supported Northcliffe on the future importance of aircraft. The Chancellor had made no secret of his disappointment with the British contribution, commenting, 'How hopelessly behind we are in these great and historic experiments!' His voice undoubtedly provided a timely and important boost to Northcliffe's persistent campaign but the 'Chief' may have pushed his lobbying coverage of aviation just a bit too far. *Daily Mail* readers were becoming confused. They did not expect to find the opinions of this annoying little Welshman greeted with approval in their favourite newspaper and an increasing amount of readers' letters were received which carried peevish complaints. Unperturbed, Northcliffe met the challenge by publishing a strongly worded response, explaining the paper's policy was 'to convince … that a new age has dawned, to rouse them to action at least, and to kindle a living interest in flight among all our citizens.'[3] The complainers were mollified. There were no more letters of protest. Sales of the 'busy man's newspaper' continued to rise. No serious damage done.

By contrast, editors of *The Times* had made very little of Lloyd George or his attendance at the Reims Air Show. Their coverage of this event adopted a serious tone which confined itself to dull despatches which carefully reported results of the various races and competitions, listing aircraft speeds, heights and other data without comment. Clearly, this editorial department was making sure there was to be no opportunity given for vulgar brawling in print over the 'Chief's' consorting with Lloyd George. *The Times* also chose to ignore the type of gossip favoured by the *New York Herald* correspondents, who had reported the attendance of the wife of the former President of the United States, Mrs Roosevelt, accompanied by the American Ambassador to France, Mr White and his wife, and a party of nine or ten people.

Readers of the *Herald*, of course, expected to be regaled by splashy news headlines and Latham was guaranteed to provide plenty of these. On 27 August, the front page banner announced: 'M. Latham establishes new records at Reims by flying over ninety-six miles in gusty weather'. But in another column, the paper aimed to recreate a taste of the frivolity being swiftly attached to the novelty of the event. The sharply observed breathless excitement of a Miss Grace Meurer, one of the younger visiting American spectators, captures the scene perfectly: 'All this makes one want to go straight away and buy an aeroplane!' she had cried, 'it looks so easy and must be the most delicious way of travelling ever invented!'

Yet behind the naivety of this 'most delicious' reaction to the circus-like atmosphere and air of entertainment of the air show there stalked the more serious consideration of how new developments in aeronautics might hold value for military use. Visiting British newspaper correspondents to Reims had been quick to comment on the heavy presence of many French government officials, army chiefs and politicians. Before the week was out, the French President Fallières and his wife had made an appearance at the showgrounds, accompanied by the new Prime Minister, M. Briand, the Minister for War,

General Brun, and M. Millerand, the Minister of Public Works and Posts and Telegraphs. President Fallières had begun his tour of inspection by visiting each of the aeroplane sheds in turn, beginning with Latham's Antoinette. Then he turned his attention to the assembled pilots. As reported in *The Times* on 24 August:

> The President inspected and had a word with each of the inventors and leading pilots. He was much struck with the Antoinette, M. Blériot, and REP Monoplanes – and the Voisin, Farman, Curtiss and Wright biplanes. This was the first time the President had seen an aeroplane in the air. The wind was strong (8 miles an hour).

The distinguished visitor was intrigued to discover that between them, the pilots presented a most unusual diversity of backgrounds and training. As the introductions were made, he began to enquire of each flyer if they were employed, or previously engaged in other commercial activities, or whether their proficiency in the air had been obtained during a stint of military service.

Louis Blériot had replied that he was an engineer, trained in the Institute of Arts and Manufactures and Henri Farman told the President that he was a former professional cyclist and now in partnership with his brother as automobile dealers; Louis Paulhan previously worked as a painter and decorator; René Gasnier du Fresne was a farmer, while Léon Delagrange, the sculptor and former arts tutor, may already have been known to the visitor through his work which had been exhibited with some public acclaim at the Paris Arts Salon. When the President turned to Hubert Latham and asked him the same question, Latham must have been stuck for an answer. He could offer neither a profession, trade nor previous occupation: 'Sir, I can only describe myself as *un homme du monde*' he had said.

English commentators who reported this exchange with some amusement usually translated the phrase to mean 'a man of the world' – but it can equally be interpreted he meant to imply he was a gentleman of high society within the narrow terms imposed by the Paris *élite*. No doubt the President completely understood. The incident, however, provides insight of Latham's view of himself – taking his position as a gentleman for granted and demonstrating a cool inbred confidence that only someone from his upbringing could carry off without appearing a braggart or casting doubts on his professionally conducted easy relationship with the other flyers.

Apart from this, there was plenty going on during that week in Reims to generate gossip about Latham and the other young aviators. Stories of *risqué* goings-on in Bétheny were soon filtering back to Paris salons with much glee. It was whispered that many of the social protocols – especially for young women – were being blatantly flouted or ignored during the air show. These daring young men in their flying machines would seem to have cultivated a dangerous reputation which generated an almost hypnotic effect on sensible girls. For instance, it had not gone unnoticed that the current popular song, '*Dans mon Aéroplane*' contained the most flagrantly suggestive lyrics: 'Oh, come, Oh, come, come up in my airplane. It's just like a bird. It stays up in the air as it should… Little old Suzanne, you'll go crazy when you've seen my little bird…'[4]

As for what else was happening behind the scenes, the scandal had already got out that, against all rules, *The Globe*'s air correspondent, Harold Lafone, had smuggled at least one English girl, Gertrude Bacon, into the aeroplane sheds where the mechanics lived and slept.[5] Gertrude was, in truth, no stranger to the unconventional nature of airmen. In recent years, having shared her father's enthusiasm for the sport, she had made something of a name for herself as a pioneering female balloonist. So, thankfully, here was one young woman who was not likely to have her head turned by the superficial glamour surrounding these popular boys.

But other incidents set tongues wagging. For instance, what kind of girl could be brazen enough to send Hubert Latham a teddy bear as a lucky mascot to accompany him in his plane at the start of one competition?[6] Was it one of those English hussies who were so keen on him? Or did it signify the girl was more likely to be an American? His every move was being watched.

Lucy White (later to be Lady Baldwin) and her brother Douglas were staying in the same hotel as Latham and had spotted him at breakfast. In her memoirs, compiled many years later, Miss White's observations on his English antecedents are almost proprietorial '… he has lived more in England than in France', she recalls, adding, '… we were to see plenty later on of that slight wiry figure with the pale resolute face.' Remarking on his triumphs at the show, she comments, 'His popularity had never been for a moment in doubt – and the enthusiastic ovation which greeted him… must have gone far to atone for that moment when the Cross-Channel flight was wrested from him.'[7]

Sensing this growing intensity of feminine revolution in the air, many of the journalistic commentators and critics had been quick to notice that a number of their own female compatriots were keen to take up flying. Was such a lady to be called an 'aviatrix', an

*Opposite:* Latham and Paulhan chat with M. Henri Deutsch de la Meurthe. (HLPP)

*Right:* Latham's sisters, Edmée and Léonie, feature with him in the fashionable journal *Fémina*, No.208, 15 September 1909. (HLPP)

'aviatress' or, perhaps, more tongue in cheek, a 'female *oiseau*'?[8] But some of the rumours attached to this latest fad were almost too shocking for words. Frenchwomen were showing themselves to be no better than the English *jeune filles* in their *comportement*. They expected to be treated just like any of the male aviators. They secretly sported laced-up breeches and boots underneath their skirts and would have abandoned the latter covering altogether if they thought they could get away with it when in public.

Back in Paris, the most important question going the rounds of mothers with marriageable daughters was whether the popularity of this new sport would actually help or a hinder prospects for a girl? One thing was for sure: it was all extremely disturbing. The claim that one could pin point the whereabouts of the most popular and eligible of all the young aviators, Latham, even when he was just walking with a lady amid a crowd of people, would seem to have been no exaggeration. The sound of spectators' box cameras being constantly clicked around him never stopped.[9] The stylish person he often accompanied was thought to be his mother, but did anyone really believe it? Those with unkindest minds firmly maintained, out of earshot, that the lucky lady was most certainly old enough to be his mother. Jealously could be very unsporting.

*Left:* Never any shortage of stylish ladies willing to pose with Latham for the camera, Reims, 1909. (HLPP)

*Opposite:* Spectators in the field had no sense of the dangers overhead: Latham's monoplane and Voisin's biplane in the air, Reims, 1909. (Royal Aeronautical Society Library)

Latham did well at Reims. His winnings, overall, must have come to almost 40,000 francs. 'Lath-am, Lath-am, the ecstatic crowd of spectators had screamed, waving hats, handkerchiefs and programmes'.[10] The Antoinette monoplane achieved a new altitude record of 512ft and he was regaled as the 'hero of the meeting'.[11] Flying ninety-six miles non-stop, he was placed second to Farman in the contest for distance. When Farman took his prize for France, the band played *God Save the King* following the normal rendition of the *Marseillaise* to formally acknowledge that Henri's father was English, although long established in Paris as the resident journalist for the *Daily Telegraph*. All week long, the competition between the foremost airmen and their respective machines had been close. The American, Glenn Curtiss, beat Blériot in the Gordon Bennett Race by only five seconds with Latham taking third place. The meeting also witnessed several dramatic moments, but the most sensational near miss of two aeroplanes directly in front of the crowded grandstand was written up by *The Times* with studied restraint. The airmen involved in the incident were two of the most flamboyant aeronauts, Latham and Delagrange.

Despatches for that day record that the less-than-good weather conditions had been a hindrance all afternoon. Pilots had had the greatest difficulty in controlling the height and

speed of their machines in the strong winds. Finally, the inevitable happened. Owing to a delayed landing of one plane, the two aviators had found themselves both in the air at the same time. As they battled against the elements, the buffeting winds drove Latham and Delagrange onto a collision course likely to end right in front of the crowded grandstand. Quick-witted action was needed. Unaware of the real danger of an aircraft collision in mid-air over their heads, the crowd was thrilled by this spectacle of daredevil flying skill. They whistled and cheered as Latham and Delagrange struggled to keep control of their machines. Only in the nick of time did each manage to swerve away from the other to avoid disaster.

The full horror of what might have happened to the spectators if a crash had occurred was only realised later. Even then, it could be said this knowledge merely added a piquancy of terror which tended to attract even larger and more enthusiastic crowds to future aviation events. Fear of a public disaster never diminished the popularity of air shows; were not Latham and other popular idols perceived as almost magical and heroic knights of the air? Cast in this role they were immune from harm, or so it seemed.

Lord Northcliffe had returned to London from the Reims Air Show in high spirits. He had been pleased by the reaction of his guests to the event; political circles had taken an interest by sending fairly sensible people; and he was only slightly peeved that the opinionated young maverick, Churchill, had not honoured his promise to attend. But this was no time for leisurely pondering. The 'Chief' was soon to be off on an extended trip with his wife to the United States and Canada and he was determined to keep his fingers remain firmly in the middle of the political pie. A crafty move to engage Robert

Blatchford, owner of *The Clarion*, had been arranged. He was to visit Germany and write a series of articles for Northcliffe with the specific aim of keeping British newspaper readers concentrated on the perceived threat of war. Campaign warning beacons must be kept ablaze.

At the dinner celebrating the closing of the Reims Air Show, Latham received a finale accolade to mark his successful participation in events: a prize of 10,000 francs, awarded by the Parisian daily paper *Le Petit Journal*, 'for his beautiful flights last week'.[12] On receiving this news, Latham was gracious in accepting 'this generous gift for the Antoinette Company and its engineer, M. Levavasseur'. Then, boosted by his successes, he agreed to take up a position as an instructor in the Antoinette Flying School, where his skills would be needed to teach would-be purchasers of the monoplane the basic techniques of aviation. One of the outcomes of his popularity was a lengthening waiting list of pretty young women who vied each other to obtain lessons in his piloting skills. Requests were flooding in from France, England and America. At the equivalent of £100 for a month's tuition, this was an excellent source of income for the Antoinette Company. The sport was no longer viewed as an uncertain and often disappointing hobby for the technical minded. It was fast becoming a most chic sporting accomplishment for young and well-heeled society people.

But it would not be long before another historic 'first' for a Frenchman came to shatter the confident world of aeronautics. It was an unsought after marker. On 7 September, the twenty-seven-year-old stunt pilot, Eugene Lefebvre, crashed and died at the controls of his plane during a routine test of a new design for the Wright brothers. Barely a week earlier he had been thrilling thousands of spectators at Reims. It was the first fatal accident of its kind. Then, two weeks later, another disaster occurred. The popular Captain Ferber was killed at the Boulogne Air Show. Their deaths had a sobering effect on those who had longed for the thrill of flying aeroplanes for fun. It did not seem such a desirable a hobby after all, but rather one which echoed the Futurist predictions of technology as a ravaging beast intent on destruction.

On the day after Ferber's death, the first ever Italian Air Show, *Circuito Aereo-Brescia*, opened in Brescia. A young and relatively unknown twenty-six-year-old writer called Franz Kafka was among the 50,000 people gathered there. This writer later wrote about this experience so vividly that Wohl, in *A Passion for Wings*, opines that: '… no other text captures in such fineness of detail and with such spare elegance of language the atmosphere of the first aviation meetings … it was all "*angst, angst*", because of the way the Italians organise such undertakings.'[13] Latham, with pre-arranged commitments to fly in Germany later in September, had not attended this show, but Kafka had sought out other prominent people there and observed how the Italian poet D'Annunzio inveigled the American, Glenn Curtiss into taking him up for his first ever flight. D'Annunzio was working on a novel with an aviator as his hero, published a year later, in 1910, as *Forse Che Si Forse Che No – Perhaps Yes Perhaps No –* and was anxious to experience the sensation of flying for himself in order to write about it. He was not to be disappointed. D'Annunzio declared flight be a 'divine thing' and equal to the 'unforgettable moments of supreme happiness', a reaction which Wohl has attributed to the poet's 'natural inclination to compare the

A celebratory occasion captured by the camera which includes the Parmentier brothers, the Raoul-Duvals and – seated on Latham's right hand – what may be a rare image of their mutual friend, Eileen Gray. (HLPP)

sensation of flying to an intense erotic pleasure'.[14] One is tempted to speculate whether the poet and Latham ever engaged in debate over this concept of flying as an extremely sensual experience when they were later mutually entertained by the habitués of certain notorious Left Bank salons in Paris – which is an aspect of Latham's social life yet to be discussed.

Another question to pose must be to what extent had the deaths of Lefebvre and Ferber affected Latham? It might be argued that he had already faced up squarely to the reality of the perils to be faced in the sport. He had already experienced many crashes and mishaps – and must have been keenly aware that he had been lucky. But there had been perils faced in other sports and spheres of adventure. His experiences of the African bush had honed his sense of danger to a fine degree; he knew the value of a steady hand and a cool head. And while his cultivation of an enduring sangfroid may have fooled some observers, in actuality, Latham took few chances that were not calculated. With the precision of a practised hunter, he studied wind and weather patterns carefully. His fearlessness in the air, particularly in stormy conditions, was no hit-and-miss foolhardiness but a strategy worked out to provide protection for pilot and machine. Yet, these immensely resilient walls of confidence were accompanied by a sense of fatalism which had been nurtured by his close affinity to the natural world and a deeply philosophical way of thinking. What is to be, will be; that was the end of it.

September days passed in quickening succession and, with the disappointments and disasters of the early summer now well behind him, Latham now threw himself into a whirl of demonstration flights and air shows across Europe. Any lingering grudges he may have harboured over the frustrations of the Channel flight were sidelined, perhaps not completely forgotten, but not an apparent cause for brooding. The partridge-shooting season was in full swing in the British Isles and gave Latham a good excuse to spend several days there with friends or visiting his Latham cousins. He then returned to the Esplanade Hotel in Berlin on 20 September for the first of a series of exhibition flights which were to take place in Tempelhof, just outside the city. These demonstration flights and choice of location, as reported by the *New York Herald*, were 'due to the enterprise of Herr Wolf Wertheim, proprietor of the *Passage Kaufhaus*, a big department store.' The opportunistic move by Selfridge to grab publicity for his new London store through Blériot's flight in July had been well noted and there were those in Berlin who were not ready to be out-done by French, English or American shopkeepers. With a star personality like Latham to boost things for Herr Wertheim, the demonstration flights would be a fine precursor of the eagerly awaited performances at the official Berlin Air Week, due to take place from 26 September to 3 October.

Since the acclaimed success of Reims Air Show, Germany was determined to show its neighbour that they could also promote aeronautical skills by offering generous prizes and the prestige that accompanied record-breaking flights. To be realistic, the organisers must have known that although there would be a total of 150,000 marks in prize money, it was going to be hard to emulate the glittering novelty and social cachet that had marked the Reims Show. Consequently, the tone for Berlin was set to be a far more serious affair. Instead of an audience of French socialites full of *joie de vivre* and out to enjoy themselves, this event was planned to be a sober and controlled occasion. Important representatives of the British naval and German military personnel were to be in attendance and the several leading manufacturing companies backing the competing aviators – notably Blériot, Orville Wright and Latham – would seek to impress spectators with the superiority of their machines for use in wartime conditions, for scouting, or even in combat.[15]

Indeed, the crowds did later reveal themselves to be reluctant to display overexcitable enthusiasm, especially for any feat that smacked of showmanship. When Latham passed the review stand waving with both hands in the air to demonstrate the stability and safety of the Antoinette's controls system, the reaction of his German audience was to conclude, somewhat grumpily, that his action was merely a 'typical Latin gesture' – and just what might be expected of these frivolous French flyers – not realising his true intent was to provide a practical 'hands-off' illustration.[16] Earlier that week, during his exhibition flights, he had risked incurring displeasure by pushing home a powerful message to demonstrate the Antoinette's potential by making a pioneering cross-country flight from Tempelhof to Johannisthal in storm force winds, battling through the air in appalling conditions which had been pronounced by experts as being unsuitable for any flights that day. Not so for Latham. As he later explained to journalists, his technique had been to take his machine up high into 'the course of the wind' where 'the currents were more constant'. It had been an impressive performance and he was greeted with unrestrained shouts of relief

Latham is given a warm welcome in Berlin, 1909. (HLPP)

on landing safely, prompting the *Daily Telegraph* to comment how even the Germans cast aside their 'phlegmatic Teutonism' to congratulate him, telling their readers that Latham had shaken journalists' hands 'with fingers that were like ice... saluting everyone with great courtesy and answering all congratulations in perfect German with the words – 'I have done nothing extraordinary'. But his cool nerve and modesty had not endeared him overmuch with his hosts. Having capped this exploit by taking a first prize for speed in one of the events and a second for height, he later made the headlines by landing in the dark, hitting a lamp-post and provoking threats of prosecution for causing damage to public property. It seems that the organisers' hope for a sober and tightly controlled show was not to be fulfilled. Efforts to clamp down with strict rules on these daring young French aviators was an impossibility.

As the Berlin Air Week drew to a close, a distinct undercurrent of dissatisfaction among the visiting aeronautic teams began to surface. There was a storm of protest when the prize for carrying a passenger was not awarded because Rougier's flight of thirty-six minutes had not been challenged by any other competitor. Then there were rumours of serious disputes over prize money being held back on all sorts of pretexts. Blériot had committed some small infringement and was being refused payment for his second day and, as bitter arguments escalated, he and other aviators were threatened with having their aeroplanes impounded by the organisers. All in all, the Berlin Air Week did not have a happy ending. When interviewed for his views by newsmen, Latham's criticism must have bemused those in London who had previously suspected him of harbouring pro-German sympathies. His frank observation that '... there was a complete absence of the slightest humanity or courtesy and quite a bit of jealousy because all the flyers were Frenchmen,' was followed by a promise that '... this is the last competition I shall take part in where the competitors are treated like schoolboys [and] ordered about by a bunch of German military officers...'[17]

Despite the acrimonious note on which it ended, the week in Berlin was a commercial success for the Antoinette Motor Company. Latham's skilful performances had brought about the sale of two Antoinette machines to one of Germany's star aviators, Dr Hellmuth Hirth, each at a cost of about 25,000 francs. The first was to be delivered before the end of the year for his own use, and the second would go to a company to be called *Albatros Flugzeugwerks* which Dr Hirth was setting up with Otto Wiener. Their chief engineer, Michael Gabriel, would take delivery of the second machine next year.[18] Did anyone wonder if the Antoinette company's prioritisation of commercial considerations might prove to be an uneasy bedfellow for Latham's sporting ambitions? In a few weeks' time, a small frisson of friction began to worm its way into his relationship with his business partners. During one of the interviews given to the *New York Herald* at the Berlin show in September, Latham's observations had carried a distinctly carping note in relation to the increased amount of pressure being put on him. Remarking that he was being 'as busy as best he could' he told the reporter that he was feeling overwhelmed by: 'an *embarrasse de choix* as many aeronautical events are being crowded into the perspective. My various engagements are being made by my company,' he had said, '[and] as I am the only member of the company who can fly, I am being used for the purpose'.[19] It was not actually a complaint, more of a casual comment. However, in hindsight, it may be easy enough to recognise that Latham was beginning to resent the extent to which Gastambide and Levavasseur took his commitment for granted.

It should not be thought that there were never any lighter moments of pleasure to accompany the Berlin Air Week's activities. *The New York Herald* – always keen to provide telling snippets of society gossip – reported how the 'French Colony in Berlin entertained the flying men' with an evening '*punch d'honneur*' during which one of the French residents recited a poem composed in honour of M. Latham. The despatch goes on to say that the 'verses were of the humorous variety, causing considerable amusement'. The evening's programme ended with a dance and it may be assumed the French visitors returned to Paris at least somewhat mollified by the warm hospitality extended to them by expatriate residents.

Meanwhile, across the Channel, one of the more conservative newspapers, the *Daily Telegraph*, was voicing predictably bleak warnings on the proliferation of air displays, tut-tutting that: 'Those engaged are running the risk of confining themselves to theatrical shows'.[20] While recognising that the crowds of spectators who turned up merely wanted to enjoy themselves by experiencing the 'thrills of shuddering excitement', it was felt that 'such public flights merely degraded aeroplaning [sic] into a kind of acrobatic performance in which those who take part gain some sort of livelihood by exposing themselves to undue risks.' This well-meaning recommendation of caution fell on deaf ears, of course. The gentlemen dubbed by the music halls in song and lyric as 'these

Latham's Antoinette flying over the cathedral at Chartres. (HLPP)

magnificent young men in their flying machines' paid little heed to the *Daily Telegraph*'s stuffy injunction that: 'there must be an international agreement as there has been in regard to automobilism [sic], so that competitions, when held, my be an indication of steady continued progress and a solemn example'. Despite the showmanship, however, by no stretch of the imagination could the progress being made be called 'solemn examples'. Flying was a fast, sometimes reckless, always scary, never dull and inevitably triumphant occupation. A young man's game – a circus.

Latham's complaint of an embarrassment of choice for flying venues was no peevishly imaged problem. The intense competition to prove leadership in European aviation was coming to the boil and an explosion was well overdue. As one *Herald* headline declared: 'Aviation Fever spreads in Belgium', the same weekend carried reports of the Aeronautical Salon at the Grand Palais in Paris, which had been opened by President Fallières. No well-known pilots had been able to attend – apart from Santos-Dumont – because the Berlin Air Week was still in full swing and not due to close until 3 October. In conjunction with the Paris Aeronautical Salon, approval had been given for a flying tournament to be held at the Port Aviation at Juvisy on the outskirts of the capital. Had the planners but known what lay ahead, preparations for this event would have been more thoughtful because, in contrast to the restrained public reception in Berlin, the enthusiasm of French people for the spectacular thrills associated with flying competitions was about to spiral dangerously out of control.

On the first day, a Sunday, the number of eager onlookers had been hopelessly underestimated. Thousands of people turned up. As *The Times* reported: 'Driving to Epsom on a Derby Day was not to be compared to the sight presented. It seemed that every motor car, taxi-cab and bicycle was making in the same direction'.[21] Not surprisingly, chaos had ensued. The roads leading out of Paris were quickly choked; the train services became swamped and stations forced to close. Soon, there was panic in the crowds when rowdy elements got out of hand and started rioting. At the Port Aviation, inevitably, the programme was hopelessly disrupted with flights delayed, rescheduled or cancelled.

The laid-back tone adopted by *The Times* correspondent in describing Latham's late arrival at his hangar speaks volumes: 'He was hot and tired, his motor car having broken down on the road caused him to walk several miles to Juvisy'. Latham would have been furious. Having dashed back from Germany in order to make a showing for the Antoinette Company, he had been due to fly at four o'clock in a new machine recently sold to a Captain Burglat, but the chaos that had ensued in the morning meant that all pre-scheduled planning had been thrown into disarray and the aviator's pre-arranged afternoon time slot abandoned. Worse was to follow. Latham's intention had been to provide onlookers with a thrill by flying his Antoinette around the Eiffel Tower. But, as he was quick to discover, the final foot slog to the flying field had been a journey in vain. Arriving at his hangar, he found not only was his machine not ready for him, its assembly could not be completed until the following afternoon. Curious onlookers were not privy to what had passed between Latham and his chief mechanic but the aviator's dark expression as he walked away without speaking to the waiting journalists was signal enough to convey his intense anger. One can only imagine his feelings when, shortly afterwards, the Comte de Lambert took to the air in his Wright's biplane and headed for the centre of Paris. All the disappointed Latham could do was watch, as one of his well-known rivals sailed effortlessly several times around the city's most prestigious edifice, the Eiffel Tower, for all to see.

The failure of the Antoinette team to have Latham's machine ready for his planned triumphal Eiffel Tower flight can be seen as marking the first cracks in what was clearly a fragile relationship. Ever since the excellent performances in Reims and Berlin, new orders for machines from cash customers had been rolling into the workshops at Puteaux and there is no doubt that this must have put a strain on facilities. Aeroplanes continued to be built by hand. It was a slow and painstaking process. Latham's success had brought about a clash of commercial expediency versus sporting opportunities. It was only to be expected. The checking and preparation of a machine before flights, which often included some repair for Latham's use in air shows, now had to take its turn, if not defer to other priorities on the production line.

Among the flying fraternity, it was generally agreed that displays of flying machines were becoming too popular for safe crowd control. And, if this was not enough to fray tempers within the commercially minded aeroplane-manufacturing sector, there was now another knotty problem for them to untie. During the last week of September, Wilbur Wright had cabled the *New York Herald* to publish a warning to anyone who might think of importing Blériot and Farman machines into the United States, declaring that the brothers would 'take steps to prevent flights in this country with foreign-made machines that are infringing our patents'.[22] The news of this request was received with predicable fury in Paris. A few days later, the paper comments that 'French aeroplane makers were ready for the patent's fight'.

In the meantime, the popularity of public air shows continued. Shortly after the debacle at Juvisy, the organisers of Blackpool Aviation Week in the north of England faced a different problem. With a meeting scheduled for 18–23 October, any spectators brave enough to turn up had to face blustery conditions that were cold and wet. Yet Latham continued to make the news. With an eye to gathering valuable orders from the United Kingdom market, he had been despatched there to produce examples of his Antoinette's capabilities. While here, Latham took up his machine several times in dangerously strong gales, earning for himself the flattering title 'Fighter of the wind'. Many years later an aeronautical correspondent was to recall how: 'in the execution of a promise to a lady he had made a circuit of the course in a 42mph wind.'[23]

Intriguingly, the identity of the lady – and why she set him this challenge – has been often regarded as a mystery. But, in recent years, Chris Aspin, a Lancastrian local historian, has discovered that the night before this exploit, Latham had been one of the dinner guests of Colonel Talbot Clifton of Lytham, the gregarious foreign explorer and traveller in Africa, Asia and elsewhere. Talbot not only owned much of Blackpool, his land-owning family had been associated with the Lancashire Lathams for centuries. Other guests included the Grand Duke Michael of Russia and his morganatic wife, the Countess of Torby, formerly Countess von Merenberg.[24] Aspin writes how the royal couple had expressed disappointment in finding that high winds had prevented them from seeing Latham fly that day. 'They were due to return to London in the morning but he urged them to stay for another day and promised that he would go up no matter what the weather might be'. A gentleman always keeps a promise to a lady. Especially one so closely connected to one of the most powerful ruling royal families in Europe. Aspin relates how, before lunchtime the following day, 'wearing a light raincoat, flat tweed cap and brown gloves' Latham was airborne in the teeth of a gale. The *Manchester Guardian* described the sight of his Antoinette's battle with the elements as being 'tossed about like a cork in a cataract'. With the wind behind him he had roared past the stands reaching the unheard of speed of nearly 100mph; he made two circuits while the crowd whooped and band played the *Marseillaise*. The Countess's wish for excitement had been fulfilled in the most spectacular way – and a mystery solved.

Two other enterprising ladies attending the Blackpool Meeting – both female aviators from less-exalted backgrounds – were also staunch Latham fans. One was an Irish girl from Belfast, Lilian Bland, a colourful personality who wrote sporting articles for London newspapers and enjoyed a reputation for 'fast' behaviour by refusing to ride side-saddle – as ladies did then – on the hunting field. Thrilled by the success of the Channel crossing and spurred-on by her studies of bird flight, she was now determined to build and fly her own aeroplane. The Blackpool Air Week had afforded her an ideal opportunity to see at close hand how these machines were designed and put together. Within twelve months she had built and flown her own model, which she called the *Mayfly*.[25]

The other young woman was the London-born, fluent French-speaking Hilda Hewlett, the daughter of a clergyman. Married to a successful novelist, her enthusiasm for

Latham engages the Baroness Raymonde de Laroche in conversation outside one of the aeroplane sheds. (HLPP)

motoring had nurtured a close friendship with a French engineer, Gustave Blondeau, who later became her business partner. She and Blondeau had motored up north together to visit the Blackpool show and the first time she saw Latham 'lifting from the ground' in one of Blackpool's ferocious gales, Hilda was so impressed by this sight, she had 'wanted to cry or shout' with the sheer excitement of the moment.[26] Hilda subsequently went on to become England's best-known 'aviatrix'; she set up a manufacturing firm with Blondeau and within two years became the first Englishwoman to hold a pilot's licence.

Blackpool's rainswept crowds had loved every moment of the thrills produced by Latham's flying expertise and the local and national coverage in newspapers was lavish. When Latham won the prize for best flight, journalists endowed him with the snappy title 'King of the Air'. However, interestingly, the *Daily Telegraph*'s correspondent took pains to emphasise that: 'He [Latham] objects to the spirit of commercialism now so obvious in the sport', explaining to readers that his attendance at the show was solely as 'an amateur' and, as such, he would refuse to sign any contract for fees but would receive expenses instead. One has to wonder what his business colleagues and fellow directors made of this statement.

On his return to France, Latham was kept busy for the next few weeks at the flying school in Châlons, teaching, demonstrating and testing several new refinements to the Antoinette monoplane. Such was the intense interest in this new sport that flying fields were quickly becoming a popular meeting-and-mixing venue for all and sundry. It was a sign of the times that female aviators were as eager for action as the men.

A Parisian girl, Elise Deroche, a former art student, who, having dallied long enough with erstwhile sculptor-turned-aeronaut, Léon Delagrange, to bear him a son, had more lately acquired the patronage of Charles Voisin, one of the aeroplane manufacturing Voisin brothers. Latham was soon destined to become a close rival in the air. The ambitious Elise was three years younger than Latham. She came from a relatively obscure background – it was said her father had been a plumber – and her early years spent in 'a drab industrial suburb of Paris where the stench of beer and creosote hung heavy in the air'.[27] But Elise had been a bright and clever girl. When disillusioned by the little episode of her liaison with her tutor in *L'Académie des Beaux Arts*, she entertained ambitions to cultivate a professional career as an actress and, having taken the route of many young women before her, had firmly set her sights on improving her social situation through influential gentlemen friends. Luck had been kind. When she became the mistress of Charles Voisin, she became the true love of his life. Through his encouragement, Elise became an expert driver of motor cars and the enamoured Charles then arranged for his company's chief engineer to teach her how to pilot an aircraft. Within a few months, the flamboyant aviatrix – now styling herself the Baroness Raymonde de Laroche – was being photographed in the company of all the better-known flying heroes, Rougier, Farman, Lebon and, of course, Latham.

Did her paramour, Charles Voisin, ever suspect the depth of affectionate *camaraderie* which, perhaps inevitably, was going to develop between Latham and Raymonde de Laroche? Voisin once added a tantalising post script to one of her postcards to Latham on which she has scrawled the message 'So that's it!' wishing him better luck in gaining a *rouge ribaud* in the next aerial competition. Voisin had added he hoped 'it' is only referring to the award and to nothing else! Had he spotted the chemistry building up between this pair? He knew she presented an easy target for her fellow aviator's notorious charms. For his part, Latham was to keep many of the affectionate souvenir messages she sent him following the air shows they had attended together. So, perhaps he, too, may have been temporarily smitten. She was soon to gain her pilot's brevet – a licence to fly – indeed the first woman to get one, and went on to become a skilled member of the Voisin team, competing with the men in many air shows across Europe.

Notwithstanding all these romantic distractions, there is evidence that Eileen Gray's friendship with Latham continued within the social round of their mutual acquaintances in Paris. Her gradual emergence as an artist worth watching was attracting increasing attention of others engaged in alternative forms of experimental artistic expression. Like

Raymonde soon featured as a member of the Voisin Aviation Team. (HLPP)

her erstwhile student friend, sculptor Kathleen Bruce, now married to the explorer, Captain Scott, she had been drawn into intimate friendship with many well-known practitioners in the world of performance dance and these friendships produce a series of intriguing, if oblique connections to Latham. There was, for example, Kathleen Scott's support for the dancer Isadora Duncan, which continues for years throughout all the ups and downs of the *artiste's* turbulent life. Significantly, in Isadora, here may be found yet another sensitive soul who was marked by a dalliance with the Aleister Crowley set and the philosophy of 'do what thou wilt'.[28] For a short while Isadora and her family had lived in the avenue d'Villers, not far from Latham's Paris apartment in the rue Rembrandt on the other side of the Parc Monceau. It was around the same time that Latham was renewing his friendship with Eileen, in early 1909, that Isadora had embarked on her affair with Paris Singer, brother of the Princess de Polignac – a family which included Latham in their social circle. The princess – formerly Winnaretta Singer – was one of the two wealthy daughters of the American owner and founder of the famous Singer Sewing Machine Company. The politely overlooked but well-recognised notoriety of this lady's lesbian affairs had not prevented her from making her mark in Paris as a formidable patron of the arts; influential doors had opened through her marriage of convenience to the ageing homosexual Prince de Polignac, whose family enjoyed status as one of the oldest surviving French feudal dynasties. Their nephews, the aviation enthusiast, Melchior, Marquis de Polignac, head of the champagne producers the *Maison Pomery* – who had headed-up the Reims Show – and his brother, Charles, both eccentric characters not without a certain 'reputation', would often have included Latham among the guest lists for shooting parties on the family estates; he was a noteworthy young man–about–town, always free to make up numbers at a dinner party, or to escort an unaccompanied lady. But to what extent could it be said he was drawn into closer contact with this social circle's more *louche* and sexually ambiguous predilections?

For answers we must turn to a curious discovery linking his name – and that of Eileen Gray, Isadora Duncan and others of note – with a notorious American woman called Natalie Barney. It is an intriguing, if not wholly explainable, relationship. With a growing reputation as a designer worth cultivating within the modernist arts movement, Gray had been taken up by the dancer and choreographer Loïe Fuller and other associated hangers-on who enjoyed the patronage of several influential and adventuresome American women in Paris. These ladies set a certain style for the enjoyment of a more tolerant moral climate which encouraged them to drift in and out of intense lesbian relationships as easily as they could their affairs with casual heterosexual lovers. The formidable Natalie Barney, self-styled 'friend of man and lover of women', featured largely in this group and, in October 1909, when she launched her own style of Sapphic salons – held in the rue Jacob on Friday afternoons – she liked to extend a welcome to a number of carefully chosen male kindred spirits.[29] While it is not remarkable to find she has included Eileen Gray among a doodled list of guests which she designed as a frontispiece for her book, *Pensées d'une Amazone*, what must be more than a little fascinating is to discover she has noted down Hubert Latham's name very distinctly in company with several men, and women, of extraordinary genius invited to these elite gatherings – writers, poets and artists – many of whom not only wavered on the margins of their own sexuality but who were taken up with a fascination for aviation themes.[30]

Certainly, Latham was a popular icon for the future of new technology destined to conquer the skies and must have been a 'catch' for any ambitious hostess. But for Barney to have placed her recollection of him as a guest in the middle of a group displaying notorious propensity for propositioning young men is, to say the least, a curious discovery. Here he is in company with Count Robert de Montesquiou, the avant-garde painter and futurist, Gino Severini and his compatriot, the Italian novelist, D'Annunzio. The list includes Marcel Proust, who would put so many of these larger than life characters of the *Belle Époque* into his novel, *À la Recherche du Temps Perdu*, and the great man himself, Apollinaire, whom Latham may have quite possibly already encountered socially by way of Le Havre's circle of arts-loving, well-heeled *haut monde*.[31] Barney has included American poet and Francophile, Alan Seeger, feminist Marie Leneru, sculptor José de Charmoy and the dancer Isadora Duncan in this same grouping of personalities.[32]

Unless Barney had later indulged in an extraordinary piece of mischief in her personal recollection of such an idiosyncratic guest list, it has to be said that the discovery provides us with a thought-provoking aspect of Left Bank Paris life and opens up the view of another strange path down which Latham's innate curiosity and need for intellectual exploration may have led him. We might reflect that there is plenty of evidence that Latham had never been short of willing female conquests, so it is very possible he and Eileen Gray were drawn into this scene because he admired certain attributes within these women by which they strove to reflect unfettered modern attitudes.

The message on the back of this postcard to Latham reads: 'Wish my thoughts would stop soaring and come back to earth'. (HLPP)

Gray's own assessment of Barney's 'Grecian Temple of Friends' as one that was 'mirrored and filled with furs and tapestries' was not overenthusiastic, being perhaps too intense for her fiercely independent spirit.[33] One of her rejected would-be suitors, Paul Leautaud, an associate of Gide, Proust and Valéry, had at one time interpreted her sexual aloofness by labelling her as one of the 'marginal souls' in Paris at that time.[34] Latham's possession of a similar trait in his nature, which often gave the impression of presenting a cool distancing from the crowd may be recognised also, perhaps, as belonging to a 'marginal soul', one that was capable of a deep empathy with an artist's sensitivity; whose instinct understood the need to seek isolation to maintain a sense of freedom.[35]

It is significant for Latham, however, that Gray's fascination with concept of flight and its attendant design applications and techniques never faded. With the help now of a Japanese-born assistant craftsman, Sugawara, she was still engaged in the slow and painstaking production of creating fine lacquer artefacts and plans for a series of ambitious wall panels were being conceived. One of these was to be intriguingly entitled '*Le Magicien de la Nuit'*. Had she drawn inspiration, subliminal or actual, for this famous piece from her previous encounters with Aleister Crowley, or more probably, a more recent meeting with him? Crowley had been back and forth to Paris several times that year and was still smarting with displeasure over the temerity of a young writer, W. Somerset Maugham, for having used him as the inspiration for the main character in his most recently published book which, coincidently, also bore the title *The Magician*.[36] Several people who had read it were now teasingly suggesting that Maugham had used Eileen Gray as his base for the girl in this story. When asked, she would always dismiss the notion as absurd. But even today, this question still hangs in the air, unresolved. One must wonder if Maugham – or any of the other writers encountered in this circle – ever considered using Latham as a role for one of their fictional characters?

By the end of November, 1909, it was announced that Latham was to take on the direction of the Antoinette school of aviation at the Châlons flying field, near the village of Mourmelon. But as the winter approached, Latham was beginning to look particularly strained and tired. The flyer's complexion had lost its summer tan and had faded to waxy paleness and it was clear that he was not as well as he might be. It did not suit him to be in Europe for the winter. Only his closest friends knew of the long-standing battle with albuminuria, which tantalisingly could give him periods of remission, only to return with a vengeance if he did not take great care of his diet and lifestyle. It was such a bore and hopelessly out of step with the fast-living, hard-drinking bohemian existence of most of his companions.

Soon after Blackpool, a rumour began to do the rounds that there were other matters worrying Latham. It was well known that the Antoinette firm had received several orders for new machines from private buyers – but those hoped-for big contracts from the French army had never materialised. It would appear that Levavasseur was the problem. Innovative, creative, yet with a volatile nature that could flare up into a tantrum at the drop of a hat, his attitude scared the living wits out of the various government agencies he was trying to negotiate deals with. This was nothing new. There had been problems with army contracts many years previously and now it seemed that young Robert Gastambide, Jules Gastambide's son and heir, had grown impatient. He had had enough of the pantomime of deference to Levavasseur's moody antics and, with Latham's support, suggested that changes must be made.

As might be expected, the elder Gastambide took Levavasseur's side in the arguments. They closed ranks. Faced by this shareholders' revolt, they threatened to pull out of the firm altogether and form a new company in England. The crunch came when the shareholders voted to install a cousin of Louis Blériot, Maurice Blériot, as a new executive manager and, with this move, the old guard's bluff was called. The elder Gastambide and Levavasseur could do nothing else but carry out their threat and promptly resigned from the company. With the bulk of the shares in the *Société Anonyme Antoinette* now held by Latham, Maurice Blériot and Pierre Chalmard – whom it will be remembered was a former managing director of the Blériot Headlamp Company – the company now needed to appoint a new chairman of the board. It had been a truly significant shake-up. They badly needed a steady hand on the tiller and Latham was persuaded by his fellow mutineers to accept the post. The question, however, as to just how much of all this coup had been master-minded behind the scenes by Levavasseur's old adversary, one-time investor and now keen rival, Louis Blériot, remains difficult to uncover.

Viewed in hindsight, it had not been wise for the younger men to challenge Levavasseur and the senior Gastambide in a boardroom battle. The former directors' first tactical countermove was to prevent any further use of Levavasseur's engines in the manufacture of future Antoinette monoplanes. This was a calculated ploy. They knew the next batch of monoplanes on the production line was awaiting the installation of their motors. Fortunately for the new board there were three machines packed and ready for the next air show due to open in Heliopolis, Egypt, in early February and these three machines were are all in perfect working order. But there was an immediate problem to be solved in finding suitable motors for all those incomplete machines left sitting on the workshop floor. Not deterred by this setback, Robert Gastambide was keen to try out out some of the new light Gnome engines. Reports on these had been good. They would run a few trials.

For Latham, his acceptance of the responsibility for chairing the new board of management was of doubtful value. It may be assumed that the need for wary watchfulness must have been unremittingly draining and the importance of the role he played in this particular episode in the fortunes of the *Société Anonyme Antoinette* is not clear. At the same time, it must be conceded that Latham's need to safely navigate the currents of naked ambition and greed all around him must have been extremely tedious. By his own admission, Latham had always tried to distance himself from becoming embroiled in the grubby under-the-counter commercial deals that appeared to be so necessary for the successful development of the aircraft industry. Only when he was in the air must he have felt completely free and detached from it all. The higher he flew, the more he felt in control of his own destiny.

# EIGHT
# Star Ascendant, 1910

Stories about the goings-on at the flying schools at Châlons were circulating the rounds of Parisian society like wildfire, zestfully repeated and embellished with shock or admiration, depending on the company being entertained. Was Hubert Latham offering a vision of the future for rich young sportsmen? He was certainly causing a stir. People were intrigued to learn he had used his Antoinette monoplane to transport himself and his guns from the camp at Châlons to a shooting party which was being held in Berru at the country estate of the Marquis de Polignac, twenty miles away.[1] Just half an hour's flying time! Arriving as lunch was being served, it was reported he had landed on the lawn outside the house, spent some pleasant hours with his friends and, at the end of the day's outing, loaded his guns and his share of the bag back into his machine before flying back to Mourmelon in time for dinner.

'Such a hoot!' thought the young people who repeated this story in great glee while the older generation shook their heads in despair. The world was getting far too fast for safety. Hunting game from the aeroplane itself was the next step, perhaps (an unthinkable barbarity), but it was being widely tipped that Latham was going to try it, anyway. He had been the first pilot to have 'shot' photographs successfully from the air with a small camera. So why not birds?

Meanwhile, across the Channel, word going round the London offices of the *The Times* and *Daily Mail* held that Northcliffe was not in good health. Different opinions as to what was exactly wrong with him were aired. Neurasthenia, inflammation of the pancreas and indigestion had all been cited – each in turn due, it was said meaningfully, to overwork.[2] It was the opinion of many that this situation could not go on much longer. He should be whisked off someplace by his doctors for a complete rest and then, as spring edged into summer, perhaps his recovery would be enhanced by a sojourn well away from London in the South of France. Northcliffe's interest in the progress of aerial flight would not be diminished by this setback. There might have to be a short pause while others took over responsibility for seeing that enthusiasm was kept up for British aviators and British events, but he was gratified that an increasing number of aerial records continued to be broken and, before he departed for his rest cure, he had issued instructions to ensure his papers' aeronautical correspondents remained aware of the serious implications of growing air power in times of war. Readers must receive stern warnings at regular intervals. Northcliffe had set the ball rolling. It must be kept in play.

The Baroness surrounded by a convivial group of aviation colleagues and rivals. (HLPP)

The New Year had slid into place quietly. It was now 1910. What triumphs and tragedies would the new decade bring? Already both Lefebvre and Ferber had been killed. The news of another fatal aeroplane accident which came within days of the turn of the year did not auger well. On 4 January, one of the most experienced pilots, Léon Delagrange, had come to grief during a demonstration flight. The tragic event was to herald the awful reality of the dangers which could only lie ahead as experimental flights grew more and more ambitious. For his friends, it was a devastating blow to have another larger-than-life personality gone from their midst so suddenly. He had been attending the official opening of the *Croix d'Hins* Aerodrome, near Bordeaux, as one of the invited stars. He had decided to use the opportunity to demonstrate his new and ingenious theory about the demands of flight and engine power and he had taken out the little Italian 18hp Anzini engine from his Blériot machine and had replaced it with a much larger 40hp Gnome. Without greater power there could be no increase of the airwaves' lifting force, he had maintained. The equation was: power equals lifting force.

Those in the know had been sceptical. It was all right for Latham's robustly built Antoinette to carry a large horsepower engine. The struts and structure of that craft were constructed like a boat. But Delagrange's little Blériot machine was tiny; its greatest asset was its lightness; the body and wings were immensely fragile; its frame and wires not designed to withstand greater levels of stress. This was not a machine built to carry weight. But come what may, Delagrange had been determined to try it, all the same.

Delegrange's crashed machine. (Royal Aeronautical Society Library)

The invited guests that day were impressed by the first few circuits. Delagrange's demonstration of his latest theory was quite a performance. The little plane dipped and swooped. Its speed increased effortlessly. He made one final dramatic turn, travelling quite fast and, to the horror of the watchers, the port wing suddenly crumpled and collapsed. The craft fell almost 60ft onto the roof of one of the hangars. On impact, the pilot had been thrown clear out of his seat. He had died instantly. He was the third French fatality as result of an aeroplane crash.

There was little time for mourning or looking back. In a few weeks time, European aviators would be heading off to the Heliopolis Flying Week, scheduled for 6–13 February and planned specifically to mark the foundation of the Egyptian Aero Club. As it turned out, desert storms and high winds, not to mention several minor accidents made it a less spectacular occasion than anticipated. The Voisin team made the best showing with Henri Rougier scooping most of the main prizes, while the Baroness Raymonde de Laroche made her flying debut with them by competing unofficially.

Jacques Balsan, in a Blériot machine, escaped uninjured from a dramatic crash and Gobron's plane caught fire. Latham had brought three machines to the meeting, but having achieved just one prize for altitude, suffered so many crashes and engine malfunctions that he was finally left bereft of any machine fit to fly. Eventually, the deteriorating weather conditions which had put paid to any planned flights over King Cheops tomb finally brought about the abandonment of the *Prix de Pyramides*. All the imaginative posters

One of Latham's Antoinette monoplanes at Heliopolis. (Harman Collection)

which had advertised the occasion with a depiction of desert scenes, camels, palm trees, and aeroplanes flying over pyramids were destined to remain firmly in the realms of their graphic designers' imagination.

The exotic setting of the Egyptian Air Show had, nonetheless, grabbed a generous amount of press coverage. One of the more newsworthy stories was a report that the Khedive – the ruling viceroy of the Sultan of Turkey – had been so intrigued by the anticipation of thrilling spectacle that he allowed the women of his harem to view the flying machines in action from a specially erected stand swathed in green muslin curtains to protect their privacy. We can only surmise how the women of the royal household may have reacted to the sight of the Baroness, who, putting comfort and convenience before fashion, adopted the jacket and breeches attire of her fellow male aviators in brazen indifference to convention. Shock and outrage may have been tempered with a *soupçon* of envy, although, it must be said, this aviatrix's award of a full pilot's licence a week or so later in France was not greeted by European male aviators with much enthusiasm, either. The emergence of competent lady pilots was being looked upon with increasing dismay by many commentators. Not unexpectedly, the straight-laced and ultra-conservative Wright brothers had always made no secret of their utter disapproval of women in this game, but now the German ace pilot, Helmut Hirth, was voicing his opinion that women did not have the physical ability to fly an aeroplane and, moreover, their very presence 'detracted from the stature of male aviators'.[3] Amid all this controversy, Latham does not seem to have had any such hang-ups over the importance of the male ascendancy and many times competed in air shows beside the flamboyant Raymonde de Laroche. In fact, if his friendly association with the Parisian lesbian and bisexual scene is any indication, he was more likely to have applauded the ladies' courage in pursuing this incursion into a male-dominated world.

Leaving aside for the moment his dalliance with Eileen Gray and whatever implications may be derived from her undisputed sexual ambivalence, one of the questions often posed about Latham at this time is his apparent lack of any permanent attachment to a member of the opposite sex. Yet, despite the unsubstantial conclusion to be drawn from Natalie Barney's linking of his name to some of the more flamboyant male aficionados of the salons, there is plenty of evidence to suggest he enjoyed many entanglements with a number of young – and not so young – women who obviously adored him. There is a suggestion of discreet indulgence in forbidden fruit. One English conquest, whose unsuspecting fiancé had left her on the loose while he went 'off to Brittany to shoot', writes to him afterwards with a sigh over the memory of 'the good times we had,' while admitting, 'I am a bad girl to write to you and my British conscience ought to kick me,' to which she adds mischievously, '[but] you can see I am making the most of my time before my marriage!'[4]

Yet standards of utter discretion were high and we are left with only fleeting shadows of the personalities involved: Elenor, Sybil, Roberta, Nina, Edith, Genevieve, Marthé and Anne. These brief *affaires*, if such, were likely to have been conducted with a generous level of secrecy. An impression lingers that that many of Latham's paramours were already married, or at least spoken for – a perfect situation for a young man who felt under no undue pressure to settle down. His successful deflection of his mother's attempts to find him a suitable marriage partner had been going on for years. In 1907, the subject even crops up in correspondence: '*Chère Maman*, as regards my own [future marriage] intentions, will you please pay attention [to the fact that] I am quite able to find someone by myself.'[5]

In any case, business matters were keeping him increasingly preoccupied and Latham's less than spectacular and occasionally disastrous performances at air shows around this time raises speculation that disturbing problems had been developing between himself and the new team running the *Société Anonyme Antoinette*. One hesitates to claim that some of the magic had left Latham, or that the company had just hit a run of bad luck. The most likely explanation is that the difficulties being encountered were due to seriously inadequate technical and mechanical backup now that Levavasseur was gone. Their clever plan to utilise Gnome engines in the 'Antoinette' monoplane may not have realised Robert's optimistic expectations, after all.

By the end of March, no one who had remained tuned into watching the turmoil affecting the Antoinette Company was surprised when rumours confirmed that the dispute which had caused the bust-up the previous autumn was being seriously reassessed by all concerned. A return to the status quo was imminent and, once their differences had been resolved, all was forgiven; Jules Gastambide was reinstalled as company chairman, Léon Levavasseur returned to the fold and Robert Gastambide, installed as a manager. In retrospect, perhaps, all that had been needed was a cooling-off period for both sides.

All parties had to concede that the crazy, if only intermittent reliability of Levavasseur's engineering skill was essential to ensure any further successes while, at the same time, the worth of Latham's coaxing touch with a motor which required sensitive handling was not to be underestimated. In addition, it is tempting to speculate that the solving of a key problem – money, or the lack of it – took a more positive turning point when an anonymous investor came forward offering 100,000 francs. This 'white knight' has never been identified.

Even so, it was not the end of the story, for whatever reality underlay the smooth function of the Antoinette Company, one thing was for certain: crashes and mechanical malfunctions which left Latham fuming and frustrated were continuing to bring disappointment with depressing frequency. Something was still not right.

By the end of April, Latham and other competing aviators were off on a round of aviation events which started in Nice during the first week of May. He was joined there by a number of English flyers who were quickly making up for lost time by entering as many competitions as possible to catch up on the superior experience of the French. Among them, one can find the name of Charlie Rolls in his Short-built Wright machine. Their friendly rivalry was boosted when Rolls managed to beat his friend Latham into fourth place in the final order of merit, although Latham took first place in the *Tour de Piste* and won the meeting's prize for highest altitude.

Nice was followed by a trip to Russia to demonstrate the flying capabilities of various machines in St Petersburg. Then the circus was back in Lyons for yet another series of aerial demonstrations. It was only to be expected that Latham's record-breaking exploits in his Antoinette would have to be eventually overtaken by others, for the technical performance of the Voisin, Farman and Blériot machines had all been greatly improved. Moreover, the Baroness de Laroche, the latest bright star in the sky, was making valuable newsworthy appearances for Voisin machines. While in St Petersburg, Elise was reported as having charmed Tsar Nicholas, although by her own admission 'her heart had been in her mouth'.[6] The Tsar's guest, Princess Henry of Prussia, Grand Duchess of Mecklenburg-Schwerin may have conversed animatedly with Latham in her own language for quite some time, but it was the Baroness who had been later invited to privately display her machine and flying costume to the Royal party. Clearly, her position as an aviatrix was now being accepted by the highest people in society.

More proof that female flyers were also the very latest up-and-coming attraction to capture the interest of the general public came soon after this, when it was announced that M. Pierre Lafitte, the well-known proprietor of the ladies' journal *Fémina*, was to offer a cup to the value of 2,000 francs (£80) to be competed for during the year 1910. The cup was quickly christened the *Coupe Fémina*. It would be awarded to a female pilot who, by 31 December 1910, had covered the greatest flying distance in an unbroken period of time.

The existence of serious competition for this type of an award brings certain evidence that there were a growing number of women intent on equalling the achievements of their male flying colleagues. One lady determined to make a bid for this prize was the outstanding French sportswoman of her day, Marie Marvingt. Her career had seen her

Latham teaching Marie Marvingt. (HLPP)

excelling in everything from competitive skiing to cycling, tennis, golf, canoeing and ballooning. Now she wanted to fly but only the best of teachers would satisfy her demands. She chose Latham. A practised self-publicist, Marvingt soon had the society magazines falling over themselves in their attempts to get photographs of them together. A photograph of her and Latham aboard an Antoinette training machine found with his private papers is signed on the back by her with a teasing 'For my Professor…'[7] Her bold signature evokes the impression of a close personal affection for the younger man. Like his friend Eileen Gray, this very individual woman was also older than him by eight years.

Meanwhile, the journals were just as keen to snap Latham with any female pupil with whom he could be linked. He was one of the most popular and eligible bachelors in the public eye and the ladies from the flying schools were for the most part all extremely chic, charmingly feminine and also glad of any publicity they could get. Dorothy Levitt, the English motor-car-racing star, was soon spotted being taught by Latham. Notorious since 1903 as 'the little secretary' who become the first woman to enter a public race, she was described rather condescendingly by a journalist as 'not a big strapping Amazon… but… the most girlish of womanly women'.[8] And the gossip columnists had swiftly identified a possible link between Latham and the attractively diminutive Hélène Dutrieu, the Belgian-born sporting rival of Marvingt, who was a close acquaintance of his friend the popular Brazilian ladies' man, Alberto Santos-Dumont.

Purveyors of gossip found the groups who gathered at the Châlons flying field were creating an air of casual bonhomie where social norms could easily be ignored. The Farman and Voisin students all stayed in the Hôtel de l'Europe in the village of

*Left:* Latham pictured with Dorothy Levitt in the journal *Fémina*, No.210, 15 January 1910. (HLPP)

*Opposite:* The Hon. C.S. Rolls at the controls of his Wright biplane. (Royal Aeronautical Society Library)

Mourmelon. Hilda Hewlett, whom Latham had met in Blackpool, was now often seen working with her business partner Blondeau in the Farman brothers' shed and a good deal of friendly rivalry existed between this camp and the Antoinette flying school and other monoplane enthusiasts who were housed in the adjacent Hôtel Marillier. [9]

As for what the more curious tittle-tattlers were to make of Latham's friendship with Eileen Gray, no one really knew in what direction that affair was heading. The gossip in Natalie Barney's exclusive circle whispered that Gray had grown tired of the men in her life and had embarked on a very intimate and long-term relationship with a rich, expatriate American girl, Gaby Bloch, who was for many years the companion and lover of Loïe Fuller, the dancer. Did this mean that Latham was now out of the scene completely?

By May 1910, news broke that a new attempt to fly the English Channel in both directions was being proposed. A well-known firm of champagne producers, *Ruinart, Père et Fils* had revived an earlier interest in promoting an award for a Channel flight by inviting competition for a double-crossing of the Channel: the Ruinart prize. A recently qualified pilot, the Comte Jacques de Lesseps, was planning to fly the Channel in both directions to win.

The Comte – another who moved within the elite of Parisian high society – was the youngest of the eleven sons of Baron Ferdinand de Lesseps, the twice-married French diplomat and engineer who made his name building the Suez Canal some forty years earlier and then lost it again in 1889 in the financial scandal that ruined the first attempt to build a similar canal across the isthmus of Panama. [9]

It was reported that de Lesseps might try to make his flight during the third week of the month, perhaps on the morning of 21 May. He was to start from Calais, taking the

same route as Blériot the previous year and it was now fairly certain that he would not be the only contender. The Hon. Charles Rolls had also announced his intention to make a bid for the prize and there were unconfirmed rumours that Latham might be also in the running. Would it be a race? Or was it just friendly rivalry?

Jacques de Lesseps moved in the same social circles as both Rolls and Latham; they were all well acquainted with each other but some correspondents believed it possible that reports of Latham's interest had been put about in the hope of stirring greater press coverage for the event. Certainly, his name was guaranteed to grab the attention of the English public. 'Fighter of the Wind', they had called him in Blackpool. He was still a hero in British eyes; his Anglo-French ancestry a matter of pride.

As it happened, the gods augured that this double Channel flight was not destined to bring about a new burst of excitement and banner headlines. Publicity for the event was just starting to build up nicely when, on the morning of 6 May, London announced that King Edward VII had died. The news pushed all else from the front pages of the world's press. Aged only sixty-two, the unexpected passing of the English monarch was shocking and almost unbelievable. It was the end of an era. The whole of London plunged immediately into deep mourning and newspaper columns concentrated on little else but the King, his illness, his life and his times. This was no time for editors to give thought to such frivolous matters as another Channel flight.

The following week, on 13 May, news of a crash involving the French pilot of a new Antoinette machine at the Lyons Air Show added to the speculation that Latham would not try for the Channel again. The owner of this recently purchased machine, who was a family member of the famous French-owned Michelin pneumatic-tyre company, M. Hauvette-Michelin, had smashed into one of the pylons marking out the course. He had been killed instantly. The catastrophe was the first fatality to have occurred involving an Antoinette monoplane and it would have come as devastating blow to the firm's confidence and prestige. The safety of this robust machine had been one of their best selling points, well demonstrated by Latham himself, who usually strolled away unruffled and unhurt from spills and minor mishaps like a cat with nine lives. But nothing was truer than the fact that the odds were cruelly and illogically stacked in this game and what luck existed mercurial.

As the third week in May approached, the gathering for the forthcoming Royal funeral was bringing half the crown heads of Europe to London. The Ruinart Prize for a double Channel flight had by now almost sunk completely out of sight in newspaper columns. The contestants had not reckoned on having to compete with the obsequies for the English monarch, but it was too late to withdraw. It was reported that de Lesseps was to fly a Blériot machine fitted with a Gnome engine and it had not gone unnoticed by some commentators that this same combination of chassis and engine had already caused the two fatal accidents earlier that year involving Delagrange and Le Blon. This factor may not have bothered de Lesseps overmuch. He could have been confident and totally inured to any kind of superstition, or merely extremely stubborn.

In the days leading up to de Lesseps's attempt, Latham had made it his business to drive down to Sangatte to convey his good wishes to his friend. Was he engulfed by a deep sense of *déjà vu* while there, perhaps? The weather was almost as vile as it had been the previous summer and Sangatte looked utterly unchanged. The same people passed him the street, nodding vaguely in half recognition. The same men sat gossiping in the cafes. The air was heavy with a broody hint of wind and approaching summer storm. There had been a mixture of hot and cold days, almost a repeat of last year's frustrating conditions and the extreme changes in temperature, inevitably, brought thick sea frets rolling in to obliterate the coastline day after day. Such weather on this stretch of coast was not unusual. Most days, the fogs would lift clear by strong and gusty winds and the sun would shine. But then, it would be far too blustery to attempt any flying. Once again, the waiting stretched patience to breaking point. A repeat of the last year's tensions; it was all very unsatisfactory.

In the preparations for his flight, de Lesseps had taken over the same garden and hut used by Blériot further along the coast at Les Baraques. The occasional journalist who might drop by in the hope of gathering extra copy found little new to report despite the air of expectancy. Not far away, up on the hillside was the site close to the old Channel tunnel buildings where the Latham camp had been set-up. Nothing there remained except the silence; emptied of everything but memories.

Earlier that month, *The Times* aeronautical correspondent in London, having nothing much to report on, had picked up a piece in the *Petit Journal* by Major Paul Renard, in which he made quite startling predictions in the wake of a flight Paulhan had made between London and Manchester. 'The future is nearer than we generally suppose', Renard had written, adding: 'we shall enter upon the third phase of aerial navigation

– that of continent to continent'.[10] It was an almost inconceivable idea. But those whose job it was to see impossible possibilities in the future knew differently. The more perceptive were ready to wager that little flights across the Straits of Dover or linking cities within a Europe would become commonplace. In certain quarters it was firmly, and, as it turned out, correctly, believed that within ten years pilots would be capable of crossing the Atlantic.[11] Like others, Latham may have entertained the dream of regular air services flying from Paris to New York carrying mail and passengers. The air industry was about to break new boundaries.

There were officials in British Government circles, especially in the Foreign Office, who conceded that such radical thinking was not at all far-fetched and it was clear that it would not be long before some method of control over the freedom of the skies would be needed as a matter of urgency. Many felt it was unthinkable that flying machines and airships could be allowed cross and re-cross national boundaries at will. But while the British War Office already harboured serious worries over the capability of German airships, their military advisors were to remain convinced for months to come that the French were right in thinking Zeppelins were far too cumbersome for use in warfare. Opinions were divisive. High-ranking members of Britain's military top brass continued to be utterly sceptical over the use of flying machines in wartime combat, despite the enthusiasm of younger staff members who argued that aeroplanes could be utilised for scouting. Sir Douglas Haig, army advisor to the War Office, had remained unmoved, holding firm on his opinion that this fashionable enthusiasm for aviation was all 'a waste of time'. 'Flying can never be of any use to the Army', he declared.[12]

Nonetheless, in the British Foreign Office there was a growing conviction that a set of international regulations should be put in place to prevent pilots flying without authorisation in what might be claimed as British skies, or for that matter, French air space, and it was being forecast that the Germans were likely to kick up a big fuss over this extremely sensitive issue. They would see any move to bring in an international agreement as another malevolent effort to squeeze Germany back into its borders. For decades they had displayed paranoid fear of encirclement by their neighbours. The Kaiser, in a speech back in 1908, had markedly referred to the continued threat of *Einkreisung* and – whether regarded as valid or not by historians or the diplomatic corps – it was a matter that would have to be thrashed out and not without great difficulty for all concerned. The same excuse had been used by the German government to explain why they had been obliged to start building their large navy some years ago. Now the coming of aviation was thrusting the arena of dispute upwards into the clouds.

Latham was not unaware of growing concern in Germany. He would have heard plenty of mutterings last year in Johannisthal, when their army chiefs saw for themselves the superior capabilities of French aircraft manufacturers and the expertise of French pilots. He understood the mindset of the military men.

As de Lesseps fretted impatiently in Les Baraques, waiting for good enough weather to make the next historic flight across the Channel, reports were filtering through to the world's press that agreement had been reached to inaugurate a conference on aerial navigation which would open on 18 May in the French Foreign Office in Paris. The result of this delicate diplomatic manoeuvring would be a meeting to try and hammer out some regulatory guidelines for international aviation. A system of monitoring traffic using the skies, such as that which existed in sea ports and dockyards for vessels, needed to be set in place.

As fate would have it, the opening of this conference generated hardly any coverage in the press because of the build-up of public interest in King Edward's funeral in London. Newspapers focused their reports on which royal personages and heads of state were expected to join the mourners. The lack of available column space meant that a great deal written about the Aerial Navigation Conference, which might otherwise have been published for public digestion, was now being spiked in newspaper offices everywhere. There had been whispers inevitably leaking out of Whitehall which hinted of serious divergence of opinion in the House of Commons – even upon the Government benches – and the British Foreign Office had thought it wise to set up an inter-departmental committee for attendance at this conference. Despite all of Northcliffe's warnings of the threat of aerial warfare, a widespread belief remained in the House that neither airships nor aeroplanes would have any really practical use in the future except for sporting events and circus-like entertainment for crowds. Yet, despite the lack of enthusiasm, several army people were more than ready and keen to purchase the Wright machine being flown by Rolls and, in due course, Winston Churchill was prompted to take flying lessons when he became First Lord of the Admiralty in the following year. But many guessed that the discussions instigated by the Paris conference to accomplish bilateral agreement on what to be called 'sovereignty over the air' would not be an easy task; they were right. It was to drag on indecisively for months.

Two days after the opening of the conference, the funeral of Edward VII took place in London. On the following day, Comte de Lesseps ran out of patience and made his attempted double crossing of the Channel. Delayed by fog on the French coast, however, he only managed to complete a single passage of the straits. A small paragraph tucked away in the extended edition of *The Times* reports how his journey had repeated the Blériot route one way from Les Baraques to Dover, landing safely in St Margaret's meadow. His flight time was thirty-seven minutes, only slightly better than that of the Blériot crossing. The planned return journey to claim award of the Ruinhart prize had to be abandoned due to strong winds.

The royal funeral put paid to any arrangements made by Charlie Rolls to make his bid for the honour because he had been required to attend the obsequies. The challenge had had to wait until some days later. Luck was not with him, either. The weather was still maddeningly unpredictable and at least one attempted take-off had to be cancelled at the very last minute. Rolls was not one to rest easy with such a reversal of fortunes. On 2 June, he made another foray, this time successfully completing the double crossing non-stop in one hour thirty-five minutes. The Ruinhart prize had been won. The Channel was once more conquered.

But amid the triumphs, the twin realities of danger and tragedy continued to stalk relentlessly in search of prey. The following month, on the second day of the Bournemouth Air Show in Dorset, in which Charlie Rolls was one of the main competitors, his specially

Roll's double crossing of the channel celebrated in a cartoon showing him being congratulated by John Bull. (From the collections of the Nelson Museum and Local History Centre, Monmouth)

adapted Wright machine crashed in front of a crowd of spectators. The impact broke his neck, killing him instantly. The Hon. Charles, third son of Lord Llangattock and founder of the Rolls-Royce Motor Company, had become the first Englishman to have died in a flying accident.

News of his death was conveyed to Latham at the Reims Show, where he and the Antoinette team of aviators were gathered in preparation for that year's forthcoming week-long programme of events. The tragedy hit hard. Although rivals of a kind since their days of mutual interest in ballooning and motor sports, Rolls had been a worthy adversary in the air and one of his most respected English friends. But hardly had Latham begun to mourn, when catastrophe struck hard again in a matter of only a few hours. This time, it was within the ranks of his own closest colleagues.

About six o'clock that evening, one of the Antoinette machines recently delivered to Reims for the show had been taken up for test flight by Charles Wachter, their senior mechanic. Wachter was still gathering greater experience as a pilot and was trying to get as much extra flying time in as possible. Like René Labouchère, he had been one of the team members to be selected to take some of the pressure off Latham. Only days earlier he had been demonstrating the special attributes of one of the Antoinette machines to the King of Bulgaria and had then flown the plane into Bétheny from Mourmelon. He was circling the field at some distance from other planes when disaster struck. On 10 July, the

*New York Herald*'s despatch described how: 'A horrified cry escaped from spectators as the machine suddenly crumpled up; the wings parted and the frame shot downwards almost perpendicular like a long white spear... The wings fluttered down like handkerchiefs a second or so later.'

As the main body of the plane hit the ground, the force of the impact created a deep hole. One reporter's graphic description records how those who arrived at the scene found the unfortunate pilot's remains were nothing but 'a formless mass'. Death had been instantaneous. To add further tragedy to the horror of the crash, Wachter had been Levavasseur's brother-in-law and his wife, Levavasseur's sister, had been watching the flight from the aeroplane sheds. It was even rumoured one of the couple's young children had witnessed the accident.

Shocked to the core, the Antoinette team gathered in a small knot around Latham. Wachter's position as their senior mechanic had been the rock-like bulwark of good sense, which could always be counted upon to temper the wilder excesses of Levavasseur's experimental genius. He had been their friend, their cheerful mentor, the good-humoured solver of all problems large and small. How could they go on without him? Their confidence was utterly shattered.

A later account recalls how Latham's leadership qualities had manifested itself at that moment: 'Without hesitation and with undisturbed calmness' he had issued orders quietly and with authority.[13] The team were instructed to bring all the remaining machines out of the sheds and to prepare immediately for flight. He would lead them out to fly the course in a circuit of respect and esteem for their dead colleague. In this way, each member could calmly mark his memory with honour.

Then, afterwards, for the rest of the week, every flight and every prize was to be dedicated to the memory of Charles Wachter. Each triumph was to be solely for him. Their only aim would be to do him proud.

During this, the second Reims Air Show, the Antoinette team surpassed all previous attainments. Latham's decision had been entirely correct. Progress was to be the catharsis. Speed and height and endurance required sacrifice and they accepted the reality that men and women were putting their lives seriously at risk, gambling with a fatalist acceptance in order to gain knowledge of new possibilities within aviation.

Within days, another truly horrific crash hit the headlines. The Baroness de Laroche, who was planning to compete for the 5,000 francs Ladies' Prize in her Voisin machine, had come down while practising in Châlons, breaking her collarbone and making history as the first Frenchwoman aviator to have been seriously injured in a air crash. Although carted off to hospital where she languished for several weeks, the irrepressible Raymonde had no intention of allowing this contretemps to end her career. Within a few months she had returned, keen as ever, to competitive flying.

By the end of the second Reims Air Show it was obvious that great all-round progress had been made in aeronautics. Nearly twelve months had elapsed since the heady excitement of the World's First Aviation Display. The acclaim for the record height, speed and endurance flights achieved at that time now seemed quite naïve. How tawdry and primitive the performance of the machines seemed by comparison. Last year the record

Poster for Second Air Show at
Reims, 1910. (HLPP)

speeds of 48mph were thought amazing; this year Morane flew at 90mph in a Blériot
monoplane and no one batted an eyelid.

Moreover, the international flavour of this 1910 show had brought about an increasing
amount of interest from the military. Russia's Grand Duke Mikhaylovich, who had already
arranged for Russian officers to engage in aviation-training courses in France, was touting
the idea that Russia was in the market for at least fifty aeroplanes. He was duly lunched
by the Marquis de Poliganc; as were the visiting Turkish Ministers for Finance and Justice.
President Fallières and his wife had again made an appearance at the show and allowed
themselves to be fashionably awestruck by the antics of Latham, who, living up to his
reputation, had taken a couple of Antoinette machines up in the air in company with his
colleague, Leymann, flying in the teeth of a gale to impress the distinguished visitors.

At the end of July, several French firms involved in aeroplane manufacture announced
a formal amalgamation to form a trade society to protect their interests. They adopted the
name *Chambre Syndicale des Industries Aéronautic*. Charles Voisin and Léon Levavasseur were
appointed to serve on the committee and they were joined by Maurice Mallet, whose
company, Zodiac, better known for manufacturing airships, had been recently making

serious moves in the direction of aeroplane manufacturing. The Comte Henri de la Vaulx, long-time friend and rival of Latham's cousin Jacques Faure, was the Zodiac technical director who had been engaged by Farman to build his new design for an aeroplane and it was believed the owners of Zodiac saw this move to aeroplane-making as holding greater potential for the future. The excellent performances of Maurice Farman's biplanes had been noted at the Reims show and, now that he had made impressive strides in proving that passenger-carrying could be improved upon, he had already received a second order from the French Government for three new machines of his own design.

Such matters held little concern for those outside business circles. Out in the streets, ordinary folk were showing markedly less interest in the minutia of individual record-breaking achievement. Expensive toys like motor cars, yachts and flying machines were all very wonderful but the public was growing bored by their novelty. People told each other that such fads were of use only to the elite. In the end, the inventors of such machines were merely in the business of making money from them. As for competitions and breaking records: rich people put up prizes and rich people won them. It was all of little relevance to the lives of ordinary people.

So the second Reims show came and went. Newspaper aeronautical columns had dutifully noted the records and awards each day and attention was already moving on to where the next aviation show would be held. In August, everyone of note would be leaving Paris for the summer and polite society would then fragment temporarily according to tastes and interests. Country estates would be visited. Keen equestrian fans travelled to Dublin for the Horse Show. Sportsmen headed for Scotland in anticipation of the grouse shooting season. The middle class took trains to seaside resorts. Europe was *en vacances*.

Although he had performed quite well throughout the year at various air shows, it was becoming obvious to many aerial correspondents that Latham's skilled piloting of his Antoinette monoplane could no longer be guaranteed to lead the field in many of the competitive events. As is often the case, he who forms the vanguard is ultimately passed out. However, there remained one notable accomplishment which Latham might still claim for his own. This was the ability to crash stylishly and without serious injury. It was as if he was under some charmed protection or surrounded by a magic aura. Experts had always believed that Latham's escapes were entirely due to the sturdy design construction of the Antoinette. With the chassis solidly built and to some eyes resembling that of a boat, it was generally thought the craft could withstand all buffets and blows; that it could ride the stormy airwaves and bob along crests of currents like one of those native canoes in turbulent rapids; that it would always be capable of gliding to safety when in difficulty. It was argued that it was Levavasseur's eccentric engine that was to blame for letting Latham down, time after time, and not the actual flying capabilities of his machine. But this opinion had held sway before anyone had witnessed the wings on Charles Wachter's Antoinette machine crumple; before the appalling, splintering smash that accompanied the Hauvette-Michelin fatality at Lyons. So what really kept Latham so coolly unperturbed and uninjured? Luck? Fate? Or was it an inner belief that he was untouchable while in the air; safe in his own schizoid-created cocoon. It was certainly uncanny.

*3. NOS AVIATEURS*

Latham's magic never failed to pull in enthusiastic crowds. (HLPP)

Consider his showing in 1910 alone: when his motor failed while he was competing in Nice in April, Latham had demonstrated his ability to glide downwards like a seabird until gently ditching his machine into the sea. He was picked up out of the water completely unscathed. By contrast, a meeting in Lyons had not brought him great successes. In fact, it had carried its own measure of bad luck. Although leading in the speed competitions there, he had ended up with another smashed machine but, again, without injury to himself. And as for his performances in St Petersburg in May – these had been more embarrassing than physically dangerous. It had taken four separate attempts to get the Antoinette airborne and, when finally in the air, he had flown for barely a minute before being forced into a heavy crash-landing. Yet all he had suffered was just a few bruises and some damage to his pride. An aviation meeting in Budapest had produced a slightly better outcome. Latham ended up with a good showing here and was well placed among the leaders for the fastest speed and longest time airborne – but it had not been gained without his usual thrills and spills and wrecked machines. It was amazing that the pundits did not begin to wonder what else could be keeping him protected besides his undoubted superior piloting skills. The more imaginative speculated on otherworld forces in play. He seemed to be touched by magic. Was he a mortal man at all?

Meanwhile, as progress in aviation had gone from strength to strength, carried along by the impact of competitive rivalry and relentless press coverage, Lord Northcliffe had continued to be seriously unwell and his London staff had seen little of him. Not being around did not mean that the 'Chief' had any lessened in any way his obsession with air power, of course, and it only highlighted the gravity of his condition that he had felt unable to personally present the Frenchman Louis Paulhan with the *Daily Mail* prize for the flight from London to Manchester. High summer had arrived. The 'Chief's' illness still dragged on and on despite messages of how eager he was to get back into harness he let it be known that his doctors had instructed him to 'take it easy': an almost impossible task, as everyone knew, for there was no letting up of his focus – no letting go of the issues nearest his heart.[14] Fortunately for those around him, Northcliffe was being increasingly swept up by his latest obsession, a desire for parliament to strengthen the imperial bond with Canada. An extended trip to Newfoundland was being planned.[15] He was to leave Britain in August and the visit would give him the opportunity to pursue this new goal while at the same time providing a beneficial holiday. As the date for his departure drew nearer, it was with some relief that his staff relished the fact that his travels would keep him away and out of everyone's hair until October.

The summer had been an exhausting one for Latham. By August he was in a downbeat mood. He seemed tired. One air show after another had been demanding of his physical and mental energy. There were lines of weariness etched round his eyes. He was determined, nonetheless, to perform well at the Havre-Deauville-Trouville meeting at the end of the month. But first, there would be participation in a number of cross-country events which were scheduled around that time. He particularly desired to make a good impression in the latter, having several times shown by example how useful a small aeroplane could be as a mode of transport for social occasions.

*Flight Magazine* would later run an enthusiastic, if not entirely accurate paragraph describing how he made use of the lawn in front of his home at Maillebois as his private landing strip – dropping in to make an unexpected visit to his mother and arriving 'just in time for dinner'. The report went on to add the impressive information that it had taken the aviator 'only one hour's flying time from Issy-les-Moulineaux, in Paris'.[16] But, while the timing was correct, the additional glamorising touch of making a landing on the château lawn was an exaggeration. The reported 'private landing strip' was, in fact, a large field in the estate, well clear of the house and its ancillary out-buildings. The enthusiast charged with writing this despatch must have been unaware that a small river bisected the ornamental 'lawn' immediately outside the château. Latham – even with his exceptional skill – would never have attempted to land in such a confined space. But the point had been made. This domestic use of an aeroplane as a transport vehicle was opening up hitherto unimaginable freedoms and possibilities. The local villagers were thrilled with the publicity his landing at Maillebois had generated. They posed proudly beside his Antoinette monoplane and a photographer from Dreux rushed a series of postcards of the scenes into print. The tiny rural community was now a part of aviation history.

As summer drifted towards autumn, headlines in the press kept public awareness of the importance of aviation alive and newspaper sales buoyant. French national journals took a keen interest in the outcome of the August cross-country events, particularly as the *Circuit de l'Est* – which would cover 782km – was being organised by the leading daily, *Le Matin*. The paper also sponsored the principal prize of 100,000 francs and, in addition, each of the six stages carried an individual prize. The first stage was Issy-les-Moulineaux to Troyes, some 135km away; the last stage was Amiens back to Paris.

MAILLEBOIS (E.-et-L.). - Le Monoplan " Antoinette " de M. Latham, dans le Parc de son Château de Maillebois

Latham's landing at the château created a historic occasion for the people of Maillebois, August 1910. (Harman Collection)

Latham serves as a sapper–pilot instructor during French Army manoeuvres in Picardy, 1910. (HLPP)

Undoubtedly prompted by the Antoinette Company's drive for sales, Latham was not slow to capitalise on the excellent publicity to be gained from the cross-country competitions, especially on the first stage, from the Paris Airfield to Troyes. The correspondent for the European edition of the *New York Herald* was sharp to pick up on the clever timing of Latham's flight, noting how it passed right over the centre of Paris and commenting how it 'coincided with lunchtime. Hundreds of Parisians witnessed the pretty spectacle and *midinettes* released from their ateliers rushed to the Tuileries Gardens to watch his flight cutting across the Champs Élysées and circling twice around the Eiffel Tower'. Some days later, the paper's correspondent reported that Latham had flown from Issy-les-Moulineaux once more, this time chased by the rumour that he had been heading for London. Instead he landed his Antoinette in Amiens to stay overnight and, on leaving the flying field the following morning, 'misjudged the distance and struck a tree before he could clear the aerodrome.' Once more, uncannily, he escaped injury but his machine was wrecked. It would seem the exhausting schedule he had set for himself had finally caught up, but there was to be no time for any long sustainable rest. In ten days' time he was once more flying in competition over the bay at Le Havre and Deauville to make his mark with six crossings of the Seine Estuary – the crowning test of this important air meeting and a feat which he doubled the following day. In everyone's eyes, Latham and his Antoinette were still the undisputed star turn. The next day, *Herald* readers were told: 'At the closing dinner held in the restaurant of l'Hôtel de la Plage there was a large centre piece in sugar representing M. Latham crossing the Seine'.

In the second week of September, Latham reported in for duty at the army camp at Briot to act an instructor for fledgling army pilots during the French Military manoeuvres in Picardy. The contribution of 'Sapper Pilot Latham' to the exercises at this time must have been regarded by the Chiefs of Staff to have been of considerable significance, for at the end of the exercises, he was informed that, 'in recognition of his contribution to aviation', his name would be included in next July's list of those to be awarded the title of *Chevalier de la Légion d'honneur*. A fitting tribute from the nation at last! But not before its time.

Duty done, Latham's next imperative was to get in some practice to qualify to be included in the French team to compete in an American Air Show which was to be held in Belmont Park, New York, in late October. Latham's first trip to the United States promised to be either a fantastic or terrible experience but, either way, it was to be a rite of passage long overdue. Another turning point, perhaps.

# NINE

# The New World Beckons

For the remaining weeks of September there was no let up of the hectic pace. The Antoinette flying school was extremely busy and Latham was being roped in more frequently to assist their regular instructor, Laffont, in the training of newcomers to aviation. As their star pilot, Latham was usually assigned to perfect the skills of some of the more prestigious clients like Prince Alphonse d'Orléans-Bourbon of Spain, some three years younger and fresh from the military academy in Toledo, who took lessons from him before going on to become Spain's first army aviator and pioneer in aerial warfare.

By this time, Latham's tutoring of France's 'Queen of Sports' Marie Marvingt was concentrating on her goal to participate in the competition for the *Coupe Fémina* – the first ever endurance test for ladies, sponsored by the French magazine of that name. Marie was the ideal candidate to compete in the *Coupe Fémina*, although, as the days shortened, flying conditions were far less pleasant. One of the greatest drawbacks attached to this new challenge was going to be the increasingly cold weather, which was difficult enough for male aviators to endure when flying in winter and quite formidable for the women because of constraints attached to what was considered suitable wearing apparel for female pilots. The wearing of goggles and scarves had come to be acceptable and the earlier practice of holding down the ends of a skirt firmly with a string tied right around which 'hobbled' the wearer was now more often superseded by the wearing of a divided skirt under which leggings and boots could be worn. In the United States, one of the first ladies to fly, Harriet Quimby, had already made a fashion statement with a personally designed purple satin flying costume which aimed to combine practicality with style. However, none of these advancements provided very effective protection against the harsher elements to be encountered in the endurance tests.

Faced with the problem of coping with the severely cold conditions for his pupil as the winter drew in, Latham had organised what he called a 'fur sack' to be made up which would envelope his pupil during her practice flights. Although remaining a novelty, its use was successful enough to subsequently allow Marvingt to come within a hair's breadth of gaining the award. In late November, while Latham was competing with the French team in the United States, she was prematurely hailed as the winner for having endured fifty-three minutes in the air while covering a distance of 42km. But the competition was

Programme for the International Aviation Tournament, Belmont Park, October 1910. (Smithsonian Institution, Washington)

keen and she was to be disappointed. She managed to hold onto this lead for only a week or so. In the last days of December, Hélène Dutrieu, a protégée of the Farman brothers, was declared the first holder of the prized *Coupe Fémina*. She had completed a flight of over 60km in just over an hour.

Latham had no problem in qualifying for inclusion in the French aviation team which was to compete in the International Aviation Tournament in New York's Belmont Park on 26–30 October. The show was being organised on Long Island under the auspices of the Aero Club of America and the French hoped to make a good showing. It had been quite a blow when the inaugural award of the *Coupe Internationale d'Aviation* had been taken by an American flyer, Glenn Curtiss, at the Reims Air Show and it would be a point of honour now for someone on their team to win it back for France on American home soil. They had a good chance. One member of the team, Alfred Leblanc, had a 100hp Blériot machine which been performing extremely well of late and Latham – who had persuaded Gastambide and Levavasseur to provide him with at least one machine powered by a 100hp Antoinette engine – was confident that several new technical improvements would allow him to fly at speeds up to 110mph. The *Coupe Internationale d'Aviation* was awarded for a machine that completed over twenty laps of a 5km course in the fastest time and there was every hope of a triumph. Things augured well for the American adventure. It would be Latham's first experience of the New World.

In early October, Latham and his friend the Comte Jacques de Lesseps were among the first members of the French aviation team to leave for New York. They travelled on a special boat train from Paris to the port of Le Havre to embark on the transatlantic liner *Lorraine* on Saturday 8 October. The party included the Comte's brother Bertram and their sister, Marie Eugénie, Comtesse de la Bégassière, who had married into an aristocratic family, owners of the château La Ville Lambert, in Brittany. She and her brother Jacques were not long returned from a successful trip to Canada where de Lesseps had not only demonstrated the capabilities of his Blériot flying machines in some style, but − in an astute move rather more to his financial advantage − had also successfully wooed and won the hand of Miss Grace MacKenzie, an heiress from Toronto and daughter of a wealthy Canadian railway tycoon. The acquisition of a distinguished foreign title was popular with ambitious North American social climbers who were willing to swap cash, or the promise of its support, for cachet. When Grace became Comtesse de Lesseps, she would enjoy an enviable social status among her peers. The gossip columnists were already reporting how this newly engaged couple planned to meet up at the forthcoming Belmont Park Air Show in New York and would then spend some time travelling with her parents in the United States before returning to Europe for a springtime wedding in London.

Latham's journey to Le Havre on the boat train was not without its moments. By the time they reached Rouen, word had got out that they were ensconced in one of the first-class carriages. A dense crowd of enthusiastic fans was waiting on the station platform and, to his companions' great amusement, and to his own growing annoyance, they found the faces of strangers pressed against the carriage windows in a hope of catching a glimpse of the celebrities. Almost the same situation came about later when visitors who had come on board the *Lorraine* to see off other passengers started rumours that the two aviators had been sighted walking around on one of the boat decks. Excited searches proved in vain. Latham had not even waited to watch the crate holding the wing sections of one of the two Antoinette machines he was shipping to the States being craned up onto the forward deck, but had retired immediately to his stateroom and would not appear again until the ship was well underway. One may only assume his patience in the face of feverishly enthusiastic admirers, on and off airfields, was beginning to wear very thin.

Arriving in New York, members of the French aviation team staying in the Waldorf Astoria Hotel soon discovered all that was novel lay just outside their door for the taking and the vibrant atmosphere of that city was like a tonic. Everything moved fast; the traffic, the people; the talk; the new buildings that soared up to dizzying height on every block. The Manhattan Life Building was twenty-six-storeys high; the Singer Building went even higher, up to forty-four floors. It was predicted that the increasing number of these 'skyscrapers', as they were being called, would eventually transform the city's skyline. Down at ground level new ways of looking at the world were accepted without question. Everything clipped down into what the Americans called 'buzz words': Life's too short; Time's money; Take it easy! No problem! It was like being permanently tipsy on a substance called optimism.

MODERN - OISEAUX

LATHAM

Latham was celebrated by many leading cartoonists of the day. (Harman Collection)

Soon after their arrival Latham and de Lesseps made a special excursion out to Long Island to inspect the flying course which was being laid out at the Belmont Race Track for what was being billed as the International Air Tournament. It did not take them very long to realise that what the organisers lacked in experience was being made up by their eagerness to display American ability to hustle. To Latham it seemed there was little evidence of thoughtful pre-planning given to the venture. He must have wondered if the organisers had taken any credence of what had been learned from mistakes made at the various European events? Had they studied the pitfalls to be avoided or the small refinements that were being introduced to ensure more safety for aviators and spectators? He feared not. The Americans had their own ideas. They would try to fix things to their own liking. When interviewed by some *New York Herald* journalists, Latham gave a forthright interview, in which he indicated his dismay on the conditions of the outer course over which the race for the Gordon Bennett *Coupe Internationale* was to be flown. 'I am pleased with the inner field, it is very satisfactory,' he told them. 'But the outer course will bar all attempts at high speed. It is the most dangerous so-called course I have seen. If the race is to be held here, it will be a very slow one. Nobody but a foolish daredevil should attempt speed on it.' When asked by the Press men if he intended to compete in this event, he replied that he would be flying, but that he would 'not try for a fast time', declaring emphatically that the course 'did not come up to the conditions laid down in the rules'.[1]

Jacques de Lesseps was quick to add his voice in support of Latham's critical assessment, commenting that: 'The race for the *coupe* should be run over a real course and not across country'.

Such forthright views really put the cat in with the pigeons. The interview with the two Frenchmen was widely aired in the next day's papers, not without some criticism and argument which hoped to justify the organisers' position. It made no use. Latham's opinion was set. Not one to leave things lie, he had made it his business to call in person to the American Aero Club's headquarters where he received assurances that the outer course would be made perfectly safe by the removal of all obstructions.

It has to be said that their intervention did not much please the American Aero Club's president, Mr Courtland F. Bishop. Behind closed doors we can imagine the gentleman's private comments were probably far more pithy than the measured tone of his reported response in the *New York Herald*, in which he continued to insist that 'Belmont Park fulfils the conditions', although he did have the good grace to admit the location was not utterly perfect, admitting that : 'It is true, in some places it would be difficult to effect a landing'. But his bland assertion that, '… by flying high an aviator can always pick out a place where he may land safely' was an unconvincing argument to offer experienced aviators. It may be taken that Latham was not impressed by the reassurances offered. These signs of conflict at this early stage of proceedings did not augur well for how things might turn out later in the week.

As the Belmont Park show got into full swing the Comte de Lesseps and his sister were kept busy entertaining his new fiancée, Grace MacKenzie, and her sisters in an unending round of social events which included taking these ladies up in a series of short flights. All the visiting aviators continually received requests from spectators anxious to be passengers and Latham did not escape similar attention. Ever since the announcement of his arrival in New York he had been getting sackfuls of mail from people – usually complete strangers – either seeking the privilege of being a passenger in his machine, asking for lessons, or requesting his opinion of their aeronautical inventions. Taken aback by such evidence of his popularity on this side of the Atlantic, he had coped with the onslaught cheerfully enough at first, but was clearly being swamped by this attack of enthusiasm. He must have deemed the problem required a spot of publicity for when interviewed by the *New York Herald* on 21 October, he admitted he was 'finding it impossible to answer the voluminous mail'. The report noted how Latham had '… laughed good-naturedly over the matter' while at the same time making sure it be known that he was 'personally not interested in the passenger-carrying department of aviation' and insisting that 'I have a racing machine solely intended to compete in the International Cup.' Pressed to expand on his views, he made it very clear that flying was no trivial pursuit: 'Neither in Europe nor here is there any royal road to learning to fly. One must be trained by experts,' he explained. As for the hopefuls who wanted him to consider technical novelties, his terse reply held a decidedly more dismissive note. 'I have no time to examine inventions, however meritorious'.

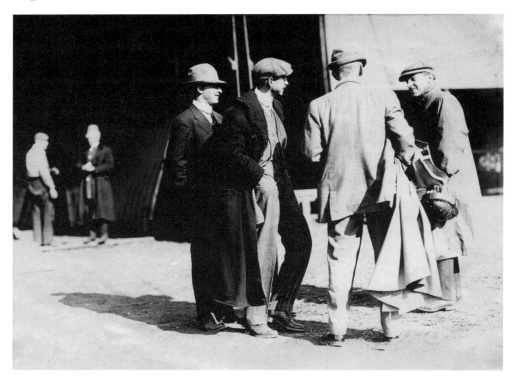

Latham chats to friends at the Belmont Park meeting, October 1910. (HLPP)

Considering all his past experience of Levavasseur's brilliant but exasperating brainstorms, Latham had probably had quite enough of coping with the wilder excesses of creative genius. Just before he left for New York, the engineer had been pestering him to consider a novel innovation he was keen to develop which would allow aircraft to be launched from the masts of ships at sea. He wanted a series of high poles to be erected at the Antoinette Camp at Châlons so that he could conduct some trials. Thankfully, the concept was still in its embryonic design stage and Levavasseur was ready to concede there were possibly a few snags still to be worked out. One is left wondering if there could have been times when Latham entertained serious doubts as to the sanity of his colleague's eccentric inventiveness?

As for the hundreds who longed to be carried as passengers in his Antoinette, Latham's argument that his machine was unsuitable for this use held good. While in New York, it would be left to de Lesseps, Grahame-White and the other members of the French and English teams to risk taking up the cream of New York society for joy rides during the aviation week.

In many ways, the social atmosphere at Belmont was reminiscent of the first Reims show. In New York, as happened elsewhere, the novelty of aviation events were attracting the smartest sets within the tight little circles of important and wealthy business families. Latham's *entrée* to New York's elite was guaranteed, not just by being the leading member of the prestigious French team, but from a number of personal introductions he had brought with him. Not only were doors open to him through the Latham and Mallet family interests in banking, steamships, rail and telegraph services but, in addition, he was carrying a letter from a good friend – very possibly Santos-Dumont – who had written to him from the Plaza Hotel, Buenos Aires giving details of several leading New York names and addresses of people 'worth looking up'.[2] The list is headed up by Cornelius Vanderbilt, described as 'a charming man', while his wife is cited as [a lady who is] 'very highly placed socially, who will introduce you to everyone'. The Vanderbilt cousins, Fred and his wife, are also recommended, the latter being another 'active woman very concerned with improving the social conditions of the masses' and the names and addresses of several bright young ladies follow, one of whom is recommended to Latham as worth pursuing, being described as a girl 'in a social situation of the first order … a great friend of mine and a pleasure to know'.

What New York offered was no different from Paris or London in this respect; word of mouth and personal introductions were the recognised conduits used by the senior members of certain elite circles and a fashionable gathering such as the Belmont Park Air Show held the promise of being chock-full of potential in the marriage market. Amid the trendsetters mingling with unconscious ease with famous sportsmen, politicians and diplomats could be found the begetters of the next generation of top people – the sons and daughters of foremost American families whose fortunes were sunk in city subways, oil and tobacco, international banking and railroad interests. The press correspondents accredited to the meeting dutifully cited the attendance of all these leading lights of society, while keeping an eye out for other titbits to write about. There was always the chance they might spot Latham chatting to the wife of the Austrian Ambassador, Baroness Henglemuller or, later, in more serious conversation with the scholarly French Ambassador, Jean Jusserand, an expert on the study of Middle English. Would Latham be found escorting some of the younger Vanderbilts attending the show with their brother-in-law, Harry Payne Whitney? Harry's wife Gertrude, great-granddaughter of the family's founder, Colonel Cornelius Vanderbilt, had studied art in Paris, so here was one person who would need no introduction to the French team of aviators. With a commission for the new downtown Pan American building, Gertrude was attracting serious attention in New York as a modernist sculptor. Like Eileen Gray, her days in Paris as an art student would have brought her in contact with many of the Parisian artists who had worked on the fringes of early experimental flight design – people like Delagrange, Henri Farman, Santos-Dumont or Levavasseur. Truly, the Atlantic Ocean had become a mere pond lying between the shores of culture and sport.

But despite all the pleasantries associated with the bright social scene in New York at that time, Latham's mood appears to have remained dark. His deep distrust of the organisers of the air show was palpable and he had been deadly serious in saying he was taking no chances when flying the Belmont Park Course. On Tuesday, which was the day for the Gordon Bennett *Coupe Internationale*, all the competitors, apart from Alfred Leblanc, flew the required laps at quite undistinguished speeds, just as he had predicted. A blustery wind was blowing and, once airborne, Latham took his turns cautiously wide.

Latham's Antoinette at the Belmont Park meeting. (HLPP)

He won the first hourly distance for twenty laps and then allowed his rate of speed to drop while remaining carefully at an altitude of only 40ft. However, despite this display of caution, the spectators who had gambled on witnessing one of Latham's spectacular mishaps were not to be disappointed. Wallace describes what happened next: after fifteen further faultless laps of the course, Latham's Antoinette had been caught by 'a sudden gust of wind … [which] slammed it straight at the crowded Belmont Park club house. Quite deliberately, Latham kept the Antoinette level, actually gaining airspeed as he roared towards the spectators until, at the last possible moment, he lifted it over the club-house roof and crashed in an empty paddock beyond'.[3] Latham's fast thinking had saved 'the lives of a score of New York's wealthy and elegant "smart set" with nerveless self-sacrifice'. A terrible disaster had been averted. The Antoinette was damaged but, as usual, Latham was completely unhurt. He was also out of the race.

The *Coupe Internationale* cup was won by the English competitor, Claude Grahame-White, flying a Blériot machine. His success brought something of a small, if wry, consolation for the French team. Having been wrested from the grasp of American aviation, the trophy could, at least, be carried back across the Atlantic by their neighbours.

The next eagerly awaited highlight of the week was a competition for a flight around the Statue of Liberty. The prize was $10,000.[4] Widely tipped to be won by a member of the French team, the prospect of being beaten in one of the most symbolic events of the whole Air Tournament was something this show's hosts did not anticipate with overmuch enthusiasm. When some dubious manipulation of the rules ensured the awarding of the prize to an American competitor later blew up into a right royal row, there were many who were not too surprised to discover how ruthless ambition had spawned the concept of winning at all costs.

With his machine smashed and undergoing repair, Latham was not able to take his place among the hopefuls for the Statue of Liberty Prize but he was still appalled by all the scandal which came to be attached to the event. Angry reverberations were to go back and forth across the Atlantic for weeks before the matter was settled. For many, it was all very disillusioning to find the underside of sporting success revealing itself to be just as corroded and fragile in the New World as it had been in Old Europe. How it had been possible for such a *contretemps* to arise?

The rules for the Statue of Liberty Prize stated that it was to be won by whosoever took the shortest time to fly from Belmont Park, round the Statue of Liberty and back again. The take-offs could only be made between 2.45 p.m. and 3.45 p.m. on Thursday afternoon, with all competitors coming in to land no later than 5.30 p.m. To be allowed to compete, each would-be competitor was supposed to have clocked-up over one continuous hour in the air during the previous week. But by Wednesday evening, only two pilots, Grahame-White and de Lesseps, had actually qualified to enter this race. Clearly, it was not going to be much of a contest, for de Lesseps had no chance pitting his little 50hp machine against Grahame-White's more powerful 100hp engine. However, the Comte displayed a sporting willingness to have a go rather than just allowing the prize to be awarded to Grahame-White by default. It was at this stage that the American Moisant brothers, the multi-millionaire bankers and import-export traders whose fortunes had originated in the coffee and sugar cane plantations of El Salvador, decided the prize could be theirs, rules or no rules.[5]

In spite of all the murky tales of exploitation attached to their business activities in Central America, Arthur Moisant (known to all as Fred) and his brother John were firmly ensconced within American Aero Club circles. John, in particular, had been determined to make his mark as a pilot and had spent a frustrating time the previous year in France in an attempt to build and fly his own machine. He finally settled for tuition at the Blériot school and purchased one of their machines. Now he was all set to show his worth and, while he had not yet flown in his native country, he was totally resolved to win the contest for the Statue of Liberty Prize. There was just one snag: he had not qualified by flying the requisite continuous hour in the air. Could the organisers not waive this rule as a special concession to their countryman?

The first inkling of trouble was a notice posted up for press correspondents when they arrived on Thursday morning, the day of the competition. This stated that the original rules relating to qualified aviators had been quashed by the committee. In the light of this decision, John Moisant could be allowed fly. Grahame-White and de Lesseps's immediate reaction was to mark their protest by withdrawing from the race. So now there was nobody left to compete with Moisant. It was to be a *fait complet*; a bit of a damp squib. What would he do?

Unfazed by the nicety of being the only contestant, Moisant's Blériot machine was duly prepared for take-off but just as he taxied it out to make a preliminary test flight, his machine was caught by a strong down-draft of wind and tossed violently into one of the parked Farmans. Both aeroplanes were completely wrecked. Wings off, struts gone: a real mess.

There was an immediate huddle of officials; a swift decision made. They could not allow themselves to be outdone by circumstances and immediately declared the Grahame-White and de Lesseps withdrawals from the race overruled. The aviators' original intention to compete must be honoured. Moreover, participation in the contest would be extended until Monday. This should allow enough time for the repair of Moisant's machine.

Finding their protests invalidated, Graham-White and de Lesseps gave in with good grace, realising that, if they had not agreed, the whole event might have to be cancelled and the blame laid at their door. They would fly around the Statue of Liberty on Sunday in the original starting time slot allotted for the competition: 2.45 p.m. to 3.45 p.m.

Flying conditions that afternoon were perfect. The race took place and, as anticipated, Grahame-White's superior speed easily out-flew de Lesseps's machine. By 3.45 p.m. the deadline for take-off had elapsed and Grahame-White was declared the winner. And that should have been the end of the matter.

But it was not. The Moisant brothers had been in no mood to be beaten. Finding John's damaged plane could not be fixed, by Sunday they had purchased a replacement. But by the time this machine was made ready it was past 4 p.m. and, according to the rules, they should have been officially excluded from taking-off. Another frantic appeal was made to attending American Aero Club committee officials who then obliged by turning a blind eye as Moisant took to the air almost twenty minutes past the deadline. Such was the confusion then that no one was quite sure afterwards what route he took, but his circuit of the State of Liberty was logged at forty seconds faster than Grahame-White's time. It was enough. The judges calmly reversed their original decision and announced that Moisant was to be awarded the prize. When the news broke, the American press corps were elated. The Statue of Liberty Trophy was theirs and hyperbole went into overdrive: 'Moisant's flight was the most superb thing the world has ever seen in an aeroplane', crowed the correspondent for the *New York Herald*.

There was more to come, of course. Under the revised rules, there was still another day left for aviators to compete and Grahame-White was not ready to concede so easily. He proposed making a fresh attempt the following day. At this, the organising committee once more moved swiftly. They coolly declared the competition to be now closed. Moisant had won the trophy and that was that. Predictably, Grahame-White's supporters immediately declared foul play. It would not end there. Outraged to a man, the Aero Clubs of England, Scotland and France declared no official confirmation of the result could be given until the matter was considered by the International Aeronautical Committee. In fairness, it must be said there were several American aviators who were as perturbed as the foreign visitors by this blatant bending and changing of the rules to effect the desired outcome. Displeasure was marked by an official boycott of the closing dinner for the Belmont Park prize winners which was being hosted by the American Aero Club at the Hotel Plaza. A swiftly arranged alternative protest celebration dinner in Sherry's was organised by Drexel and it is significant to find Latham representing the indignation of the French team at this gathering. Had he not also fallen foul of what may have been skulduggery behind the scenes during another competition – the 1909 Channel Flight Prize?

Moreover, it is noteworthy that Latham's other companion at dinner that evening was none other than his cousin Jacques Faure, who had travelled all the way down from Canada to join them, having just finished competing in an International Balloon Race. It may be recognised that the arrival of Faure, who was well respected on both sides of the Atlantic as a distinguished sportsman, must have lent considerable weight to suspicion that the Statue of Liberty Prize result had been rigged. What was later described as a 'monumental dinner and drinking party' that evening provided a splendid platform for those backing the hard-done-by Grahame-White.[6] Both Latham and Faure spoke at some length during the evening's declamations of outrage.

Their protests turned out to be well justified. Within a few weeks, a panel of International judges announced that American Aero Club's spurious claim to the prize had been axed. The official pre-set rules for a competition must stand and Grahame-White would take the Statue of Liberty Prize for Britain, as deserved.

Despite what the papers said in praise of the success of the New York aerial tournament, Latham's first taste of the American experience had been flawed by this display of unsporting behaviour. New York had been a bad start. If there was one thing Latham abjured, it was any hint of deviousness or lack of fair play. Undeterred that forthright views might create adverse publicity, he had never been loath to speak out in public when he felt straight talking was needed and, while not over concerned about his popularity on that side of the Atlantic, he must have been hoping things were going to turn out differently at the forthcoming show in Baltimore.

Perhaps sensing he might be teetering on the knife edge of another serious deterioration in his health if did not keep close watch on his diet, especially when in the company of his hard-drinking British and American colleagues, Latham had been careful not to let himself to get too tired or stressed these past few weeks. Since arriving in the United States he had deliberately cut short his attendance at the many social events put on by society hostesses. The chief *raison d'être* behind the rounds of parties, dinners and dances for the foreign visitors was dangerous ground and he was in no mood to be snared by some ambitious mother with a marriageable daughter bent on capturing a rich young man. So, when faced with the more rapacious advances of determined hostesses, he had made stiff excuses and raised not a few eyebrows when asked by a lady reporter in Baltimore if he thought their local girls were not far more attractive than those in New York by replying that he 'never noticed the ladies'.[7]

Yet, despite this gaffe, Baltimore newspapers found much to their liking in Latham's visit to their city and he received by far the best press coverage of all the foreign pilots – a factor calculated to lift any aviator's spirits and good humour.

The Baltimore show was a great success. Excited spectators turned up in their thousands to view aerial demonstrations of height, speed and manoeuvrability despite Baltimore's police department's threat to arrest anyone who violated the Sabbath by the act of selling tickets to the public. Despite a report in the *New York Telegram* that eight people had managed to get themselves arrested, all these grumpy rumblings had been largely

LATHAM IN HIS BEAUTIFUL "ANTOINETTE" HALETHORPE, MD.

Latham at Halethorpe. (HLPP)

ineffectual. On the first day of the show, crowds of spectators were thrilled at the sight of Latham taking his machine up to a height of 2,100ft. On the following day he flew over the city, making certain to pass directly over one ailing multi-millionaire citizen's mansion, whom, it was rumoured, had provided $5,500 for this privilege.

It was generally agreed among the participants that the more prominent visitors to the Baltimore show were significantly of a more serious disposition than those in attendance at New York's Belmont Park. The presence of leading politicians and many more army representatives indicated increased eagerness to investigate the possibilities of using aircraft for waging war. Press reports noted that the eminent visitors from Washington included the Postmaster General, Frank Hitchcock, and the Chief of the Army Signal Corps, General James Allen. The attendance of the American Secretary of War, Jacob M. Dickinson, and the President of the Army War College, General Wm. Witherspoon and Count Zeppelin were also commented on. Other worthies showing keen interest included the well-known author and soon-to-be diplomat, Thomas Nelson Page. When demonstration of aircraft capabilities in warfare were mounted for spectators drawn from the armed services, Latham's skill in the use of small arms for shooting targets while in the air produced an impressively high score. There were also simulated bomb-dropping exercises undertaken from the height of not less than 100ft, using bags of flour. In one report, New York's *Journal of Commerce* takes pains to emphasise how some of Latham's best scores were dropped from double this height and against a rising wind, while one – designated as an example of a bomb aimed down into the funnel of a battleship – rated as a bullseye.[8]

Excited spectators watch as Latham flies over Baltimore. (HLPP)

Latham's Antoinette does a circuit of the port at Baltimore. (HLPP)

In the meantime, an event in the Wright brothers' home-town of Dayton had produced an intriguing *Herald* headline: 'First Aerial Goods Van Breaks a World's Record'.[9] The despatch reported how a consignment of silk, weighing 45lb had been transported sixty-five miles in a Wright machine. The time taken for the journey was only sixty-six minutes. The concept of 'air freight' had been born. Immediate reaction was low key. It was thought that – if such a term could ever be coined – the use of cargo planes would be expensive and confined to the carriage of small amounts of lightweight goods. Surely there was no real challenge to railways and steamships? Only the most perceptive were prepared to leave the question open.

The Baltimore show closed on 13 November. No rows or disputes had flared up to mar the atmosphere, everyone was well pleased with the outcome and several members of the French team returned to New York to make their farewells to friends. In a week or so, Latham would set off for California. Jacques de Lesseps was leaving for Canada with his fiancée Grace Mackenzie and her parents, in order to finalise plans for their forthcoming tour of Mexico. The Comte's sister, the Comtesse de la Bégassière, was returning to France on the transatlantic liner *Lorraine*.

Before leaving, the Comtesse gave an interview to the *New York Herald* in which she announced that her brother had made a decision to forego aviation for a while. Private nods might well have concluded his abandonment of a flying career had been the price the Comte must pay for the acquisition of an heiress, but in those days no prying pressman would dare to make such an opinion public. Other considerations were in play, in any case. Suggestions were being tossed around that an aerial survey of the isthmus of Panama during its construction would assist plans being made for the future fortification of the Canal

Zone.[10] The building of the Panama Canal was still a sensitive issue for the French – given its traumatic history – and one does not need to surmise too much that de Lesseps's graceful retirement from the aviation scene at this juncture bears all the hallmarks of excellent timing. He would have been keen to put some distance between his family name and any lingering memories attaching his late father's scandalous financial failure in Panama.

Not surprisingly, there is no record of Latham or any other European aviator showing ambition to fly in Central America. One of the civil engineers consulted, Lewis T. Haney, had made no bones about the dangers of such a mission, predicting that a pilot would have not only have to contend with tropical heat, but would be faced with unpredictable wind eddies and cross-currents which swept over the surface of the jungle and swamplands on both sides of the canal.[11] It very much looked like American aeronauts would have to handle the Panamanian aerial survey for themselves.

With the formalities of competing in New York and Baltimore now behind him, the dark and brooding mood that had hung over Latham since his arrival in the United States was lifting. It was as if some anticipated impending menace had not materialised. There had been no ghastly tragedy. No really serious trauma. The aviator was now much more relaxed. The excellent publicity given to his Antoinette monoplane's performance in Baltimore could not have been better and he was now looking forward to the air shows in Los Angeles and San Francisco with greater hope of enjoying himself. His crew of mechanics had already set off for the West Coast ahead of him and the Antoinette had been crated up for the journey. Nothing signalled the onset of deep sorrow that was about to strike him down in just over two weeks' time.

It was now December. Latham was still in New York, making final preparations to leave for California when a cable reached him bearing the most terrible news. Jacques Faure, his beloved cousin, friend and mentor, had died suddenly and quite unexpectedly in Canada from an attack of typhoid fever. There had been no warning, no hint. Latham must have been devastated with shock. It was barely a few weeks since they had supported each other to fight for Grahame-White's entitlement of the Statue of Liberty Prize. When they parted, his cousin had been anxious to get back to Canada as soon as possible to catch up with his friend, Walter de Mumm, a champagne manufacturer, fellow balloonist and, more recently, the owner of an Antoinette machine, who was to join him on an expedition to hunt moose. Faure would have been edgy, impatient to be away and his adieu to Latham may have been brisk; perhaps with a promise to meet up again in the spring when they were both back home in France. And now fate had dictated otherwise.

By Saturday 3 December the news had reached the world's press. Newspaper obituaries were lavish in their praise of Faure and spoke of the esteem this well-liked sportsman had enjoyed. Émile Dubonnet, a member of the French aperitif family, described as one of his close and intimate companions, recalled how Faure 'had made no enemies in life, only friends'.[12] Left with the memory of so many shared adventures – the yacht and motor-racing, the ballooning and hunting – Latham must have found the loss of his long-time mentor hard to bear. The disturbing omen of doom that had bothered him so deeply ever since his arrival in the United States had revealed itself be justified. It had threatened to envelope him and now it was here. These were black days, indeed.

# TEN

# 'Kingpin Man-Eagle'
# Thrills the Yankees

Setting off for California with a heavy heart, Latham would not have anticipated that the tedium of a long railroad journey – across a whole continent east to west – was to have its own healing value. But it had given him time and space to mourn the passing of yet another of his good friends and had allowed quiet moments to mull over the vision of the future they had shared, one that was becoming less and less improbable. The coming of air links – city to city; state to state; nation to nation – to bring mail, goods and people just as efficiently as railroads and steamers would create lines of communication on a global scale. It was breathtakingly simple.

What a boon it would be in the colonies! Crossing the Sahara in hours, or flying over the bush, the aeroplane would triumph in places which previously could only be travelled by river, on foot or with pack animals. Some of the most difficult routes he had traversed three years ago in Abyssinia, each of which took him several weeks to complete, might be covered within days, if not hours.

Of course, Latham was not alone in this thinking. At the time of his leaving for the United States, a report had appeared in the *Paris Journal* which indicated that the French Colonial Army was well ahead in making plans to build aerodromes in Algeria on the edge of the Sahara.[1] The despatch even mapped out several sites in North Africa that had been surveyed and earmarked. Airfields at Oran and Blida were to be followed by air links between Biskra and Tougourt and eventually a service running south between Timbucto, Agadar and Tchad. An adequate budget to the Colonial Office was already on the cards and potential for expansion into French Equatorial Africa and the Congo a possibility. There was only one snag in this plan: top brass, in the form of General Bailloud, was still considering whether, instead of using air links, a wireless telegraph system might prove more advantageous and much less dangerous.[2]

With time on his hands as his train rolled across the vastness of American mid-western prairies, Latham may have mused at length on this report. Was the time right for him to return to Africa to conduct covert aerial surveys of colonial terrain? The concept was not as far-fetched as it sounds. Rumour mills were hinting that the British authorities were entertaining similar intent and had already shipped off several different models of aeroplanes to British Colonies. Two Sommer machines were en route to Bombay – if not already there – and a pupil of Henri Farman was currently showing off his flying skills in Singapore. Reports in *The Times of India* maintained these Farman demonstrations were poised to continue – first in Saigon and then in other locations throughout Indochina. Farman's next move would probably be to seek out markets in South Africa and South America. Latham must have wondered whether he might see not his way to have a word with some of the French Colonial Office people on his return to Paris. Interesting opportunities lay ahead.

However, being realistic, he knew that many of the new technical improvements currently being developed in aviation were more closely focused on refinements for active military service and not for geographical ordnance or commerce. Already there was acceptance of aeroplanes for reconnaissance of battlefields or enemy troop movements. And now, as had just been demonstrated in Baltimore, trained pilots could fire guns and drop high explosives accurately on targets. The awful realisation was clear: devastating destruction was going to be the inevitable and ultimate outcome of all these years and months of cheerful aeronautical rivalry and sportsmanship. It was going to be a veritable enactment of those Futurists' wilder predictions.

Latham should have sensed he was being sucked into a vortex. His old friend Santos-Dumont had seen it all coming with an increasing personal dismay that made no secret of his utter abhorrence of airborne armaments. When, earlier that year, this stylish and courageous early pioneer of aviation had had to finally abandon flying for good because of the onset of an incapacitating disease – multiple sclerosis – he had made sure to convey his feelings on aerial warfare to everyone, vowing that on his return to Brazil he would devote the rest of his life to promoting the peaceful benefits of aviation in commerce and communication.[3]

By the time the long coast-to-coast train journey to California had been completed, Latham would have been rested and more cheerful. He had left behind him the chill-to-the-bone sharp air of New York which was already bracing itself for the onslaught of harsh winter weather. Left behind, too, was the unfettered rawness of the metropolis; the dog-eat-dog striving for success; the constant noise produced by man and machine; a glimpse, perhaps of Marinetti's disturbed vision of a future world. When he emerged from the downtown Los Angeles railroad station it was like turning back the clock to a gentle late summer day. The sun shone; the light breeze was balmy and flowers bloomed in profusion. Behind him were those dark days of mourning for his beloved cousin Jacques Faure. It was high time to move on.

How his heart must have lifted with the realisation that he would soon be back in the air. The Antoinette team of mechanics had travelled out earlier and they had had plenty of time to make sure his machine was behaving perfectly. Moreover, the Californian Aviation Association had set up a fund to run the Los Angeles Air Meeting – with the profits going to charity – and, in response to a request from the chairman for a subscription, Latham had sent them a donation of $1,000.[4] It had been received graciously and had the advantage of putting him in good stead with the organisers. With the show not due to start until Saturday 24 December there were several days of relaxation to enjoy and, as the Americans would say, everything was just dandy. It was the ideal time to turn his thoughts to the eager response he had received in reply to cabled enquiries about the possibility of a spot of novelty duck hunting. The result proved almost too easy to arrange.

Two days before the opening of the air show, on the invitation of a prominent member of Los Angeles's sporting set, he took his machine and a twenty-gauge gun into the air over the Bolsa Chico hunting grounds, ten miles outside the city. The following morning, 23 December, the audacity of the exploit made headlines on the front page of the *New York Herald* which declared: 'Mons. [sic] Hubert Latham bags one duck on first aeroplane shooting trip. He pursues the birds miles out over the sea: stirs up thousands.'

The jaunt had been an inspired introduction to the West Coast. Not only had he conducted the world's first duck shoot from an aeroplane, he had also made the inaugural flight of an Antoinette monoplane on the Pacific coast. The journalist who wrote the report described how the throb of the aeroplane's motor caused consternation among the snipes, mud hens and ducks and went on to explain how, for twenty minutes or so, Latham had chased the flock of startled birds out over the ocean until more than three miles from the shore. He had 'emptied both barrels of his shotgun and at least one bird fell'. When interviewed later, Latham comments that had he brought a heavier, twelve-gauge gun on board, he would have done better with some of the long range shots. In due course, a week or so later, it was arranged for him to present the duck he had bagged – now preserved by a taxidermist for posterity – to the members of the exclusive, semi-Masonic, all-male Bohemian Club, which had recently re-opened its luxurious re-built premises on Post and Taylor Street in San Francisco. Latham's welcome into their midst had been a rare honour bestowed to mark a unique sporting first.[5] Things could not have got off to a better start. The exploit had made a piece published in the London magazine *Sketch* ten days earlier sound prophetic:

The Sporting Aeroplane:

Mr Hubert Latham has offered to make a five-thousand-dollar bet that he will shoot antelope and grisly bear and other big game from a monoplane. If Mr Latham wins his bet and is able to prove that a monoplane can be kept sufficiently steady to admit of a sure aim being taken from it by a man with a rifle, big-game shooters will begin to take an interest in flying-machines, which they have not as yet evinced. A tiger in the long grass, one of the great wild-cat family, lying on the branch of a tree, a rhinoceros in reeds, buffalo and lions in the scrub, all conceal themselves from an enemy approaching on the level; but none of them give a thought to an enemy coming from the sky; and broken ground and thick undergrowth will cease to be obstacles if the flying-man can become a shooting-man as well. Of course if something should go wrong with the propeller or with the wings, and the sportsman, instead of shooting his tiger, should fall onto it, the odds will be greater in favour of the tiger killing the man than of the man killing the tiger.[6]

Purists were outraged. Others were mildly amused by that final tongue-in-cheek comment about the airman literally falling prey to a tiger instead of vice versa. But – in reality – there was no point in shielding the public from the dreadful truth that men

# Mons. Hubert Latham Bags One Duck in First Aeroplane Shooting Trip

### He Pursues the Birds for Miles Out Over the Sea.

## STIRS UP THOUSANDS

### Warmly Complimented by Mr. Curtiss, Who Declares Feat Opens New Field for Airships.

[SPECIAL DESPATCH TO THE HERALD.]

LOS ANGELES, Cal., Thursday.—Mons. Hubert Latham, the French aviator, in his Antoinette monoplane, flew from the aviation field to-day to the Bolsa Chica hunting grounds, a distance of ten miles, where he killed one duck.

This is a world's record for duck shooting from an aeroplane and the first flight of an Antoinette on the Pacific coast.

When the big monoplane flew over the slough, where the best shooting is on the preserves, water fowl rose by the thousands. The throb of the Antoinette's motor caused consternation among the snips, mudhens and ducks, which frequent this place.

Mons. Latham's craft was in the midst of a flock of ducks before they could get away and he emptied both barrels of his shotgun. One bird fell

HUBERT LATHAM IN HIS MONOPLANE

man, and aeroplanes can be constructed that will be better adapted to the sport."

## AERO CLUB SANGUINE OVER MOISANT CASE

"They are not fighting a mere handful of men in New York, but the whole organized aviation interests of the whole United States. They are fighting America, and our opponents will find our position, as presented before the federation,

Latham's flying duck shoot in Los Angeles headlined in *The New York Herald*, 23 December 1910. (Author's Collection)

and flying machines constituted a dangerous combination which could cause tragedy in whatever circumstances. It was to be starkly demonstrated on American soil only too soon. The Los Angeles Air Show had been in full swing when two horrifying aerial fatalities blighted the optimism of the New Year celebrations. Both accidents occurred, albeit it in different locations, on the day the Michelin Altitude Trophy was being competed for in Los Angeles on 1 January 1911.

Latham and Archie Hoxsey – who was the most popular of the Wright brothers' fearless pilots – were considered by everyone to be the leading contenders in the Michelin event. Hoxsey was confident of a successful record-breaking flight. Just before take-off, he had announced to the attending press correspondents that his ambition was to reach the unprecedented height of 12,500ft. It seemed an impossible and foolhardy feat to attempt in the face of the stiff and gusty winds that were blowing. Significantly, Latham was still nurturing the low-key cautious mood that had enveloped him since his arrival in the United States and he had more or less indicated that he did not expect to break his own altitude record that day.

The event got underway without any hitch and, for over an hour and a half, the spectators watched in amazement as Hoxsey's machine rose higher and higher until but a speck in the sky. His machine's barograph later revealed that he had reached over 7,000ft when, without warning, his machine began a spiralling descent downwards. At first, the watchers thought he was deliberately making tight circles as he made his descent. Then it became obvious that all was not well. The machine never pulled out of the spiral but plunged inexorably earthwards to crash with horrifying impact. The chilling details, as reported in the *Daily Telegraph*, describe the crash:

> The cracking of the spars and ripping of the cloth could be heard as the machine, a shapeless mass, came hurtling to the ground in a series of somersaults… when attendants rushed to the wreckage they found the body crushed out of all semblance to a human being.

The cause of the accident was never satisfyingly diagnosed. There was speculation that Hoxsey may have suffered an attack of 'Mountain Sickness' similar to that experienced by a climber whose heart action becomes almost paralysed from the effect of great heights. It was later deemed an inadequate explanation, although Latham was inclined to concur with this theory because he had been flying not too great a distance from the doomed machine and had had a clear view of Hoxsey from the air at the commencement of his fatal descent. It seemed to him that the aviator had made no move to control his craft, almost as if he had already lost consciousness.

Later that same day, if Hoxsey's demise was not enough, stunned aeronautical journalists learned of a second fatality at a flying field near New Orleans. The American flyer, John Moisant, who was still embroiled in dispute over the awarding of the Statue of Liberty Prize, had lost control of his Blériot monoplane as he made preparations to land. At a height of about a 100ft, a sudden gust of wind had caught the tail of his machine and up-ended it. Moisant had been pitched completely out of his seat onto the ground, breaking his neck on impact.

In the days that followed, the loss of these two leading American airmen provoked a spate of critical commentary on the safety of flying machines and the real dangers to be faced in performing hazardous stunts to please crowds. As one American pilot put it: 'We shall all be killed if we stay in the business. It is only a question of time. The spectators desire sensation and the aviators strive to please them'.[7] Debate raged as to how to eliminate feats of recklessness while it was generally agreed that if progress in aeronautics was to continue, test pilots must undertake risky experiments. There were no comforting answers to be found.

One way to cope with the danger inherent in this game was to ignore it. The tragic deaths of Hoxsey and Moisant had to be put firmly out of Latham's mind in order to concentrate on the opportunities being offered by the forthcoming San Francisco meeting. He made it no secret that he was keen to fly his Antoinette over the Golden Gate Park, having been assured that this section of the Pacific coast had spectacular scenery ideal for viewing from the air. He and one of the British team members, James Radley, had agreed to undertake some circuits of the area as soon as they arrived there.

In an interview for the *San Francisco Chronicle*, on 8 January, Latham offered an ecstatic summing-up of his first flight over this stretch of the Pacific coast and city:

Latham's Antoinette over the city of San Francisco. (Smithsonian Institution, Washington)

> It was the finest flight I ever made and you are to be congratulated on your beautiful climate
> which allowed me to see every object beneath me. It was a beautiful sight and I only wish
> that every person in San Francisco could see the city as I saw it… Sailing through the
> cloudless sky in brilliant sunshine in the heart of winter is an experience which I had thought
> until now could only be obtained in the South of France.

A compliment indeed.

The San Francisco Show opened on 7 January to a large gathering of spectators. A special train service to the airfield had been laid on, and the organisers had cleverly pitched the aim of several advertisements to stir up the notice of a younger generation. 'See the Birdmen FREE', advertised the *Chronicle* excitedly, going on to urge:

> Boys you can easily earn an entire day at Aviation Park. You can be an official messenger at
> two dollars a day and take twenty friends to Children's Day. You can see Latham, the kingpin
> man-eagle with his giant Antoinette – the man who flies rain or shine because he loves to
> fly.

Despite the colourful description of being a 'Kingpin man-eagle' and his apparent disregard of the weather, Latham and his monoplane were still at the mercy of unpredictable flying conditions. The following day, although bright, saw what was described as dangerous cross-currents of winds sweeping across the peninsula. The flights over the Golden Gate Park might have been successful twenty-four hours previously, but now neither Latham nor Radley could get their machines airborne. It was a pure piece of luck that these cross-currents did not hamper one of the later highlights of the day's events, later explained to the readers of the *New York Daily Tribune* as 'a sham battle staged between soldiers of the 2nd battalion of the 13th United States Infantry and two aviators flying Wright Biplanes'. From a height of 400ft the Wright aviators dropped mock bombs on to the soldiers who were 'defending' themselves shooting with blank cartridges.

Fortunately, the setback to the Antoinette's participation was only a temporary one. Two days later and once more in the air to thrill the crowds, Latham had flown his machine past the grandstand while the band played the *Marseillaise* in his honour. Without question he was viewed as the hero of the hour. But fate, as ever, was once more ready to strike with unforeseen disaster. Headlines next day in the *San Francisco Chronicle* reported woeful news: 'Latham's beautiful Antoinette is wrecked in collision with a barbed-wire fence. Daring Frenchman is uninjured.' Every detail of the accident was described in the press coverage:

A little gust of wind and rain had come over the hill from the sea. Before it had passed over the field Latham had started [his take off]. He cleared the knoll on the north of the hollow, flying low. Then the gust caught the big wings and those who watched saw him turn and go down the east slope of the hill just clear of the ground. Crash! It was the barbed wire fence in the hollow that caught the rubber tyre bicycle wheels and tore them ruthlessly from the shaft. The impact toppled the graceful machine to the ground and in an instant it was a wreck. When the flying squadron of infantry, Army ambulances and Press photographers reached the scene, Latham was standing beside the dead bird smoking a cigarette in a long amber mouthpiece and giving utterances to pure Parisian French that may have been emotional, but had a very calm and dignified sound, '*Très mauvais*'. That was the extent of his observation.

The inside section of the same day's newspaper also made much of the crash in its gossip column, with a report which expanded on the accident with glowing admiration for Latham's renowned sangfroid:

The coolest and apparently least annoyed man over the accident which put the Antoinette machine out of the meet for good, was aviator Latham. After the accident he returned to his hangar and slowly divested himself of his flying uniform, replacing it with his overcoat and hat. As he left the hangar he was approached by several friends and fellow aviators who sympathised with him on the loss of his machine. Waving his inevitable cigarette, Latham said: 'It cannot be helped. I said all I wanted to when the accident took place. Now I will watch you all and be a spectator'.

Significantly, this incident brought rather more than usual disappointment to Latham. Plans had been made for him to take part in an important experiment later on that same

Latham landing during the San Francisco Air Show. (Smithsonian Institution, Washington)

day, during which his Antoinette would be carrying special equipment to test out the use of wireless while airborne. If the results of this experiment had proved successful it would have enhanced anticipation that air-communication links across difficult terrain were more feasible when supported by some form of radio telegraphy. Latham must have been well aware that such a system might be particularly useful to expedite the French army's proposal to establish a string of flying fields in Saharan Africa.

Under the headline 'Upper air currents stop wireless tests', the *San Francisco Chronicle*'s aviation expert, Paul Beck, had been careful to comment that:

> Had Latham not met with this unexpected accident… the demonstration in wireless telephonic and telegraphic receiving would have been a success. The entire apparatus was ready, the details of the experiment had been arranged with Latham and he was in the act of making a preliminary flight to warm up his engine and try aerial target practice with a view to taking up the more serious wireless work when the unfortunate accident occurred.

It might have seemed to some that Latham accepted the failure of the wireless experiments with more than usual sanguinity. But this attitude only underlined his calm acceptance that the operation of an aircraft could not be relied upon when safe landing places were not correctly installed or the weather did not co-operate. As to the loss of the Antoinette, the setback only meant he was unable to bring his machine with him on his journey home via China and Japan, a route which may have been planned to include the possibility of generating a few sales there. Japanese military sources, in particular, were known to be keen buyers in the aviation market.

The West coast of the United States was keeping a wary eye on their neighbours across the Pacific. Reporting on the air show, one *Chronicle* journalist voiced unease at the sight of 'a car-load of Chinese gentlemen' seen watching all the flights in each event with absorbed interest. The despatch hinted that these people might be on official business for their government. However, suspicions were allayed – perhaps not without some relief – when it was discovered the gentlemen were merely merchants from the city's Chinatown.[8]

The San Francisco's aviation meeting came to a close without further incident and as people began to pack up and head home, the New York correspondent of the *Globe* sought out Latham for an interview. Latham's co-operation with pressmen was usually good. He was forthcoming, attentive to any questions put to him and normally tactful in his replies. However, on this occasion he may have felt it was appropriate to voice some of things that had caused him the most displeasure. Some straight talking was due before he took his leave of the United States and there is a more than hint in the report that suggests he may have been tired of being diplomatic and polite. A headline in the *Globe* on 16 January 1911 set the tone:

'M. Latham's Plaint'

> The foreign flying men … are on their way home, all of them more or less disgruntled with their experiences here. They complain they are not treated with the same personal consideration here as in Europe, that flying meetings here are mismanaged, and often the sport is made needlessly dangerous by the local arrangements. M. Hubert Latham, one of the discontented migrants, says his machine was wrecked at San Francisco on Wednesday solely through the monstrous carelessness of the managers of the local gathering in leaving barbed wire fences on the course…

Latham had gone on to say that, with his own plane now damaged beyond repair, he would do no further flying because he 'would not trust himself to any American-built aeroplane'. He had also thrown repeated scorn on the sensation, just lately announced, that an American aviation expedition was going to fly across the isthmus of Panama. This was not the first time he had expressed contempt for the foolhardiness of such a project – a view that would hardly have found much favour with his interviewer. Clearly rankled, the American pressman's report went on to comment waspishly that:

> M. Latham is thought to be rather ungrateful. It is contended that he has been rather well treated during his stay in this country, and it is estimated that he will take back with him to France material consolation for any lack of American politeness in the shape of at least $50,000 in good American money. For the rest, flying has undoubtedly gained popularity in this country through the performances of foreign experts, and the business of making aeroplanes is becoming quite a respectable industry.

In the carp about the money, the reporter had been reasonably correct in estimating Latham's American earnings to have been $50,000. Such sums were not anything untoward. *The Westminster Gazette* had calculated that Latham must have made about

Widely distributed as postcards, images of Latham created international publicity. (Harman Collection)

262,159 francs in fees and prizes altogether since mid-1909 and that someone like Paulhan would have earned almost twice this amount, perhaps even as much as 410,000 francs.[9] Very little was ever left over from these vast sums to show a working profit for individual aviators, however. Fees and prizes were swallowed up by the huge expenses incurred. To those in the know, it was no surprise that Blériot expected to command 75,000 francs per day. He would have needed it. Compared to flyers with a generous private income like Latham, he and some of the other practitioners who were trying to build up a fledgling business in this new form of transport on stretched capital outlay were not immensely rich men. They needed every prize they could get. The *Globe*'s journalist's transparent display of pique in the reference to 'good American money' and the lofty declaration that aircraft manufacturing was now being considered 'respectable', would have struck anyone trying to make a living out of aviation at that time as being as a most naïve remark.

Some time later, in a letter home while still en route back to France, Latham would write that he had been disappointed by the United States and its people. His exposure to both East and West Coast culture had been raw and invigorating but he does not seem to have been over-awed by the hustle to impress, the eagerness to embrace change for change's sake or the attempts to throw out much of the stuffy convention of European etiquette in order to reinvent a new set of rules for social behaviour. His curiosity may have exposed him to the latest jazzy music rage called Ragtime or to some of San Francisco's exuberant new dance-floor routines with outrageous names like the Turkey Trot, but what had he made of it all? Whether he loved it or hated it intensely, there is the certainty that he could not have come away uninfluenced from the New World, one way or another.

On Saturday, 28 January 1911, the *San Francisco Chronicle's*, 'Water Front News and Maritime Intelligence Notes' describes how the strains of the music being played by a Filipino band on the deck of the Pacific Mail Liner, SS *Korea*, had drifted across piers 41 and 44 as the vessel made final preparations for cast off at 1 p.m. The liner was bound for its regular ports of call: Honolulu, Yokohama, Kobe, Nagasaki, Shanghai, Manila and Hong Kong. It was to be a leisurely, pleasant trip for the hundred or so cabin passengers. Among those earmarked for disembarkation at Yokohama, the paper dutifully notes an 'important passenger, Hubert Latham, the French aviator, who puffed cigarettes and watched the preparations for going to sea with a careless gaze. His is on his way home to Paris after an eventful career in the United States'.

When he wrote to his mother from the Hotel St Francis, San Francisco, a few days before his departure, Latham had outlined his plans to return home by way of the Caribbean and Japan. The journey was to take about five or six weeks. The first port of call was Honolulu in five days' time. He is elated with news received that he has been elected to one of the most prestigious clubs in Paris, the *Rue Royale*, and he is eagerly looking forward to his return home. Yet, despite the up-beat mood, the letter is careful to make her aware that a bitter cloud of dispute has been gathering over his relationship with the *Société Anonyme Antoinette*. Since his arrival in the United States he had been pestered by several letters from his cousin Jules Gastambide over the matter of costs accrued for the installation of the big 100hp engine in his Antoinette for the Belmont Park show and the expense of additional insurance cover incurred. With increasing displays of testiness, Gastambide had sent several statements of accounts to him since October. These had been accompanied by letters addressed to Latham's Paris apartment and, as Gastambide did not know his whereabouts in New York, with copies despatched to him care of a firm of accountants who could contact him in the United States. By the time Latham had reached the west coast, these communications were being followed up by urgent telegraphs demanding payment. Exasperated by all this hassle and wanting to wait until his return to Paris to sort out several disputed details in the accounts, Latham had responded finally from Los Angeles with a cheque for 10,000 francs which was only in part payment of the full amount. The gesture had thrown Gastambide into a fury. And Latham's laconic telegraph '*Impossible pas d'accord*' in reply to one of his cousin's more incensed and angry demands to pay up in full merely provoked even greater ire. Gastambide's earlier letters may have complained peevishly of being hurt and wounded to the core by Latham's tardiness, now things had turned more serious: he was threatening to sue.

Latham's letter to his mother from San Francisco clearly reveals his laid-back attitude to all this kerfuffle. He informs her that, in his opinion, his cousin and the other directors of the firm appeared to be completely 'wicked or stupid' men – perhaps both – by making such threats. And he goes on to further warn his mother to ignore Gastambide if he tried to make any either direct or oblique approaches to her for money. He writes that he will sort all the difficulties out on his return and tells her very firmly that she must not allow herself to get involved in the matter.

In the meantime, Latham was determined to enjoy a leisurely journey home via the delights of the Orient. It may be assumed that when Latham made his stop off at

Yokohama, he had not intended to meet up with any possible Japanese purchasers of the Antoinette monoplane. Things might have been different if he had been able to ship a machine with him with which to make some demonstration flights. But, as it was, both his machines had come to grief. He had nothing to show. In any case, he may have been aware that other manufacturers had already cornered this market. Only a few weeks earlier, on 14 December, two Japanese army captains, fresh from training in France and Germany, had made the first public demonstration of aircraft at an Army Parade ground at Yoyogi, just outside Tokyo. They flew a machine bought from Henri Farman. The Japanese army had already taken delivery of two German-built machines, a Blériot monoplane and a Wright bi-plane, and plans were in hand for a special military commission from Japan to visit Buc, near Versailles, to inspect some Maurice Farman biplanes. Clearly, the Japanese had been swept with enthusiasm for several of the more successful rivals of the Antoinette machine.

With his experiences in Indochina still relatively fresh in his memory, Latham had treated this latest foray in the East as a holiday. His close association with Eileen Gray and her obsession with Oriental lacquer-work had heightened his appreciation of Japanese art and culture and it must have made good sense for him to take the opportunity to see as much of it as time permitted. But he could not dally too long because he had to return to Paris in time for the nuptials of his old friend Léon Parmentier who was to be married in April. Eventually he wrote home from Kyoto to say that he was boarding the German boat, *York*, to travel to Hong Kong where he would transfer to the French mail boat *Le Tonkin* en route to Europe via the East Indies. In a wry comment – perhaps a bit tongue in cheek – he tells his mother in this letter that having spent such a long sojourn in the United States he is '*si dégoûté*' (fed-up) with Americans and everything foreign and cannot bear the thought of having to endure a long sea voyage home in anything except a French vessel. He is even willing to wait around for a couple of weeks in Hong Kong until he can catch the right boat.

It is worth noting that although Latham had been away for months and many thousands of miles distant from Europe, such was his continued popularity with his English and French fans that his movements abroad were constantly under scrutiny. In mid-March, *Flight Magazine* ran a paragraph informing readers that the popular aviator Latham was on holiday in Shanghai. Almost a month later, the same journal reports his return to Paris. He had arrived home from the East Indies, exactly as planned, having travelled back on the French mail boat *Le Tonkin*.

The news waiting to greet the traveller on arrival was disturbing, but not, perhaps, unexpected. From the increasingly frantic tone of Gastambide's letters he must have suspected the *Société Anonyme Antoinette* could well be facing into a serious financial crisis. His own expenses still had to be sorted out to everyone's satisfaction and the trip to the United States had brought about no discernible benefit to the fortunes of the firm. No sales had been generated, either there or in the Orient. What did the future hold now?

# ELEVEN
# Meanwhile Back in Europe, 1911

It is unlikely that Latham entertained a great deal of thought about friends and events at home during his absence in the United States. Now and then he may have come across a newspaper despatch describing the spates of miserable weather affecting northern Europe through the late autumn and winter of 1910. Paris had been swept by almost incessant rain storms which left the city shrouded by dark and dreary clouds for weeks. Everyone and everything there was being described as gloomy beyond belief. Even when the river Seine eventually broke its banks and swirled foul-smelling water into low-lying streets and basements of the capital, this calamity brought about a barely perceptible *frisson* of excitement to lift the heavy lethargy the dreariness of those dark days created. For Latham, such depressing reports would have only enhanced his enjoyment of the balmy climes of sunny California. Paris and its problems would have seemed delightfully remote.

Meanwhile in Europe, the avid interest of English and French newspaper readers in the spectacle of men taking to the skies had been gradually waning. The number of record-breaking aeronautical achievements reported during the past year had lessened their novelty, except to those with either a vested business interest in the development of the aeronautical industry or in the ominous potential of aircraft use in warfare. Instead, a new arena for heroes of adventure had come under the focus of the general public. The race for the South Pole was on again and the latest expedition to the Antarctic Circle was being led by Captain Robert Falcon Scott. During the summer he and his wife, Kathleen, had travelled together as far as Cape Town and by the autumn he was setting up his base camp in New Zealand for the first leg of his journey to the South Pole. Kathleen then returned to Europe, stopping off at Marseilles in the New Year in the hope of seeing her friend Isadora Duncan before arriving back in England. She was to be disappointed. Isadora had moved away to go and live with Paris Singer, the father of her second child, Patrick. With two children to care for and an apparently stable domestic relationship, Isadora was less in need of Kathleen's nurturing support, but it is interesting to find that the dancer's disturbing link with Aleister Crowley had not been broken. That autumn, the magician had been a guest at one of Isadora's 'famously exotic' parties in London.[1] As for Kathleen, she was about to embark on a work which would renew her connection to many of her old acquaintances within aviation circles. It was a commission for an 8ft statue of her recently deceased friend, Charlie Rolls.

When Latham arrived back in France from the Far East in late March 1911, his most pressing social engagement was Léon Parmentier's forthcoming wedding, which was to take place in Orléans on 26 April. In the meantime, there was an urgent need for him to hasten to the Antoinette manufacturing works at Puteaux. Things here were looking grim. For months, there had been only a trickle of orders for new machines – mostly for private patrons – and, although two new monoplanes were ready for Latham's own use in the coming season, only a couple more were on the production-line. The reason for this state of affairs seems to have been that Levavasseur's concentration was now totally focused on the manufacture of a radical new concept – a three-seater Antoinette that was specifically designed with armour plating for wartime military use.

The potential to win valuable army contracts had accelerated earlier that year with the announcement in March that the French Government would hold an open competition, a *Concours Militaire*, to select the best military aeroplane suited to their needs. The trials were to take place in Châlons in the autumn of 1911 and Latham was still on the high seas en route home when Gastambide and Levavasseur made the decision to enter a new version of the Antoinette for these competitions. As the construction of a prototype started to take shape, the mechanics who worked on it began calling it 'The Monobloc'.

There was something ominously depressing about this name. It conjured up a sense of brooding heaviness that was more suited to a creation that was earthbound. No hint remained of the dancing dragonfly attributions of former Antoinette models. But if Latham had had any opinion on their choice for the new design's appellation he would have probably left it unsaid. The sensitive matter of his settlement of the balance of his outstanding account for the American adventure was still to be resolved and Gastambide's fury had gathered like an unlanced boil. It was left to Latham to argue that additional expenses should have been anticipated; he had kept his part of the bargain by providing splendid publicity for Antoinette, but without the 100hp engine and all the ancillary repairs necessary, his showing would have been at best mediocre and, at worst, quite disastrous. The reputation of the Farman, Wright and Blériot machines had gone from strength to strength and every aeroplane would soon carry a 100hp engine as standard. Their Antoinette was in danger of being left far behind in this race for superiority.

Some sort of compromise must have been hammered out, for whatever the outcome of this dispute, the truth of the matter was that if the company was to stay solvent, they had to increase sales. Much would hang on landing the security of an army contract and their hopes now lay in the success of 'The Monobloc'. The new machine had nothing of the sleek lightness that had allowed Latham to flirt teasingly with wind currents. The pilot now had an enclosed cockpit; the struts and braces on the wings were to be made significantly stronger and the wingspan, increased by more than a metre, would stretch to 15.9m. The dragonfly had grown into a truly different sort of dragon, a tough fighting machine, whether called the Monobloc, Antoinette Blindé or Armoured Antoinette: it was now far more rugged and a great deal heavier animal.

Strangely, problems attached to the additional weight of armoured plating seem to have been temporarily sidelined. Levavasseur was not going to use the more powerful 100hp engine with which Latham had performed so successfully in the United States, perhaps because of worries over its hefty size. Maybe the engineer was confident that a solution to the increased heaviness of the machine would be found before the French Army trials began?

By the start of 1911, British aviation manufacturers were beginning to watch the development of military aircraft in France a mite more anxiously. Some saw it as provocative that the French nation claimed to hold the 'superiority in the air'. Worries were voiced in several journals and one or two thoughtful pieces pointed out to their readers that there were: 'people in France as well as in England and other countries [who regarded] the presence of M. Declassé, Minister for the Marine and M. Berteaux, Minister for War in the Monis cabinet, as a danger for the peace of Europe'.[2] It was also written that: 'the attitude of the German press is, on the whole, rather calculated to strengthen that impression'. By the same token, it was held on good authority that the German Kaiser was convinced it was the intention of the British press to stir up bad feelings between France and Germany. He described reports in the *Daily Mail* and *The Times* as being 'most hostile'.[3] If Germany and France were ever to 'come to blows', to use his own words, then he would blame Britain and her newspapers.

Popular journalism on all sides was going to have to answer for an awful lot. Sentiments expressed recently by the French War Minister in *Le Matin* were even considered serious enough to have been picked up and repeated by the British journal, *The Field*. The colourful description of the new French Minister for War as someone with a 'fervent partisan passion for the development of military aviation', indicates the kind of sore temptations that were laying in wait for any keen journalist working on this hot topic.[4] It was all talk of war, the possibility of war and the preparedness for it. When interviewed by *Le Matin*'s correspondent, de Jouvenel, Minister Berteaux had spoken passionately of 'the aeroplane as a prodigious instrument of war in the hands of the French ... absolutely indispensable in scouting in front of an army on the march and [in giving] marvellous results in explorations'. He had then gone on to mount a rhetorical soap-box of enthusiasm, assuring *Le Matin* readers that, 'In attacking, aeroplanes will constitute a force, the formidable effect of which is still impossible to estimate. I look to the aeroplane as the most admirable engine of modern warfare. We cannot give it too great practical development. France is a great military and naval Power, but she must be the greatest aerial Power.'[5]

The Minister's arrogance was not altogether misguided. No less than 138 machines had been entered already for the forthcoming French Military trials in October. Every aviation manufacturer in France was exerting all-out efforts to be in at the fray. The Antoinette Company would find the going very, very tough.

Latham's view, if shared with that of his friend Santos-Dumont, the soon to be disillusioned pacifist, may have been ambivalent. He was all for progress, but the concept of men waging war against each other in the air – already prophesied by Marinetti's Futurist vision, 'we hunted death like young lions...' promised no joy, only despair.

Keeping an eye on all this from London, Lord Northcliffe's enthusiasm for his newspapers' aeronautical column never flagged. But things were running a bit less smoothly for those working in *The Times*'s London office. Everyone's equilibrium had been upset by the antagonistic undercurrent of dispute which had deepened between the 'Chief' and the paper's editor, George Buckle. Their views were at odds over the reporting of political and parliamentary matters and while this was nothing new – it had always been a volatile relationship – it was now disturbing that the editor-in-chief was convinced 'the independence of *The Times* is being tested'.[6] Some feared the 'Chief' was squaring up to turn the paper into a deluxe version of the *Daily Mail*. If this happened, the promise of non-interference in editorial matters would be gone for good.

The loss of their managing director, Moberly Bell, who had died at his desk in early April, had brought even more gloom into the newspaper office. Bell's appointment at the time of Northcliffe's purchase of the paper had been a real link to the old days. It was he who had fought for the retention of their high ethical standards – the paper's championing of Latham at the time of the Channel flight competition was a case in point. Without the steadying hand of Bell, Buckle's position as editor was looking even more shaky.

In the second week of April, a young French aviator called Pierre Prier flew a Blériot machine from London to Paris. This non-stop flight constituted a record, but there was no hullabaloo and only a few subdued headlines in the press. How quickly the extraordinary could become mundane. But Northcliffe may have viewed this exploit as an excellent publicity opportunity squandered and the 'Chief' set about the promotion of another novel air contest which would once more excite the hearts and minds. It was to be a *Daily Mail* Circuit of Britain Race, to take place later on in the summer; the contestants would fly 1,010 miles. The prize was worth £10,000. Englishman Grahame-White, fresh from his triumphs in America, was sure to accept the challenge and it was thought Latham might decide to compete because cross-country flying had become very much his forte of late. Moreover, a certain amount of curiosity about Latham's future plans had been whetted by the air of mystery surrounding a short report which had appeared in *Flight Magazine* on 20 May. The despatch indicated that a London Credit Finance company had become involved in the affairs of the *Société Anonyme Antoinette* of Puteaux. A transaction had taken place which indicated there had been a partial sale and transfer of assets. This suggested some rearrangement of Gastambide's share holdings may have occurred. Moreover, the advertising section of the journal carried the formal announcement of a newly registered English-based firm called Antoinette Ltd. The news was reinforced two weeks later by commentary in a rival journal, *The Aeroplane Magazine*, which was confidently predicting increased sales of Antoinette machines in England.

But the uncertainties carried by this news had not much pleased some aeronautical journalists who liked to think they could keep well abreast of events. If Gastambide had sold out, who might now be assigned to do the selling of this machine, they asked themselves?

With the approach of summer, Latham had been seen more frequently in London, so perhaps it was he who had been making the push to find new English buyers for the Antoinette. He had the advantage of having many loyal fans and supportive family connections and his name continued to be ranked among those who were now gathering

The aircraft sheds: the location of each competitor in an air show was always clearly identified. (HLPP)

in increasing numbers at facilities like the flying field attached to the Motor Racing Arena near Weybridge in Surrey. Founded in 1906 and known as Brooklands, it was quite the 'in' place for gatherings of aviators as well as attracting a coterie of leech-like society hangers-on. Gossip columnists soon noted that Captain Scott's wife might often be seen among the enthusiastic ladies who liked to attend events at this venue.

Her acceptance of a commission for a statue of England's first air victim, the late Charles S. Rolls, had allowed Kathleen Scott to resume building up her reputation as a sculptor of worth. It had not been an easy task. Rolls had been one of her circle of close friends and she had found the work a traumatising experience, especially when she had to find a willing young man to pose for her in the dead man's flying suit. But, by May, she had completed and displayed a small plaster cast of her design. The finished 8ft-high bronze statue was destined to be erected in Dover.

This piece of work had renewed her contact with several young aviators and a photograph of her visiting the Brooklands flying field had appeared in an aeronautical magazine. Although the accompanying caption had discreetly omitted to reveal her identity she had been instantly recognised by friends - and talked about – which did not much please her family, especially as the more tactless of the gossips were spreading word that she was spending more and more time airborne with several different young English aviators. Malicious tongues wagged.

With more than his fair share of French and English paramours to keep him busy, it is unlikely that Latham came to be featured in this idle gossip. He had more important things to do. English buyers had started to show greater interest in the Antoinette that summer and Latham had brought over two machines to demonstrate their capabilities on the spot.

*Above:* Kathleen Scott's memorial statue of Rolls was unveiled in Dover in April 1912. (From the collections of the Nelson Museum and Local History Centre, Monmouth)

*Opposite:* Surrounded by the ladies – Latham could never complain of a shortage of female companions! (HLPP)

In June, on Whit Bank Holiday Monday, an impressive gathering of aviators from far and near had gathered at Brooklands to thrill and entertain spectators. There was the usual mix of English aviators and foreign visitors. The morning had seen Horatio Barber flying over from Hendon in his Valkyrie machine, while Sam Cody came across from Aldershot, carrying a passenger on board. After lunch, Graham Gilmour made an impression by putting a big military Bristol through its paces on a short flight, despite a rising wind which had buffed him about, as one journalist put it, 'like a small boat in a rising sea'. James Radley and C.V. Roe were there, as were Blondeau and Drexel and several other well-known names.

According to the several reports of that day, it had been about 5 p.m., when Latham took up an Antoinette machine. He performed a few banked turns over the main block of sheds and then flew out over the racing track. The machine was performing perfectly.

As he neared the track he made a sharp turn and a sudden eddy of wind caught him unawares. The turn was tight; too tight. One of the wing tips came in contact with the roof of a shed at the end of a row of buildings next to the track and the machine spun into a cart-wheel, landing with a loud crash onto the shed's roof. The tail was up in the air at an angle of 45 degrees, the chassis was upside down, the nose was buried deep into the roof beams. As everyone watched in horror, the Antoinette's wings folded forward and the rudders dislocated, dangling down under their own weight. Latham was left hanging, helplessly suspended upside down by his safety belt. As spectators rushed forward, the rivet holding the belt to his seat suddenly snapped from the strain. They watched, transfixed, expecting the aviator to tumble headfirst through the broken roof-space to the ground below and certain injury. But it did not happen.

With a typical Latham-esque stroke of good fortune, he slid quite gently down onto the tangled mass of wire wing stays, strong enough to bear his weight and which held his fall, much as it would the inside of a spring mattress. He was quite unhurt. By the time would-be rescuers arrived on the scene he had managed to disentangled himself and was already scrambling down from the roof, cool and collected.

As rescuers rushed to help, a dozen or so aviators took a few minutes to climb up to the wrecked machine by way of the waterspouts, poles and ladders to see for themselves what had caused the crash. Argument ensured: had it been the wind, or had it been a broken warping chain? On balance it was thought the wind was most possibly the culprit together with, perhaps, some element of misjudgement of those tight turns by the pilot. Whichever it was, Latham had remained unfazed by the incident. Within fifteen minutes the second Antoinette machine had been wheeled out and his colleague, René Labouchère, was in the air. In an hour or so, Latham himself had taken his place behind the controls and, to the cheers of onlookers, was once more airborne. He was still a star.

The long hot summer dawdled on. In July, to Northcliffe's great disappointment, Grahame-White failed to win the *Daily Mail*'s Prize for the Circuit of Britain for England. Instead, the prize went to a clever young French Naval-Lieutenant who flew in a Blériot machine under the assumed name of Beaumont. Latham had not competed.

Meanwhile, anyone who was anyone in Parisian society was thinking only of the forthcoming summer *vacances*, but because Latham had been back and forth to England so often, he may have made no plans to be away from Paris for any length of time. He was now paying some attention to a new conquest whom, it would seem, had taken quite a shine to him. An up-and-coming young actress called Nina Myral had sent several postcards addressed to Latham at the rue Rembrandt: 'Hail to the King' she writes; and on another, 'See you later'. Latham may have had an unerring eye for latent talent. Within a few years, Nina was to be launched into a long and successful career as one of France's brightest film stars, famous for her lead roles in a string of memorable screen dramas.

Was he still in contact with Eileen Gray? It was unlikely. Her creativity had taken a lateral move and she had set up a Moroccan-inspired rug-making business in partnership with a friend, Evelyn Wylde. The new venture looked like becoming a commercial success and Eileen's fascination with the concept of flight found a new outlet in rug designs which carried minimalist abstract themes suggestive of aerodynamics. At the same time, she had not abandoned the slower and more painstaking production of creating beautiful things in lacquer work. In the autumn of 1911 she finally made a start on the ambitious blue and red lacquer panel she planned to call *Le Magicien de la Nuit*. It had developed from a doodle and, perhaps still believing herself to be in the thrall of Crowley, this uninvited image of a powerful sorcerer may have been conjured up from her subconscious.[7] It was to turn out to be one of her finest pieces.

That year the Princess de Polignac, otherwise Winaretta Singer, having tired of the affections of her late husband's niece, Armande de Polignac, was flaunting her current affair with a supposed love child of Edward VII, Olga de Meyer, the opium-addicted

Latham's crash onto a roof at the Brooklands flying field, 1911. (Royal Aeronautical Society Library)

wife of a society photographer. Unorthodox attitudes and mores were accepted with a shrug within the circles in which they moved. This was the Parisian *mode* and these the people whose lives swirled around personalities like Latham and the flamboyant heroes of the air. The dawn sun of a new century was now well up in the sky. There was nothing considered unacceptable behaviour any more except, perhaps, bad manners.

September had brought news of the death of another of Latham's long-time aviation acquaintances, Charles Voisin. He and the Baroness Raymonde de Laroche had been motoring along a road en route to Lyons to visit his parents, when a vehicle collided with their car at a crossroads. Voisin was killed outright and the Baroness received terrible injuries in the crash. Despite the seriousness of her accident, Raymonde once more drew on her reserves of strength; as soon as sufficiently recovered, this determined lady was once more in the air.

Autumn days rolled on and all was busier than ever at the *Société Anonyme Antoinette*'s works in Puteaux. The French army trials for military contracts were about to commence and, fortunately, their firm had drawn one of the last days allocated for the demonstration flights – the second week in October – so time was on their side. Levavasseur could not later complain that his final preparations had been too rushed. Rumours that the performances of Blériot and Farman machines had already been rewarded by large orders from the military authorities must have presented a challenge to confidence all the same.

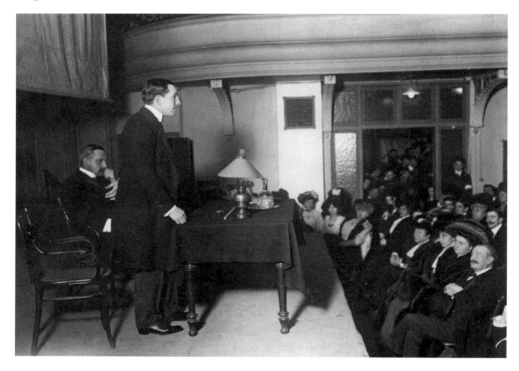

Always much in demand for lectures on flight, here Latham is seen addressing a meeting of air enthusiasts. (Royal Aeronautical Society Library)

Levavasseur and Gastambide both knew that the success of their new model in gaining an army contract was crucial to the future commercial survival of the *Société Anonyme Antoinette*, yet accounts of what happened on the day of their demonstration flight now read as an incredible tale of ineptitude, ill-preparedness, or even downright stupidity. The increased weight of the Monobloc could not have been ignored as a real problem but Levavasseur appears to have been stubbornly insistent that all would be well on the day. If there had been secret and worrying failed field trials then the results seem not to have been conveyed to Latham, despite the fact that he was to be the pilot. How strange, but this seems to have been the case.

On the day of their presentation to the judges of the *Concours Militaire* the demise of their hopes ran its course like a black comedy. The machine had been wheeled out on the morning of the trial. The engine was started. Latham took his seat at the controls and he gave it full throttle. The Monobloc had lumbered forward. It had gathered speed and for a moment or two, imperceptibly, it seemed the nose was beginning to lift – but then … no. There was insufficient momentum. A second run was made. It was the same story. This new version of Latham's Antoinette had made a few feeble hops but failed to take off. It was hopeless. The fragile beauty of an airy dragonfly had metamorphosed into an ugly soil-hugging reptile. This militarised creature was now, indeed, too heavy to fly. Levavasseur's insistence that a heavier 100hp engine was not needed to power lift-off had been a very bad mistake. So, what was to be done now? Latham's fury could not be assuaged; he had been made to look a fool.

1911 was drawing to a close. In the past twelve months the formerly exciting world of aeronautics had become acceptable, even mundane. A flying machine no longer created awesome drama every time one of these strange-looking contraptions rose high into the air over people's heads. To view the soaring climb of a pilot until but a tiny speck in the vastness of a blue sky had quickly lost its novelty value as a circus sideshow for gawking spectators. While it was still popular as a stylish sport for rich young men and saucy women, it was now realised that the coming use of aeroplanes for military and commercial purposes was inevitable. Whether this was an augury for good or for evil remained debatable. The editor of *The Field*, a magazine popular with 'hunting, shooting, fishing' upper-class readers, now wrote how:

> Aviation is rapidly settling down to a steady, ordered progression and adaptation to various useful services; and each year marks a welcome decline in the vogue of the flight 'hero' with all the mischievous concomitants of newspaper notoriety, vainglory and sensation-mongering. Each year witnesses a further transference of aeronautical personnel to the normal, the level-headed and the authoritative.[8]

Clearly, outrageous showmanship had had its day. There was little left now of the glitzy glamour that had been nourished by an appetite for risk-taking and almost impossible aspirations.

By the end of November word had reached Mme Latham that her son was contemplating another trip to Africa. Friends and family might have assumed that he was thinking of heading off once again for the Sudan to attend to some unfinished business out there. A parcel of land near Khartoum which he had purchased a couple of years ago through an English agent called Lynch was still something of a mystery to everyone and, while they knew he had a particular affection for that part of the world, no one was sure what he might have in mind to do with this investment. The papers relating to the sale, together with the deeds and registry in his name, had been languishing in the Bank of Egypt, Khartoum, waiting for his decision for far too long.[9]

It must have been quite a shock when, in a letter to his mother on 5 December, Latham revealed his destination was not to be the Sudan but to the French Congo. He tells her he is going out to West Africa to engage in some big game hunting. He does not plan to be away for very long – perhaps just four to five months.

As word spread, it occurred to people that his intention might be to ship out an Antoinette machine to assist in making aerial surveys of uncharted areas. The expectation was not unreasonable. It had been talked about before and the French Colonial office was at that time in a position to consider such a proposal with a degree of seriousness.

The summer of 1911 had seen France sorting out several problems involving its North African colonial protectorates. These were interesting times for European colonial control of Africa. A deal was being hammered out with the Germans over Morocco and, while diplomatic negotiations over the Algeria and Tunisian borders still remained volatile and were plagued with problems, the focus of the French Colonial Office was now more intent on finding some way to provide a corridor of improved communications which could link the Sahara with their Equatorial African possessions. The building of a rail-line had been mooted and the army had sent off one of their infantrymen, a veteran of desert expeditions, Captain Cortier, on a fact-finding trip. [10] Not yet shelved were earlier plans which envisaged building airports as far south as Fort Lamy and Bangui in the French Congo.

Of particular significance was the fact that this region was not too far from the border which divided the French Equatorial territory from the German-held Cameroon. For some time talks had been held at diplomatic level to agree on a mutual realignment of the territory and redrawing of a small stretch of frontier between French and German occupied land in the Congo. Since 1905, France and Britain had been eyeing German ambitions in Africa with increasing unease, but by diplomatic mutual consent it was felt another crisis similar to the one in July 1911 over the Moroccan port of Agadir should be avoided at all costs. Since October, those in the know had been confidently suggesting that an honourable end to the dispute – settled by way of an agreed trade-off of a small section of German-occupied Cameroon which could be ceded to France – would be of ultimate benefit to both countries. To many minds, this was a splendid and equitable solution. This new piece of French territory would fruitfully expand and consolidate the district now designated by the French Colonial Office as the Oubangui-Chari–Tchad. On paper, it looked excellent; but the sad truth was that this was an unhappy place with an unsavoury reputation.

For decades, the respective Belgian and French colonial administration of the Congo had been appalling. Officialdom had allowed foreign concession companies trading in wild rubber to terrorise the indigenous populations of this part of Africa. [11] Atrocities abounded; licensed foreign agents starved and beat natives into paying 'tax' which they had to raise by harvesting rubber growing in their areas. Savage punishments, such as cutting off the hands of a recalcitrant native, continued to be tolerated and, when villagers abandoned settlements and fled into the jungle 'to escape being kidnapped by government agents or forced to serve as porters', their once-fertile plantations of maize and other subsistence crops were abandoned and the land reduced to a wilderness. [12] For the inhabitants of the adjoining German colony in Cameroon, the conditions were no better; if anything they were rather worse.

In Europe, many concerned agencies, Church missionaries, Quakers and bodies such as the Congo Reformation Association – founded in 1904 – had been raising protesting voices over colonies in Equatorial Africa but the introduction of reforms had been slow. It was still a territory that bore the terrible scars of a very brutal past and the region remained a rough and primitive frontier country, ruled by torture, beatings and unbridled cruelty. One historic account famously describes how, not far from here, the behaviour of two French administrators at the military post of Fort Crampel a few years previously, had 'sunk to the level of the most bestial Africans'. [13] Official punishments meted out by the authorities for such infringements of the law had been derisory and reports that exposed faults in the system had been swiftly and efficiently repressed. With a legacy of a

A victim of a widespread punishment meted out in the French Congo – a young man's hands have been severed. (HLPP)

simmering undercurrent of resentment towards all white colonialists, this was no place for a European traveller to seek a pleasurable venue for a hunting safari. The fact that this was to be Latham's intended choice of destination poses the question: why? Why select such a benighted and unhappy place as the Congo when there was no shortage of alternative remote, well-stocked and uncrowded sporting locations?

Several scenarios may be picked over for clues. Leaving aside the potential offered to the Minister for the Colonies in planning a chain of flying fields to link the Northern Sahara to Tchad, the scandalous exploitation of Equatorial Africa was now being targeted by European humanitarian activists.[14] Up until recently, the French Colonial office had not been too concerned, but now, with the eyes of the world's press about to be more closely focused on the Congo in coming months and with the suspicion that the military garrisons had all but lost control of these regions, a covert, unbiased and independent report might be a useful knowledge-gathering exercise. An approach may well have been made to Latham as a man very suitable to undertake this job. The issue was a sensitive one. It was difficult terrain and a ghastly climate; only a seasoned traveller, well used to the

African bush and willing to undergo rigorous hardships would fit the bill. Latham certainly had the attributes needed. Moreover, the Colonial Office were aware of the reputation of his brother-in-law, Dr Paul Armand-Delille, and his involvement in humanitarian issues. The doctor's medical career was geared towards progressing a number of well-publicised philanthropic projects. He and his associates had worked among the deprived poor to bring about improvements in children's health and welfare and the provision of further education opportunities for the working classes. It is not too speculative to suggest that Armand-Delille also numbered among those who were vocal in their concern over the rumours emanating from the French Congo, which hinted of continued atrocities and military inadequacy. He would back anything Latham might uncover.

Official movement to expedite improved communication links to Central Africa may also be considered a compelling reason why someone like Latham should be despatched to the furthest reaches of the Oubangui-Chari–Tchad district. Almost twelve months previously, when Latham had crashed and wrecked his plane in San Francisco, he had been poised to take part in an experiment using wireless technology for communication. Since then, he had had time to reflect at greater length on the feasibility of the use of radio in conjunction with airfields in remote locations. It was no great secret that a number of French business consortiums whose investors had family connections to Latham may have been keen to have the potential of what was termed 'radio electricity' investigated – especially in regard to expansion in French Equatorial Africa and a personal report from the region to the Ministry for Colonies could pave the way for immense progress in this direction. Moreover, as matters at this level of diplomacy were of the utmost delicacy, it could be ensued that no hint of any such consultations could emerge within the public domain.

To Latham's advantage was his fluency in German and English, in addition to a smattering of Arabic and other African languages. He had experience of expeditions in uncharted territory and – since his surveys and geological reports of his 1906/07 expedition had proven to be of inestimable value to the Minister for War – an impressive track record. The suggestion that their man travel to the Congo ostentatiously for big game shooting was entirely consistent with Latham's reputation as a sportsman. It was the perfect cover story. It could be arranged for him to telegraph reports from the region using recognised coded channels while there, and if Latham could be persuaded to embark for the Congo without delay, certainly before the end of the December, the Ministry would ensure that every facility be provided.

The setting up of such a fact-finding mission would require one crucial caveat. In the event of any untoward mishap, the military administration of the area would be expected to ensure that Latham's presence in the region would not be construed as being in any manner noteworthy. There must be nothing which could cause any security scare.

As might have been anticipated, the civil service bureaucracy's carefully constructed layers of secrecy soon sprang a leak. However, Latham was already well on his way to Africa by the time a British journalist, writing in the aeronautical magazine *The Aeroplane*, suggested that the aviator's decision to travel to the Congo had followed meetings with the Ministry for the French Colonies and that he would be 'acting on their behalf in a matter that is not disclosed'.[15]

Speculation had not ended here. *Flight Magazine*, while also featuring the story of the hunting trip, added the suggestion that Latham was bringing his Antoinette monoplane with him. The sighting of large crates being loaded onto his ship at Bordeaux had probably triggered this rumour, fuelled by whispers that Latham was up to something. In fact, the speculations had come within a hair's breadth of reality. The idea of shipping an aircraft had been possibly discussed at official levels. This is clear from his letter to his mother from Paris on 5 December, in which he tells her he has decided *not* to bring either an aeroplane or a motor car with him to the Congo but would bring a simple motor '*carnot*' – possibly a semi-portable outboard motor which could be attached to an open boat or canoe. Nothing more was ever heard of this piece of equipment in the coming months, so he may have changed his mind about shipping it. What Latham failed to reveal to his mother – as may be expected – was anything which carried hints of a hidden agenda attached to this journey or the location of his exact final destination. Yet evidence exists which confirms he was carrying several important letters in his luggage addressed to business interests and senior army administrators in that northernmost outpost of the military controlled French territory in Equatorial Africa, Oubangui-Chari-Tchad.[16]

There is something odd about these letters. At least one communication, a short note of introduction written by an official with a Bangui address, bears the date 18 December 1911 – twelve days before Latham had left France and some weeks before his actual arrival in the Congo. Several other officially stamped communications (which remain among his papers, still unopened in their envelopes) were addressed to senior official government administrators in the Chari-Tchad district. He also carried a letter addressed to a French colonial trading firm in this area and, rather more interesting, another intended for delivery to an enterprising French firm in Tchad which specialised in systems for electric wireless. Fate would ensure that none of these communications would ever reach their intended recipients.

That December, Latham's announced intention to travel abroad could not have gone down well with his fellow directors in the *Société Anonyme Antoinette*. With the last of the outstanding orders for Antoinette machines delivered and no army contracts forthcoming, the Monobloc debacle had delivered the fatal blow. Levasseur's stubborn streak had ensured he hung on until too late to put in a rescue package and the onset of bankruptcy was inevitable. The engineer took the impending setback with a shrug; it was not the first time he had seen his grandiose ideas disintegrate and it would not be the last. He would soon be poised to start up again with fresh ideas and a fresh set of investors.

Although Latham's other sources of income and personal finances were in no danger from the collapse of the *Société Anonyme Antoinette*, there was, nonetheless, too much Latham family finance tied up in various oblique ways to abandon the aviation business completely. Two of his young first cousins, Jean and Pierre Latham from Caudebec, near Le Havre, had developed an interest in the potential of aviation and may have at this point begun to consider whether or not the family firm should buy up anything that could be salvaged from the looming bankruptcy. Their firm, *Latham et Cie Société Industrielle de Caudebec*, later called *Hydravions Latham*, became involved in building flying boats during the First World War.[17]

'It may have been his last mortal flight.' (HLPP)

Not everyone was happy. There were others who, when they heard Latham was off to Africa, firmly believed he was just running away from all these problems. Some genuinely held the opinion he had lost heart, later writing poignantly that 'At the end of the year he flew in loneliness for two hours in a very high wind at Mourmelon. It may have been his last mortal flight.'[18]

By Christmas Latham was ready to leave for the Congo. Packed carefully in his luggage were three small books which were never to leave his side throughout his final journey: one was Rowland Ward's *Records of Big Game Hunts*, a classic reference book for all serious game hunters; the second was Robert Service's popular *The Spell of the Yukon and other verses*, which was included, perhaps, for lighter moments. His third book was a distinctly practical necessity: *Adams' Codex*, an international telegraph manual – essential for the sending of commercially coded messages.[19]

If, indeed, a covert mission had been undertaken, it must be asked whether he had been made truly aware of the complexity of issues which lay behind the Congo's terrible reputation as a place ravaged by violence and stinking of corruption? Was it possible he never anticipated the nature of the difficulties that lay ahead, or of the shocks to come? In much the same way as he had set his face into the challenge for the prestigious Channel Flight Prize, there is one fact which remains certain: when he left for French Equatorial Africa in December 1911, he knew he was taking off into the unknown to face hardship and hazards. This was not running away.

# TWELVE
# The Final Chapter? 1912

Following the trail of Latham's final weeks by way of his letters home and the meticulous notes he compiled each night in his African journal would appear to be a formula which, at first glance, should lead us on a clear-cut path to the final *dénouement*. But it is not so. The unruly territory he traversed was still gripped by savagery and unrest and the official reports, later coordinated by the military authorities to describe events, neither indicate the difficulties he encountered, nor the dangers inherent in the region.

Latham's personal journal for his 1912 expedition can guide us through those last troubled months of his life, although it is possible to wonder if he may have been deliberately circumspect in recording these private thoughts and impressions?[1] A verse of a poem he had jotted down on a spare back page of this journal has nothing to indicate whether or not these lines were his own composition or something he had come across or remembered from another's work:

> *Mes feux de campement sont un semis d'étoiles*
> *Dans la nuit du passé que je hante souvent.*
> *Et leur scintillement illumine ses voiles*
> *De la douce lueur d'un souvenir vivant.*

> The showers of sparks of my campfire are like seedling stars, planted
> In the night of my past, which I often haunt.
> And their sparkle illuminates its veils
> With the soft light of a living remembrance.[2]

One gets the sense of a curtain being lifted briefly to reveal an inner self that reflects gentle regrets. Of what? For whom? He does not choose to say.

Latham embarked for the Congo at Bordeaux on 29 December 1911. Travelling on the Réunis Line vessel, *L'Afrique*, he reached the West coast of Africa just over two weeks later. As he prepared to disembark at the port of Matadi on 13 January, he found a moment to write a brief letter home to say he will be continuing to Brazzaville by train and will telegraph from Bangui, adding that before he leaves the port he will pack up his London-tailored tweed 'wool suit' for despatch back to Bordeaux. He will collect it on his return to France.

His first task on reaching Brazzaville was to obtain an official permit for the import of arms into the French administered region several hundred miles to the north which was to be his final destination. Formed by the merging of the middle Congo with Gabon and Oubangui-Chari-Tchad two years earlier, this district had been re-named *Afrique Equatoriale Française Colonie de l'Oubangui-Chari-Tchad*. He was bringing in an Express 500 calibre hunting piece, a .20 hunting rifle and a 9 mm/bore Manlicher (one of the best and most expensive Austrian–made elephant-hunting guns), and a supply of ammunition consisting of 300 cartridges for the Express, 2000 rounds for the rifle and 10,000 cartridges for the Manlicher. No difficulty arose over the importation of this weaponry and, by 19 January, the permit had been granted and signed. Interestingly, this document described Latham's occupation as 'Aviator'. There is nothing on it to say he was visiting to hunt big game.

Before leaving Brazzaville, Latham wrote to his mother once more, this time to tell her that he will be leaving the next day on a steam packet heading up river. He will transfer to canoe at Ouésso in order to navigate up the Sangha river as far as Nola. After that, the rest of the journey will be trekking overland to Fort Archambault. He reckoned, 'I may be able to start my return journey around July or August' and promised, 'I will write as often as possible'.

Latham left Brazzaville on 22 January 1912. The first night out on the river marked the start of a careful pencil-written log of each day's events in his journal. For the next six months, not a day would be missed, not an incident unrecorded, and it is very evident from comments made in the first couple of entries that his approach to this adventure was to be typically laid-back. At the close of the first day's log he had declared: 'No mosquitoes, or only very few'. But by the morning, he has had to add an amendment: 'They arrived, all the same'. Fearing he may have been bitten already, his immediate concern was to provide himself with a mosquito net: 'Bought one for 5 francs.'

The progress of the paddle boat's journey upstream had been leisurely and Latham and his fellow European passengers, all seasoned travellers, soon befriended the 'idiotic but charming' captain and crew. After dinner, evenings were spent pleasantly enough – playing poker well into the small hours. It had been a good start.

On reaching Ouéssa, which lay on the border between the German, French and Belgian territories, Latham made contact with the local under-administrator who confirmed that his proposed trek northwards would be very easy to arrange. His letter home from here on 3 February was optimistic, telling them that he has engaged a native who will travel with him as a cook. 'His name is Tchitembo – he speaks good French'. He has also engaged another 'boy' as a personal servant and asks his mother to let Edmée know that he has met up with a doctor – posted out here by the military administration – who 'was interested to learn I am the brother-in-law of Dr Armand-Delille'. The doctor had told him Paul was tremendously admired for his excellent reputation in the medical world.

In a day or two, having been assured that the country ahead was good for hunting and abundantly provided with a diversity of game, a line in his private journal marks the first inkling of something unexpected and, to some extent, disturbing. Having gathered together a team of porters, and *pagayeurs* (canoeists) for the next leg of his journey up river, he had

Latham was a hunter with years of experience. (Parmentier Collection)

been warned that he must report to the officer in charge at the military post, in order to expedite these arrangements. On writing this up in his journal, Latham had observed 'It seems he [the army officer] is the person to whom one must go to for everything in this region'. Latham's surprise at having found such reliance resting in military hands suggests he may not have been fully appraised of the true situation in this part of Africa. Had he not known that the whole area to the north of here was still a virtual war zone?

Three weeks later, by which time he had reached Nola, another letter home comments that the weather had been good. He has seen a number of hippopotamuses, antelopes and large gorillas but, in his opinion, the countryside on either side of the river was in a very poor state. Their boat had been 'constantly surrounded by many crocodiles'. Ahead lay the jungle of the equatorial forest. From here on, he planned to leave the river to proceed on foot, guided by pygmies. 'I have never seen such small people,' he remarked, adding 'I hope I can take some photographs of them.' Subsequently, this tribe tracked down several sightings of gorillas for him to observe climbing trees and eating fruit – and he was able to take more photographs.

Latham's use of his camera as frequently as his gun reflects his adherence to an emerging concern among sportsmen hunters that the coffers of nature they stalked were not boundless booty. While it was true that many previously unknown new species of flora and fauna were not yet discovered and identified, and the strict rules of animal conservation that conscientious wildlife enthusiasts would put in place were still many decades away, certain individual hunters had begun to curtail their activities in a number of small ways – and using a camera instead of a gun was gaining favour. Hunting licenses imposed some restrictions for each territory and, like the Parmentier-Latham expedition of 1906/7,

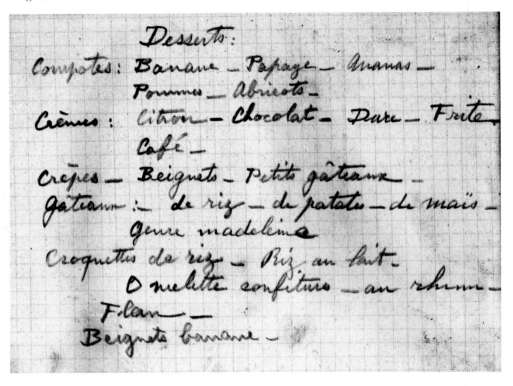

Latham has scrawled a list of favourite desserts in his African journal, 1912. (HLPP)

parties now trekked with smaller caravans. But horns and ivory were still rare and valuable commodities which Western markets sought. With prices fetching record heights, most expeditions relied on this bounty to cover their expenses. Latham's trek was no different from others in this respect. Apart from the obligation to provide sufficient game to feed his men, the proficiency of his gun would have been crucial to his balancing of the books.

For his own dietary needs, his carefully accounted check list of the western delicacies packed for the trek included sardines, magi soup, sugar, coffee, tea, curry, corned beef, peas, cheeses, macaroni and noodles, rice, tapioca, raisins, jam and biscuits, and so on. But one gets the sense that the deprivations he anticipated were carefully balanced by some well-deserved compensations. Never a man to stint on the finer pleasures of his table, his porters had also carried a generous supply of champagne – *Pomeroy*, naturally – and he has made sure to pack several bottles of dubonnet and whisky.[3] On a spare back page of his journal, a list of favourite desserts have been jotted down. These may have been instructions for Tchitembo, his cook. Or, perhaps, more likely an indulgence of nostalgia for home-made *compotes, crèmes, crêpes* and *gâteaux* with flavours of *citron* and *chocolat* – to which he had added a distinctly Proustian note by including those sweet confections known in France as '*madeleines*'.[4]

The impression one gathers from reading his daily log is that the team Latham put together at Ouéssa had got off to an excellent start and that his relationship with the natives had been good. On taking to the water on the first day out, he has described how one man would be selected from the *pagayeurs* to lead the chanting pace of the paddlers. They worked in time to the stroke of the chant and later, one by one, the 'caller' was replaced by another, so that each man was given a rest in turn. Some days later, when he had to order his grumbling *pagayeurs* back onto the river before they could consume any more copious amounts of palm wine being offered by a hospitable, but over-bountiful village headman, Latham himself generously opted to take one of the paddles for a while, 'to repay them'. He may have found this stint more physically demanding than expected. On writing up that day's activities, he observed, 'It [the paddling] is easy and not too tiring for men who are used to it'.

But the sense of friendly camaraderie, so carefully created, was not to last. Very soon, there were hints of problems ahead. His team complained that the posse of military men designated to guide the party had taken (- or stolen?) all their rations. The incident must have made Latham wonder at the worthiness of the strict advice given to him not to travel without a military escort. But Latham had no choice but to give his men eight days' ration as a replacement even though their story could have been just a ploy to gain extra supplies. His confidence in the 'good' advice meted out by region's under-administrator was then further lowered when his new cook, Tchitembo, revealed that this official – the cook's former *patron* or master – used regularly beat him with his '*chicotte*' (a whip made from hippopotamus hide). Clearly, Latham found this information disconcerting. He ended that day's entry in his journal by asking himself bleakly, 'Is this how I have to do things around here?' It is a sharp and acutely accurate observation. French administration still favoured deploying discipline harshly. As Pakenham later put it, '… twenty strokes of the *chicotte* were considered a handy way to keep the Africans under control'.[5]

As the weeks went by, it may be seen that Latham's aim to mete-out fair and considerate treatment to both his team and the native population became increasingly difficult for him to maintain. The villages they had been passing through were still undergoing the transition from German to French administration. Many were deserted – for their inhabitants had fled into the bush. In one place, a party of Germans had recently killed a man – he did not record the actual circumstances of this incident – but the news of the atrocity was badly unsettling for his men. Latham wrote in his journal that he 'did not blame his *pagayeurs* for being reluctant to stay in this place'. They moved up river to the next village where they received a more friendly reception from its inhabitants, but he found it worrying when word got back to him that some of the natives were spreading it around that he was German. It was not safe to let a rumour like this linger on.

The practical organisation of Latham's trek followed the customary procedure of shooting game en route to feed a team of porters and other men, and it was quite normal for a party of hunters to be welcomed into an area by the inhabitants of local villages, keen to get fresh meat in exchange for fruits, eggs or chickens. The existence of several European trading companies in the Congo who were also willing to buy meat always ensured that there was an alternative dimension to this simple bartering procedure, and it goes without saying that Latham had found himself being eagerly entertained by resident agents representing French, Dutch and Portuguese companies. All had been keen to do business with him for the sale of any surplus bush meat – either fresh or smoked – which his gun could provide.

A group of Congolese pose for the camera, 1912. (HLPP)

Latham soon struck a deal with a Dutch company who agreed to supply him with a series of horses – which he later described as disappointedly lame, wheezing or otherwise broken down – to carry him on some of the overland sections of his trek north-eastwards. Around this time, his log reveals that he was thinking of selling his .20 rifle and planned to replace it with another type. He may not have been having much luck with his guns, because by mid-March and six weeks into the journey, he was reflecting that he must set-to to 'apply myself with greater dedication to the hunting when the rains have gone'. His eye had to be kept firmly on expenses. The trophies being gathered en route had all been carefully conserved – the elephant tusks, rhino and antelope horns and, from time to time, he had arranged for these to be measured and weighed by agents to assess their worth. He was still being escorted by the military but he writes home in a cheery enough mood about the beautiful flowers to be found in the deep jungle and how he had encountered several large elephants which he also hoped to photograph. His light-hearted observation that the locals eat what he calls 'bizarre fruits' – and that 'they also consume toucans with some relish', was almost certainly aimed at entertaining everyone at home in Maillebois.

And then, in late March, things started to go wrong. Corporal Moussa Koulibaly of the 6th Company of the Artillery Reserve Regiment for French Equatorial Africa had arrived on the scene. On 27 March, a note in Latham's journal merely states that he 'has had a chat' with Moussa – but within three days a decision had been made to engage this man as his personal gun bearer and team leader. It may be taken that some form of official permission must have been obtained from the corporal's military superiors – and perhaps the recommendations Moussa brought with him had been backed-up with assurances that here was a man of long experience who knew how to get things done. As will come out later, the corporal had completed his army training in Tchad and would seem to have been a man with an ambition to further his army career. His knowledge of Arabic, for example, had been already recognised as an advantage and he was being occasionally called upon by the French authorities to act as an interpreter.[6]

The unsettling relationship that was about to develop between Latham and this senior member of his team would soon become a key factor in the outcome of ensuing events. Within a few weeks of their setting off on the next leg of their trek, disquieting comments linking the name of Moussa to a number of disturbing incidents, start to appear in Latham's daily log.

The initial indication of Latham's unease comes with his private observations on the behaviour of the military escort. It was deteriorating day by day. Writing up his journal late one evening by the light of his candle, Latham had been consumed with outrage at the violence of the soldiers' behaviour on finding the inhabitants of one of the villages they passed through had not paid their taxes. These men had 'taken' a woman (an implied euphemism for an act he does not wish to expand on) and seized chickens and two panniers of chickpeas. Moreover, such was the fear of what the military might do at the next settlement some three kilometres away, the chief or headman of that place had taken the precaution of offering them not only gifts of salted meat but two more women! Rounding up his account of that day's events, Latham had observed wryly that the military had told him he can expect their party to be attacked that night in revenge for these raids. For the first time since setting off there is a note of cynicism in his journal: 'How charming!' he has scrawled.

And the situation does not improve. The next day, he has heard that Corporal Moussa was being heavy-handed towards the people in another nearby village. His men have told him that Moussa was 'forcing' the natives to supply their party with food – often from these people's depleted and meagre stocks. Deeply troubled by this information, Latham had offered to go out the next day and shoot some game which he ordered to be given completely gratis to the villages in recompense. He would have been well aware that none of his party could have been in dire need of supplies because they were travelling with a plentiful amount of basic foodstuffs and at least seven of the crates carried by his porters contained a very adequate – even luxurious – supply of dry stores, tinned goods, cooking oil and so on. While occasional extra supplements of fresh fruit, eggs and milk were always welcome, it was only to be expected that such commodities were not always easily available in remote areas. Moreover, to cater for the diet preferred by his team of men, Latham's skill with his gun had always ensured that they had had a regular provision of fresh meat.

April drifted along, but it did not bring an improvement in Corporal Moussa's violent behaviour. Quite the contrary. If anything, Moussa had become worse. His belligerent mood had rubbed off on Latham's 'boys' and the accompanying team with whom Latham had previous enjoyed such an excellent rapport.

Nonetheless, there were many good days when Latham had managed to get in some successful hunting. Writing from Bozoum, he reported finding antelope, elands, buffalo and elephants. But there were other times when things had not gone so well. Expecting

Latham used a small diary to keep tally of his food stores, May 1912. (HLPP)

his 'boys' to come forward to attend to their work of retrieving tusks, horns, skin and meat from a fresh carcass, he often found them gone missing, out of earshot, or taking their time in dawdling back to the location. He suspected they were lazing around with the military escort, getting drunk. Several times, while out tracking, they had made so much noise from the excitement of finding game that they caused the quarry to stampede out of range. He had tried to discipline them – not by whipping the culprits as was recommended by the officials and agents who gave him advice – but by curtailing the men's ration of meat. It would prove to be a totally ineffectual exercise. A short time later, on their discovery of a beehive of wild honey – a bushman's prime treat – the find had stirred up everyone into such a frenzy that all thought of attending to their duties to him had evaporated. On writing up the incident in his journal, Latham's fury had been palpable. Yet, rather than resorting to violence as a form of chastisement, he had merely confiscated the honey from the men as a punishment for their insubordination. Well-meaning or not, clearly, the pursuit of this policy only guaranteed that his patience was to be stretched to its very limit.

To make matters worse, the steamy equatorial clime was beginning to take its toll on Latham's health. For weeks the pattern of his days had varied little. As a rule, he rose early so as to be out of the camp, sometimes before five a.m. Around noon, he would stop to rest, eat and sleep. The heat and humidity in the forests was stultifying and he had suffered several bouts of fever. He complained of feeling tired and there were troubles with his digestion. He was also plagued on a regular basis – not by the recurrence of an exotically rare tropical malady – but by attacks of a decidedly unglamorous disability, diarrhoea. We might now speculate that these complaints were all symptoms of malaria. Having no option but to resort to self-medication, he had dosed himself with various remedies, placing his trust in purges, Epsom's salts, or a shot of stiff whisky laced with quinine. There were times when he could barely move from his tent – often for days at a stretch. Worse still, his cook, Tchitembo – the French-speaking interpreter charged with translating his orders to the men into their local language, had kept making mistakes and was growing forgetful, claiming that he had not understood his clear instructions. Utterly exasperated, Latham's logged entry was frank: 'I regret I don't have the authority of the military to deal with my cook more sharply'.

Finally, one day, while rebuking Tchitembo for once more distorting or disobeying the plans for the day's hunting, Latham's patience snapped. He lost his temper and '*flanque un coup de pied*' – angrily aimed a few kicks in the cook's direction. Tchitembo had muttered a rude retort and Latham threatened to send for his horse's '*chicotte*' (whip). What happened next – '*phénomène imprévu*' – his words – was something quite unforeseen. 'Suddenly my cook turns into a savage and springs forward at me shaking a spear, crying "If you beat me – I will beat you!"' Not without wry humour, Latham's comment afterwards was that: 'my position was a bit ridiculous, standing there with this idiot threatening me with his weapon. So I walk towards him to stop the dangerous game he is playing'. His cool reaction may have unnerved Tchitembo for the 'boy' had dodged away before Latham could grab hold of him. 'I was sure he was going to attack me again', wrote Latham, 'so I went to find one of the military to get a gun to defend myself with'.

Things must have come to a pretty pass to make this move and it was fortunate that the soldier Latham met up with had solidly refused to release hold of his gun. He had merely apologised '… sweet as a lamb, saying "sorry, sorry" – hands together in an attitude of prayer'. Latham's summing-up was laconic, 'I think he was on the side of the cook.'

Following a warning to Tchitembo that he could be put in prison by the soldier if he didn't behave himself, Latham later recounted how Tchitembo had begged for forgiveness: '[he] flung himself into my arms [but] … the *chicotte* had already been sent for' and the furious Latham had found himself with no choice but to set about using it 'two or three times…' adding the caveat '- but not too hard'. He must have felt he was letting himself and his high ideals down badly – although we might remember that the use of corporal punishment on miscreants – and the young – was still considered quite a normal practice in Western society.

In a curious way, a semblance of honour seems to have been restored on both sides following this incident. Still frightened of a military arrest, Tchitembo had run away from the camp that night, but Latham's men caught up with him at the next large village, where he was detained for a day or two and then quietly released from custody on the payment of a fine.

Latham's final reflections on this incident in his journal were thoughtful. He had just heard that the men in the next village were in revolt and were threatening to abandon their support of the French administration; to which he added 'The military are rumoured to be in total sympathy with them and have it in their minds to desert…' But it was Latham's closing remarks on an exceptionally trouble-filled day that strike as the most illuminating. He was quite resolved to prepare a seriously critical report, adding the observation that he found the behaviour of the military to be bad. 'And I shall tell everyone exactly what I think'.

It has to be recognised that it was not in Latham's nature to ever balk at 'speaking his mind' when he felt it absolutely necessary. He had always said what had to be said following disputes at air shows on many occasions: in Berlin, in New York, in San Francisco, and in his arguments with Levavasseur and Gastambide. The question now must be: how seriously was Latham incensed by the state of affairs in this French administered region – and to whom was he referring as 'everyone' who should hear what he had to say about it? Had his intention been to send a scathing report into the Governor's office in Brazzaville, the administrators of *Afrique Equatoriale Française Colonie de l'Oubangui-Chari-Tchad*; or – more significantly – would he have made direct contact with the officials in the French Ministry for the Colonies in Paris?

Twenty years earlier, Irish-born Roger Casement, a conscious-stricken young assistant consul working in British held Nigeria had been faced with an almost similar situation and had alerted the world to the horrors being perpetuated by the colonial administration there, writing later of it as '… a tyranny beyond conception … come what might to myself, I should tell the whole truth'.[7] And public dismay had been loud when the even more atrocious exploitation of the indigenous population in King Leopold's Belgian Congo was exposed for what it was. That Latham may have been about to submit a report about conditions in French-held Equatorial territory was indeed timely. But he would have been appalled, had he any way of knowing it then, that, despite many similar findings by others like him, nothing was going to be done to bring about change in the French equatorial territories for a very long time to come. It would be well over a decade – 1927 – before the French writer, André Gide, who had 'innocently set out on a tour of the Congo', also became so outraged by the discovery of tyranny that he mounted a protest to ask why 'this frightful regime, this shameless exploitation still survives after the harmfulness has been recognised?'[8]

Although, clearly, Latham's journal entries voice the complaints he intended to make, it has to be wondered when and by what means he envisaged being able to send a despatch on the appalling conditions discovered? We may assume he anticipated that the next place capable of sending secure letters or cable messages would be Fort Archambault – still several weeks of journeying away.

Weeks earlier, when planning the trek, Latham's intended route had been to travel to the environs of the Bénoué river, a tributary of the Niger, close to the border with Cameroon and not far from a stretch of territory over which the French and German governments had been conducting negotiations. In one of his previous letters home, he had suggested that, when finished in Goré, he was probably going to spend some time here. He may well have suspected more evidence of instability and acts of atrocity – probably even worse – were still to come.

In the meantime, having arrived at the next military post, his journal describes what he found there as 'in a real mess'. The officer in charge was slowly recovering from having been attacked and wounded in the chest by his 'boy' and there was a distinct atmosphere of ill-will and fear. Unable to do anything but observe, Latham could do nothing but take note of the situation before continuing on towards the territory north of Goré.

On reaching the environs of a place called Kan, he found the countryside around him presenting an all too familiar sight. It had been laid waste; the villages were deserted or

A typical village in the French Congo, 1912. (HLPP)

burnt to the ground, sometimes by the local chiefs, and nearly all the people had fled. Latham's reaction was stark: 'The military have pillaged and burned their way through this district'. It was by then mid-May and things were clearly out of control. The few natives who remained were in a hostile mood.

To add to his troubles, serious problems with his team-leader, Corporal Moussa, had been accelerating. For some time, Latham had noticed that their supplies of bush meat were becoming inexplicably diminished. It had been a puzzling and annoying discovery. On many occasions, he had found there was not enough surplus meat available to fulfil the sales bargains he had pre-arranged with the agents. It should be pointed out that, throughout the trip, Latham had been particularly meticulous in keeping account not only of his stores and his collection of tusks and other trophies, but the number, type and description of all game successfully hunted. Suspicions aroused, Latham had concluded that the canny Corporal Moussa must have set up a system calculated to deliberately steal some of the meat to sell off for his own benefit. Not without some misgivings, he had confronted the miscreant. The outcome was not altogether satisfactory.

On being asked to explain how such an amount could have gone missing, the corporal had insisted that the loads had become too heavy for the porters and that a lot of the meat had had to be abandoned in the bush. It was a story Latham knew could not be true. He had calculated the weight of the loads and Moussa was palpably lying. The men's rations of salt had been also mysteriously depleted. When the corporal asked if he could buy some more salt for them from their stores, Latham had swiftly countered the request by insisting that Moussa should go to the army for any extra supplies. Later that night, as he logged the daily report, Latham's equivocal conclusion that: 'I have decided I do not like this man' says it all. He would have to watch the corporal very carefully. The man was not to be trusted.

By the end of May, the party accompanying Latham numbered twenty-eight military, forty porters, and ten boys and women. This leg of Latham's journey was almost completed. He was due at the next military post within days and a messenger had arrived bearing a letter of welcome from the commandant of Fort Archambault, Captain Pierre Cros, *chef de la Circonscription du Moyen Chari*. The army base was, by then, only a two-day trek ahead.

Since leaving Brazzaville in January, Latham's journey north-eastwards through the Congo had lasted over four months. He would have been looking forward to reaching Fort Archambault, his last stopping place before Fort Lamy which lay further north in the military controlled territory of Tchad. Fort Archambault was considered to be one of the more important military posts in this district and Latham must have anticipated finding the base well equipped with improved communication facilities to link it with the outside world. Bearing in mind the atrocious conditions he had witnessed in recent weeks, it is not too presumptuous to suggest he was anxious to despatch a few coded cables to alert the recipients of his intention to submit a more detailed report on the conditions had had encountered en route. He was patently unhappy with the behaviour of the military and the apparent ineptitude of their superiors to curb their excesses and his earlier determination not to shirk from speaking his mind still held: 'I shall tell everyone exactly what I think'.

In addition, there was a less urgent, but nonetheless important duty needing his attention as soon as he reached Fort Archambault. This was to despatch a telegraph message to his mother to say all was well. He probably also intended to write another letter for everyone at home because, although all were addressed *Chère Maman*, the correspondence would be passed around to his sisters and read out to small nephews and nieces. Throughout the trip, his letters have described the animals and the native people, the forest plants and the curious insects his brother-in-law Paul has asked him to find. He had told them about the wonderful photographs he was taking and the names of the places he was going be passing through on the next stage of his journey, and it can only be expected that these letters, aimed to ease their worries, conveyed nothing of the horrors or the hardships encountered. A month had passed since his last communication. Dated 3 May – and written when he was in Goré – it had been on the point of reaching Maillebois by the time he arrived at Fort Archambault in June.

There were to be no more letters. Latham's arrival at Fort Archambault had brought about some terse entries in his log. Frankly dismayed, he had discovered the base had no direct facilities for sending either cables or mail. All communications had to be first brought by canoe up river to Fort Lamy – another 200 miles or so to the north – from where they would be despatched to the outside world. Had he found this situation strange – shocking – even bizarre? In view of the volatile atmosphere of the unruly region he had just been travelling through, he must have questioned this apparent military communications black-out. Perhaps the explanation given to him was that this was just a temporary malfunction? There should have been no reason why the Fort was cut-off from outside communication and it was hardly a deliberately orchestrated breakdown. He may have had his own suspicions, nonetheless. It would have felt more prudent to put off writing his next letter until he reached Fort Lamy, by which time he would be on the point of starting his journey home with all the sadness, danger and despair of the Congo left far behind. Such hopes were not to be realised.

Apart from meeting up with a visiting officer called Lancrenon, a member of *l'Artillerie Coloniale*, who had made an appearance shortly after his own arrival, Latham had remained fairly aloof from most of the regular personnel stationed at Fort Archambault. Captain Lancrenon was the officer in charge of the district's communications network, the *Mission télégraphique du Tchad* and, while it could be construed that it was entirely coincidental that he had been sent there to fix the inadequacies of the Fort's communication facilities, it is also possible to ponder whether Lancrenon's encounter with Latham might not have been entirely accidental? It should be remembered that Latham was carrying letters addressed to firms who were engaged in setting up 'radio electricity' communications in the military zone of Tchad; his ultimate destination.

Latham's comment in his journal, 'Lancrenon has arrived', suggests to us that this signals officer might have received some prior knowledge of the nature of Latham's intended business up there. They may have had an appointment to meet and, certainly, Lancrenon later claimed he had enjoyed Latham's company 'at table'. It is a bland enough observation which tells us nothing, however, and Latham does not mention this bit of conviviality in his journal because it had coincided with the onset of several days of severe sickness for him – later described as a fever by Lancrenon – but which was, in reality, a return of the diarrhoea. We know this because Latham's habitual detailed chronological note-taking of events was reduced to just one line for each of the days he was incapacitated. Only one of these entries had an additional scrawl to note that he has sold his horse to Lancrenon. We can take this to have been a transaction of no particular significance; Latham would have had no further use for a mount on his next, final push northward to Tchad. The last leg of the journey was to be up river by canoe to Fort Lamy.

Latham's journal certainly contains evidence that he had some other European company while at the base. There are short references to two civilians: one was an Englishman called Buckley, with whom he 'spends two days' and the other, 'an afternoon with Dr Nicoud', who was the resident medical officer. The doctor, in a letter to Latham's mother, will afterwards claim to having enjoyed quite a *rapport* with the visitor during his stay, but his recollection that her son 'had been cheerful and in good health with plenty of energy' seems to have been a doubtful diagnosis, if not a downright inaccurate one.[9] Viewed in retrospect, the four or five final days of Latham's sojourn at Fort Archambault had seen the visitor clearly quite ill. He may have been in denial over the symptoms of malaria and it is always possible that he had concealed his true state of health from the doctor, although the debilitating effect of his complaint must have made him drawn and lethargic. He had lost weight and was less than robust. Certainly, at that time, Latham was not a candidate who might qualify for a later description of being 'healthy, cheerful, and full of energy'.

Yet, from the journal entries, we know that despite all the hardships endured in the past months Latham was nonetheless anxious to enjoy a few hunting forays before taking his leave from the Fort. This military post had acquired a reputation of offering its visitors a good variety of game and his keenness to sample what was on offer was apparently still undiminished. It should not go unremarked, however, that he had noticed how the natives local to this area showed signs of great nervousness if any military escorted strangers came near their villages. This sullen hostility was something very familiar to him. It reflected everything he had discovered in all other districts he had visited on his way here. A disconcerting thought.

The arrival at Fort Archambault had marked the point for most of Latham's team to be dispersed, and for the duration of those last few days there, having already gained a good measure of Moussa's untrustworthiness, Latham had been treating his gun bearer very warily. When the corporal had come into him with a further demand to purchase salt for the men, Latham was anticipating, not unreasonably, that the man was once more acting deviously. It had not helped that the timing of Moussa's fresh approach carried a deliberately calculated insult – for he arrived at a sacrosanct moment – an effrontery underlined by Latham in his notes '… *enfin, terrible*! He comes in while I am at dinner!' Notwithstanding this dreadful *faux pas*, Latham received the corporal courteously and the request was heard, but, once more, Latham stalled him. If the men were short of salt he was happy to give each of them an extra supply. But he will not sell it to Moussa under any circumstances. *Touché*. But, the clash of wills must have left uneasiness in the air, all the same.

The past few weeks had seen disapproving comments about Moussa's behaviour developing into a regular feature in Latham's daily journal entries. The corporal had been throwing his weight about in front of Latham's servants, expecting them to be running around, fetching and carrying for him and answering his shouts of 'boy'. Latham, of course, had viewed this behaviour as being totally out of order and had finally firmly remonstrated with the corporal, telling him that he has no right treat the house boys in this manner and he must call them by their first names. Only their *patron* or master – in this case Latham – had the right to use the term 'boy' in calling for a servant. But the impudent Moussa had been in no mood to accept this instruction in colonial social etiquette. His retort was audacious – Latham called it arrogant – claiming how he was well accustomed to having servants of his own at home whom he calls 'boy' whenever he liked. The belligerent challenge of this answer was left hanging between them, once more unresolved and more than a little menacing.

Clearly, the dilemma facing Latham was that he had no one on his team who could replace Moussa as an arms bearer. He would have to bide his time. Latham's daily records reveal how the gun bearer's surliness often reached its peak when they were all out together on a hunt. The corporal had long stopped calling him 'sir' and would turn his back with palpable insolence while being spoken to. Moreover, of greater importance was his failure to instruct Latham's team of men to stay close when he had moved ahead of them, stalking or targeting prey. Often, the men were missing just when he needed them. Finding himself abandoned on several occasions after a successful kill, Latham had been left shouting and letting off rifle fire to alert them of his location for quite a length of time before Moussa and the others made an appearance to give assistance. One night, after recounting yet another instance of the corporal's attitude – 'he is very arrogant, rude and nonchalant' – his comment in his journal was thoughtful: 'I shall have to do something about rectifying this situation,' he wrote.

Latham was well aware of the importance of the protocol employed by a well-trained team during a hunt. When facing a wild beast, the hunter is alone. The others will have withdrawn from sight but they remain close at hand because he must rely on them for instant attentive support after the first shots are fired. The sound of his gun should bring his bearers running immediately to his aid. They may be needed to produce a diversionary tactic to distract an animal momentarily while he re-loads his gun; he may be relying on a gun-bearer to hand him a freshly primed weapon. Certainly, the responsibility of their role is clearly understood and must be meticulously adhered to for the sake of everyone's safety. Even at the most simple level they should remain within earshot even though they may be only needed for the task of dealing with the carcass of a despatched animal. These were the rules. But the rules were being broken.

Soon after Latham's arrival at the Fort there was a spate of nasty weather which brought unpredictable and violent rain storms. This made the going difficult while out hunting and very much increased the danger. On 9 June, the inevitable happened. A potentially fatal accident was averted only by a stroke of pure luck. Latham's comment in his journal for that day's excitement was matter-of-fact. 'It is a miracle I am still alive.'

When writing up the details of the incident, he described how he had been waiting to get a good, clean shot of a male hippopotamus, when the animal suddenly started to move away. Latham's first bullet only wounded the animal, his second shot missed and, for his third, the beast was far out of range. He says: 'We then went after him – or, rather, he came after us'. He had aimed and fired again, without success, and then, as the animal began to charge towards him, he had turned away in order to reload his gun, slipped on the muddy ground and tumbled forward with hands outstretched in an effort to save his fall. Afterwards, he complained regretfully, 'I lost my ring [in the fall] and could not find it again'. He had worn this signet ring on the little finger of his left hand for years.

Luckily for him, the tumble had also dislodged his pith helmet. It had rolled away towards the charging animal – and the hippo had stopped in its tracks on seeing this strange object coming towards him – perhaps thinking it was a decapitated head. It was the moment for Latham to stay cool. He had remained motionless – playing 'dead' until the hippo turned away, believing it had seen off the danger. Latham later writes that: 'the beast was mean, but not vicious.' Nonetheless, the animal had suffered one gunshot wound and, as it was the recognised code of hunters not to leave a creature seriously wounded in pain to suffer a lingering death, the journal entry goes on to note how he has ensured his team later tracked down the hippo to put it out of its misery.

This incident was only the start of a generous ration of excitement for that day. When the animal had gone, Latham had begun an unsuccessful search for his lost signet ring. The significance of it having become so loose on finger as to slip off easily during the fall points up that he must have suffered considerable weight loss from the successive bouts of sickness during the long and demanding trek to this outpost. Distracted by this task and possibly assuming his team of men were close by keeping a watch out for other lurking beasts, he was suddenly confronted by a rhinoceros which, as he put it, had 'come out of nowhere'. It spotted him and started to charge. Torrential rain storms had made the scrubby ground tacky and unstable – and, as he dodged out of the way, he lost his footing again. This time he was not so lucky. A glancing blow of the animal's horn caught him on his left calf – but, although thrown to the ground, he managed to fire four bullets in quick succession to despatch the animal. With one of his typical understated remarks that it was 'no worse than a fall from an aeroplane' his journal entry states that his injuries were only superficial. But the hunter, like the pilot, is ultimately reliant on the efficiency of those around him to provide essential support structures. These two near-disastrous encounters demonstrated only too plainly how the escalating insubordination of Latham's team had been consistently letting him down. Apart from having suffered the effects of recurring bouts of illness which affected the efficiency of his marksmanship, having been increasingly left isolated and at risk will eventually prove to have been the greatest danger Latham had had to face.

Latham's bout of sickness had confined him to bed for several days after this incident but as soon his health had recovered sufficiently he had taken leave of Fort Archambault. He was probably glad to see the back of it. He had set off on Saturday 22 June to continue on the final leg of the journey to Fort Lamy which he planned to have reached in a few days' time. On a page in his small personal diary, a scribbled appointment indicates that his intention had been to meet up with a Lieutenant Levoy there on 1 July, but what adds further interest is that another name was jotted down beside this entry – Cros, the commandant at Fort Archambault. The juxtaposition of these names may have been merely an *aide mémoire*; the commandant's name could have been the contact for introducing himself to Levoy; or it may have been a reminder to discuss some mutual topic of interest concerning Cros which Latham wished to raise with Levoy; or maybe not. We shall never know.

Latham's sojourn in this part of Africa was now almost completed. The piece of business with the Electric Radio Company in Tchad he had been entrusted with was to be attended to very shortly and, once this was done with, he would then have been able to start preparing for a choice of route home. He had already procured an introductory letter addressed to a M. Otto, a local agent in that territory, who could arrange for transport by canoe as an alternative to a camel train for the trek to the border with the British territory in Uganda. Evidence suggests this was to be his proposed route home. The composer of an unsigned commentary found deposited among the Latham papers has concluded that Latham was hoping to traverse up the other tributary of the Oubangui river in a north easterly direction in order to cross the border into English administered territory. From there, it would seem he planned to head for Khartoum via Bahr el Gazelle. It was all of six years since he was in the Sudan with the Parmentiers. He would have been looking forward to seeing it again; a place full of memories.

Latham had left Fort Archambault in a relaxed and anticipatory mood. All he needed for this last leg of his journey were his porters, *pagayeurs*, and 'boys' to bring him up river by canoe to Fort Lamy. By six o'clock that night they had set-up their first camp on the river bank and they were off again early the next morning. Stopping for lunch on the second day out, he took a couple of hours off to hunt for a hippopotamus – without any

Latham's last camp at the confluence of the Chari and the Bahr Salmet, June 1912. (HLPP)

luck – after which they were back on the water. By late afternoon, they had set up their next camp on the wide sandy bank of the sludgy confluence of two slow-moving rivers, the Chari and the Bahr Salmet. It was a flat, uninspiring, and undistinguished-looking landscape with a scrubby hinterland covered with high grass, thorn bushes and scattered groves of spindly trees. On arrival, Latham immediately went into the bush to find some prey, perhaps some small buck or antelope which could provide enough provision to feed the party for the next day or two. He had moderate success. His entry for that day notes that he had successfully despatched a waterbuck and some other small game. But his terse remark that his men, as usual, had left him – 'they ditched me' – speaks volumes. All was still not as it should be.

Latham was up early the following morning, 24 June. His brief account of that day's events – the last entries in the journal – record that he had successfully tracked down a buffalo – but it had not been a clean despatch. At the moment of encounter a heavy rainstorm had forced him to take shelter and the wounded animal had escaped. He writes that he will go out and search for the injured beast in the morning. His final log for that day, 'shot a reedbuck' would seem to indicate this had been a chance encounter on his way back to the camp at the end of the day. It was the last entry in his journal.

Neither he nor the wounded buffalo could have rested easy that night.

The official report, drawn up three days later by the military authorities to describe the events that followed, claims he left the camp very early the following morning, 25 June 1912.[10] He had brought with him two hunting pieces, his Express 500 and the Manlicher. His sole companion was one of the *pagayeurs*, a man called Koogoun. In less than two hours of their leaving the camp that morning, Latham was dead, although it will take almost three weeks before the news filters through official channels to reach the outside world. When the story broke in London and Paris on 17 July, the tragedy was announced in *The Times* by a terse headline: 'Death of M. Latham: Killed by a Buffalo.'

Latham's final entries in his journal, June 1912. (HLPP)

The task of hastily convening an inquiry into the circumstances of Latham's fatal accident had fallen to Captain Pierre Cros, the Military Commandant of Fort Archambault, who would be acting on behalf of M. Merlin, the French Governor General for the Colony. Captain Cros was a forty-two-year-old professional soldier from the South of France, who had seen campaign service in Madagascar and Tchad before arriving in the Moyen-Chari region here two years earlier.[11] He had soon gained a reputation for ruthless efficiency. In retrospect, it may be wondered if it was an altogether uncanny coincidence that a citation for his 'brilliant decisions in executing operations' during the military campaign described as a 'war' by his superiors during the previous year was officially added to his military record on 11 July, 1912, almost exactly two weeks following Latham's death. By December this same year, Cros was decorated as a *Chevalier de la Légion d'honneur*. Here was a man with a military career on a decidedly upward curve. One is left with the impression that the clinical efficiency shown by this officer in dealing with the embarrassing death of a well-known – and well-connected – white hunter right on his doorstep in disturbingly compromising circumstances was nothing short of masterly. Given the reputation of the Captain, perhaps this was only to be expected.

At face value, the report on the death of Latham prepared by Cros was a simple and tidy piece of administrative business which swiftly reached a conclusion from evidence given in an oral deposition gathered from the sole eyewitness – the *pagayeur* called Koogoun, who had accompanied him that morning. Koogoun was a thirty-five-year-old Niellim farmer, native to this district of Moyen-Chari. He was interviewed with the help of two translators to clarify his evidence because the man did not speak French and could communicate only in Arabic or in his obscure and dying-out native tongue which had no written form.

When his evidence is examined more critically, Koogoun's chronicle of events on the morning of the accident contains some strange ambiguities, although, at the time, the hearing produced sufficient satisfactory testimony to allow Cros to confirm conclusively that Latham had met his death on the morning of 25 June, following an attack by a wild buffalo.[12] The witness had related how the animal had charged; how Latham's gun had failed; and how the enraged beast had tossed him with his horns three times. It was assumed Latham had died instantly.

It is at this point that one can identify the first of several shadows which cast unease over the reporting of these proceedings. One of the translators recruited by Captain Cros to interpret the truth of the evidence bears a name that has become very familiar to us. It was none other than Corporal Moussa Koulibaly of the 6th Company of the Artillery Reserve Regiment. Latham's own words 'I do not like this man' must surely have haunted the scene of the official evidence gathering.

From out of the shadows, too, the peripheral correspondence which coursed their way from one military observer to another – sometimes for some time to come – carry other questions to be addressed. And answers can be found.

# THIRTEEN
# Unravelling the Mystery

Two or three almost throwaway observations – a mere handful of words – in one of several statements prepared during the inquiry, hold the key to uncovering a little more of the truth surrounding the story of Latham's last hours. In addition, there will be alternative and more compelling, if disconcerting, evidence to raise further questions – although these darker undercurrents did not rise for several years to come.

The first clues can be found in accounts of events written in a letter to a colleague two days after the incident by the *Chef de Mission télégraphique du Tchad*, Captain Lancrenon.[1] It will be remembered that Lancrenon had met up with Latham some days earlier, perhaps by prior appointment. (Latham's matter-of-fact comment 'Lancrenon has arrived' certainly indicates an expected encounter.) The captain was one of several officers from the military posts at Fort Archambault and Fort Lamy who were pulled in by Captain Cros to assist in sifting through the evidence – such as it was – for the report on Latham's death.

Lancrenon begins by displaying anxious concern to discredit some earlier depositions which he says had been taken from Latham's *pagayeurs* and which he insists should now be disregarded. He hints that the information initially proffered by these men to explain the tragedy may be firmly dismissed as 'fiction' for the reason that they 'could not have been eyewitnesses and had merely put their imaginations to work during the night', adding that 'the story of the ambush was very plausible but was not true'. His statement brings us up sharply. Ambush? What ambush? There is no mention of any incident of this nature in the official report which explained Latham's death as a hunting accident involving a buffalo, and why should Lancrenon concede that the *pagayeurs*' missing information had produced a 'very plausible' story?

It would be well to remind ourselves that this northernmost outpost of French Equatorial Africa was still trying to establish some semblance of stability following a series of colonial and tribal wars since 1910. On paper, the French had won control of the area. In reality, as Latham had found out for himself, the mechanics of military administration were dangerously overstretched; the headmen of neighbouring communities were being deliberately set against each another by rampaging military patrols who were still terrorising any settlements found to be laggard in paying imposed taxes. It was a hair trigger situation. Ancient jealousies and deeply embedded tribal rivalries were being stirred up. Beset by such a climate of uncertainty, if some outrage had been perpetrated – such as an ambush of a visiting white hunter by the inhabitants of a Niellim village in the area – it went without question that the military investigation would feel it prudent to whisk such an incident away swiftly out of sight.

Lancrenon had taken some care in preparing his analysis of Koogoun's evidence in his letter but, little by little, disturbing questions may be seen to be rising on the surface of his concern. For one thing, he had not been able to clarify what exactly had caused both of Latham's guns to fail on that fateful morning. Theories abounded, but nothing could be put to the test: both guns had gone missing.

Lancrenon's account of Koogoun's evidence was meticulous in its detail: the *pagayeur* and *patron* had left camp early. Latham was carrying the 500 Express shotgun and the *pagayeur* bore the Manlicher rifle. Their first sighting of a quarry was a rhinoceros. Latham aimed and fired – but the barrel of the 500 shotgun burst apart. Latham had quickly grabbed the second weapon from him, the Manlicher. He despatched the animal with two shots. They had stopped briefly to examine the dead rhinoceros, but then continued on in the search for the wounded buffalo. Suddenly, the beast emerged from the long grass directly in front of them. Latham had swiftly taken aim and fired a shot, but it was a badly placed bullet which only caught the animal in the shoulder. The enraged buffalo started to charge and, according to Koogoun, Latham knelt down to reload his gun while the frightened *pagayeur* scampered off to climb up the nearest tree. It was from this vantage point he claimed to have seen the buffalo tossing Latham three times in the air. The beast then had made its way to the foot of this tree – sensing that Koogoun was hiding up in the branches – but the wounded animal had exhausted its reserves of strength and settled itself down underneath the tree to rest. The *pagayeur* was trapped. He started to shout loudly for help and, after a short while, some local Niellim men appeared in response to the noise he was making. They saw the buffalo lying in wait and they, too, climbed up into some nearby trees for safety until the animal eventually roused itself and moved away off into the bush. They were then able to come back down to the ground to go and inspect where Latham lay in the clearing. In his evidence, Koogoun had said he noticed that the Manlicher rifle was lying open beside Latham's body with its chamber empty. Then, most extraordinarily, he claims that he had picked up the rifle and handed it to one of the Niellim men with the instruction to 'take it away'. He had then set off to get help from the rest of the party in the camp. And, perhaps as puzzling, there is nothing in his evidence to explain what became of the earlier damaged 500 Express shotgun.

In concluding this résumé, Lancrenon gives his own opinion on the malfunctioning of the shotgun, which Koogoun claimed had burst its barrel. Lancrenon theorises that on the day before his death, during which Latham encountered two heavy rain storms when out hunting, he may have dropped his 500 into muddy sand. It was possible that one of the gun barrels or chambers could have become blocked up with this material. He then further speculates that Latham may have failed to clean out this gun when he got back to the camp and, therefore, when he set off the next morning, the weapon was already unusable. But Lancrenon must have known that this was an unlikely scenario. All experienced hunters check their weapons at the end of a day out. The task of cleaning a hunting piece was an essential routine which never varied and Latham was meticulous in his attention to procedures.

Lancrenon goes on to write that he is puzzled why the second gun, the Manlicher rifle, also let Latham down. One opinion being made – by whom, he does not say – had suggested that the failure was due to it having 'jammed'. Lancrenon summarily dismisses this notion as impossible, commenting that such an excellent weapon could never fail in this way – a surprising observation for any army man to make. Most experts are aware that any make of weapon can do this, and often for an inexplicable reason. Lancrenon is also curious why Koogoun should think Latham was trying to reload the rifle when he stood his ground to face the charging buffalo. The native may have been mistaken – he was a canoeist and not a gun handler – but, in any case, how did he know this detail? By his own account, he was running away to climb into the nearest tree, so he could not have had a clear view of what was happening behind his back.

Lancrenon finally comes to the conclusion that Latham had knelt down to take careful aim because he must have believed he had two or even three more shots at his disposal and he justifies this by arguing, 'If Latham had known otherwise he would have taken cover to give himself time to reload his gun.'

Lancrenon's assiduous concern over Koogoun's deposition contains two obvious omissions. He has made no comment as to why the *pagayeur* removed the Manlicher rifle from the scene so swiftly following the fatality. Perhaps this piece of strange behaviour was one embarrassment too much. And he does not ask what became of the broken shotgun. There is a note of desperate justification in his report's final comment which certainly rings hollow; Latham had come to the region 'only to hunt', he writes. One is left wondering just how much classified information this signals engineer had gathered about Latham's proposed business mission in Tchad and how vocal Latham's criticism of belligerent military patrols in the colony had been during their conversations in Fort Archambault. Would there have been serious repercussions from Latham's threat to 'say exactly what I think' at the end of his journey? One is tempted to conclude that Lancrenon knew far more than he cared to admit to and, like Cros, he was hastily covering his tracks.

According to the official report on the incident prepared by Captain Cros for the Governor-General, by the time Koogoun had reached the camp to report on the incident, he found that, in the meantime, two members of the local military – an adjutant and a sergeant – had recently landed there. They had been passing by on a transport canoe and one might think it quite an extraordinary coincidence – if not suspiciously fortuitous – that they should have thought to stop off at the camp just then. They immediately sent word to Fort Archambault by canoe and, while they waited for a response, the adjutant claims he ordered some of the natives in the camp to go in search of the wounded buffalo. The beast was soon tracked down and killed and, following its dismembering, a photograph was taken of the beast's huge head by someone using a camera, possibly the one Latham had brought with him. That evening, several Europeans arrived from Fort Archambault by canoe. They retrieved documents and various other personal items which Latham was carrying with him and inspected the scene of the accident. It was claimed they found blood splattered on the branches of nearby bushes to the height of three metres.

These observations may be compared to another account written up by a M. Martineau, who was administrator from the military garrison at Fort Lamy. That lunchtime, while on the river, he and a colleague, M. Combescure, a *Commis des Postes*, had met a party of natives in a canoe coming from Fort Archambault to collect the body of a white man who had died. Martineau writes, 'When we reached the campsite, one of the natives told us the white man had been wounded by a lion. We set off with a stretcher and medical orderlies and when we got to the place we saw with our own eyes the spectacle of the corpse lying under a massive thorn bush. The body was gashed and all the clothes torn. We did not know the name of this unfortunate victim and didn't discover who it was until we arrived back at the camp with the corpse and found a letter addressed to M. Latham in the pocket of his khaki jacket.'[2]

It is at this point we must leave the scene in 1912 to consider a startling version of events surround Latham's untimely death which was published on 16 January 1914 in the *Le Havre Journal*, almost two years later. It appeared on the day after Latham's funeral, juxtaposed to reportage covering the obsequies following the repatriation of his body for reburial in France.[3] This astonishing despatch carries no byline:

> Two or three hours after Latham's death, the adjutant-commandant of the nearest French army post arrived at the scene of the drama. He found the body already cold. Latham had a massive wound to his head, his pith helmet was lying beside him, as were his empty rifle and some spent cartridges. The officer noticed that the ground where he lay showed no signs at all of having been disturbed by the trampling of a raging animal, which it would have been if, as reported, he had been tossed and gored by a wild buffalo. Apart from a single wound to his head, Latham's body was intact. In this officer's opinion it looked more like he had been killed in an incident of foul play.

There is nothing ambiguous in the use of the term 'foul play' here and particular note might be made of this account's reference to a 'massive wound in the head'. Whoever voiced this opinion was determined the victim was not to be laid to rest without awkward questions being raised.

This piece of evidence prompts us to return to Captain Lancrenon's own careful setting out of the evidence in 1912. There is another sentence in his letter which now strikes as indicative of some nagging worry. He wrote, 'We brought Latham's body to Fort Archambault where it was examined by the doctor who confirmed there was no wound to the head.' Why, one must ask, was Lancrenon so keen to make this point about an apparently non-existent head wound unless it was an attempt to suppress doubts that the fatality was caused not by the buffalo, but from injuries sustained from an entirely different set of circumstances?

A photograph exists – another of the murky prints of the camp that were later repatriated with the body – which shows the close-up head and torso of the corpse enveloped in a cotton sheet lying amid thorn bush branches. Latham's face is clear and unmarked but the cloth has been carefully wrapped to form a hood-like covering to swath the top and sides of the head. There would appear to be no sensible reason why the folds of the shroud-like cloth should be arranged in this way. Unless…?

The military inspect the scene of Latham's death, 25 June 1912. (HLPP)

As if to underline a point, a small pencilled note accompanies this fuzzy print. It draws attention to an indistinct smudge low down on the exposed torso, claiming this is the injury that was sustained from the horns of a rampaging beast. Offered as confirmation of the evidence given, 'tossed three times', it fails to impress.

So what are we to think? If, on the one hand, the suggestion that a local band of disgruntled Niellims had mounted an ambush on Latham seems altogether far-fetched, it might be considered, alternatively, why the official inquiry so easily accepted one single witness's account of the incident. No blame for the 'accident' appears to have been attributed to Koogoun, the man who accompanied Latham although – highly speculative as it may seem – it is possible to construe an argument that the canoeist, being inexperienced in the handling of firearms, may have accidentally discharged the Manlicher at some stage during that morning's outing, fatally wounding Latham from behind. The mystery of why the 500 shotgun barrel burst apart could be attributed to malicious sabotage, if the fact that the barrel was blocked with sand is accepted and if a suitable reason for this piece of wickedness can be found. The only person who would seem to have reason to hold a grudge against Latham was Corporal Moussa and, while his role as official translator during the military inquiry rankles, no one seems to have asked any particularly awkward questions over it. Moreover, it beggars belief that no one asked why Latham's firearms – two extremely reliable weapons – should have both malfunctioned with such disastrous effect on the same day. Who or what had caused them to be so quickly spirited away after the incident? On the face of it, it seems that neither questions nor explanations were offered – except that in this instance a small, but interesting postscript can be added to throw a sharp spotlight on this incident. It will be necessary to shift the focus of the time frame once more forward – well beyond two world wars – to more than forty years later.

In 1955, a retired Irish medical officer by the name of Ridgway, who had been attached to the British District Commissioner's Office in Uganda at the time of Latham's death, wrote to a BBC broadcaster in response to a radio talk on Latham which had been aired in August 1955. The doctor's letter contained some very curious information. He wrote to say that while stationed in Uganda at the time of Latham's death he had been told that '… a white man had been badly wounded by a charging buffalo in the Belgian [sic] Congo. I at once got ready to cross the Nile to go to him but later heard he was dead, and it subsequently turned out that it was the late M. Hubert Latham, and his gun bearer was trying to sell his gun, but was detained by the District Commissioner.'[4]

He had added that by an 'extraordinary coincidence' he had been a house doctor working at the local hospital in Dover in July 1909 on the day of Latham's almost-successful second attempt to make a Channel flight. When Latham fell into the sea outside the harbour at Dover, this doctor had been called out to attend to the aviator who was sitting in one of the hotel rooms with a badly cut face which required nine [sic] stitches.[5] As the radio commentator adds 'some coincidence!'

One is left wondering what reason would prompt the unknown person – described as Latham's 'gun bearer' in this account – to make a long and difficult trek as far as the border with British Uganda to sell one of his guns in another jurisdiction, unless there was something underhand attached to the disposal of this weapon? And was this gun the missing Manlicher? The only possible explanation is that if this rifle had turned up in French-held territory there would have been too many awkward questions raised.

We are left with the thought that whatever could have, might have, or might not have happened, what is certain is that the military administrators were not prepared to allow themselves to be left facing anything blameworthy concerning the suspiciously violent death of a white European in their territory. Careers could be ruined for less. Only one conclusion can be arrived at with safety, which is that the circumstances surrounding Latham's death had been very efficiently and successfully handled. Whether, in reality, there had been a fatal confrontation with a wild buffalo, or alternatively some kind of native ambush, a revengeful sabotage or an unpremeditated accidental shooting – it made no difference – the smooth patching-over of events had not presented too many difficulties for Commandant Cros and his military colleagues.

Cros was a career military officer who had already gained approval for his 'brilliant' execution of duties. All that was needed was an acceptable and civilised explanation for this tragic death. He would see to it that one was provided. He had Latham's own written

The head of the buffalo is displayed at the camp for a photograph, June 1912. (HLPP)

evidence of intention to track down an injured buffalo that day – what better and most likely cause of the fatality?

Over two weeks after the official findings of the inquiry were drawn up, a cablegram from the office of the *Gouverneur General de l' Afrique Equatoriale Française*, M. Merlin formally announced the news Latham had been killed in an accident involving a charging buffalo. Within another two or three days the report hit the world's newspaper headlines. There were various versions of its content published, some were more garbled than others, several had bits of journalistic embroidery added, or confusion over names and dates. All essentially carried the same story. Aeronautical correspondents rushed into print with laudatory obituaries and news columns revisited Latham's former triumphs on both sides of the Atlantic.

On reading the reports of her son's death, Mme Latham had made contact immediately with the editor of the *Daily Mail* to ask, not without understandable agitation and unbelief, for the name of the correspondent who had written the despatch. The editor had replied courteously that the report had been supplied by *La Presse* in Paris – but added that the paragraph signed with the initials H.H.F. had been written by their own Hamilton Fyfe, in London, 'who had known your son'.[6] But Hamilton Fyfe was disadvantaged, like all the other journalists, in that he could only base his commentary on the official report to hand. One hundred years later, the truth of what happened remains almost – but not quite – as elusive.

The business of conveying the news of the tragedy to Latham's immediate family can only be described as a disaster created by faulty communication technology. Latham's brief letter to his mother, written when in Goré some seven weeks earlier had been his last-but-one communication with home. This letter was delivered to Maillebois on 13 July, eighteen days after his death and just one day before his mother received the official notification of the fatal accident from the Ministry for Colonies. To add a further ironic twist, the telegram Latham had composed on 4 June announcing his safe arrival at Fort Archambault had been also delayed. Presumably, it had been sent up to Fort Lamy – but it had then not left for at least another week. Stamped Nguigni, 20 June, the wire was eventually delivered to Maillebois on 28 June. The distressed family only realised later that its reassuring content had reached them a full three days after the fatality.

Outside of official channels, the half-spoken suspicions over the circumstances of his death remained unresolved, and the coming to terms with the disturbing inconclusiveness became a long, drawn out and distressing saga for his family and friends. The tidy official explanation was never easily accepted by those that had known and hunted with Latham in the past. In particular, a claim by Cros which cast doubts as to the efficiency of Latham's guns, the accuracy of his marksmanship, his carelessness and lack of experience in going after a buffalo was a theory that particularly rankled. A distorted picture had been constructed. But Cros had done his work well in rallying the support of colleagues in Fort Archambault with the story that Latham put himself in imminent danger by his preference to hunt alone without the support of a team: a patently untrue spin on the story which could be easily rebutted from the evidence of Latham's own words in his journal notes. Even the medical officer, Dr. Nicoud, in his letter of sympathy to Mme Latham, confidently referred to her son's penchant to hunt alone as being due to some incident in the past while hunting on the estate of Maillebois.[7] How could he presume to suppose this? And why did he not convey to her the true severity of Latham's last bout of ill health during his time at the Fort Archambault, pretending instead to have found him 'with plenty of energy'?

These disturbing and hurtful false imputations that Latham himself was only to blame for his untimely death were later publicly refuted by the most loyal of all his friends, Léon Parmentier, who wrote in *L'Illustration* that this was '... *une version erronée et que jamais ils n'ont admise*' (a wrong opinion which should never have been accepted).[8] In his opinion, Latham, a crack shot who had spent many years engaged in hunting in the wild, was incapable of being other than meticulous and careful. He had hunted buffalo successfully on numerous occasions and was well aware of the dangers. Léon was devastated at the thought of this 'brave man who had risked his life in many ways in the pursuit of science should die in obscurity and without glory'.

The newly married Léon Parmentier's first daughter had been born that same year and his grieving over the loss of his dear companion of old must have cast a blight of sadness across a time which should have been devoted to the enjoyment of his own personal happy family circumstances. Right up to the end of his life Léon was to remain convinced that Latham had fallen victim to some unspeakable wickedness at the hands of the Congo natives. As for his brother, Jean Parmentier, the suspicion that the real truth might never come to light had brought nothing but the frustration of an unsolved problem and may well have come to colour the increasingly cold intensity of his own exactitude of integrity within his career as a government administrator.

At the time of his death, Latham's remains were immediately transported down river by canoe to Fort Archambault. From here they were transferred to the military cemetery in Bangui, some miles south, where a temporary interment took place on 30 June.[9] In order to comply with the colony's regulations, Latham's body would not be allowed leave the territory for repatriation to France for at least another eighteen months. The coffin arrived home from West Africa for burial in the family vault in Le Havre on 13 January 1914. The military representative of the French colonial administration who accompanied the body was a young Senegalese army courier called Guillaume Moustey. His responsibility included the carriage of all Latham's personal effects which had been carefully stored until such time as they could be repatriated to Mme Latham. With his assiduous care, all these items together with documents and reports were lovingly gathered together in Maillebois. The inventory included Latham's journal, his camera, wallet, cigarette case, cigarettes, books, letters and maps and, rather more gruesomely, leaves and earth from the ground where he had laid, together with a bloodstained handkerchief and the bullet which it was claimed had been retrieved from the shoulder of the wounded buffalo.[10] Mme Latham's gratitude to this army courier for the care he had given to all these precious relics was understandably profuse and, when the intervention of the First World War delayed the young man's return to the Congo, he was given the use of a small house on the Maillebois estate. While there, Guillaume Moustey wooed and married a local girl from the village of Blévy with whom he raised a family. It must be asked if his task of returning Latham's body had a connection with the forthright commentary on the circumstances of this death which appeared in the *Le Havre Journal* the very next day? And it has to be conceded that this cannot be verified. One of Moustey's surviving children, now an elderly lady, maintains he never spoke about events concerning Latham's death in the Congo to his family.[11] He died in Senegal in 1949 following a car accident shortly before he was due to return to France, and his children remained in Blévy with their mother and grandmother.

Within a few years of Latham's death, the main street in his home village of Maillebois was renamed in his honour and, to mark his flying career, a bronze statue created by Georges Verez was incorporated into a monument which was erected on the coast road just outside Sangatte, the scene of the Channel flight.

However, the historical memory of Latham was destined to be overshadowed by fast-changing times. As international conflict escalated, the world he had known was to be shattered by the outbreak of hostilities. By 1914, the easy-going and optimistic years of *Belle Époque* were gone forever. The bright young men whom he had trained to fly for the joy of life were destined to fill the skies they had conquered with new weapons of anger, despair and death.

The construction of 'what if' scenarios offer a multiplicity of choices which Latham's future might easily have embraced if he had lived. If he had reached Dover successfully on 19 July 1909, his name and not Blériot's would be now enshrined in the history of the first Channel flight. Had he not died so soon after the triumphs of his aviation career, the acclamations he received for his role as the most challenging pacemaker for height, speed and daring might now be more clearly remembered. If he had not gone to the Congo in

The Latham Memorial, Sangatte. (HLPP)

1912, but had returned to the Sudan to take up the options proffered by his land purchase near Khartoum, might he have encouraged more contemporary French colonists to take up residence in the highlands of Ethiopia? This place and its settlers might have become as commercially successful – or as notoriously risqué – as the Happy Valley set in British Kenya. And what if he had made it safely up river to Fort Lamy in 1912 and thence home to France with his damning report of the conditions in the French military zone of Moyen–Chari? Is it likely that his findings would have been acted upon any more speedily than of those who came after him? Probably not, but would French influence in Equatorial Africa have taken a different path if he had successfully negotiated the setting up of a wireless system to link the flying fields of the Sahara to Tchad and Bangui? Such speculations are not without merit.

However, there is little doubt that had he lived another two years, Latham would have answered the call to arms as a French army reservist. His expertise as a pilot would have drawn him into the aerial combat of the First World War to meet another new challenge charged with violence. Like others of this generation fated to lose their lives on active duty, the unfolding of history might well have brought a different, but equally early, tragic end to his story.

In real life, however, it may be argued that Latham's contribution as an important player in that fast-changing world of the early 1900s, while short-lived, still deserves to be acknowledged as historically significant. As a wealthy young man of leisure and one of the most tantalising and enigmatic personalities of his day, his life and times might be seen as reflecting the ambiance of a *fin de siècle* era which is perhaps too often dismissed as a frivolous decade. We should acknowledge that Latham made his mark. Let his endeavours be remembered as a brief burning out of brightness in the sky; a shooting star on a dark night which suddenly illuminates the mercurial quality of its special place in time and space. To paraphrase the poet:

> He heard the challenge - and responded to it;
> He learnt the lesson – and triumphed over it;
> And he paid the cost that destiny dictated.

His story has been told. May his bright spirit *requiescat in pace.*

Latham – *requiescat in pace.* (HLPP)

# Epilogue

What the future held in store for some of the other protagonists we have encountered in this story may be worth final comment.

Two weeks after the announcement of Latham's death in the Congo, the long-suffering editor of *The Times*, Buckle, was finally outwitted by some clever manoeuvring by the 'Chief' and forced to resign.[1] But Northcliffe's Machiavellian change of editorial crew brought little luck in its wake. Within ten years, the controversial Press Baron's newspaper empire was to crumble when he finally succumbed to illness and a serious mental malady. The 'Chief' died in 1922, aged fifty-seven. On receiving the news, Lloyd George was moved to comment, '… he may have done a lot of good things, but the truth is he had a bad effect on the public mind.'[2]

Léon Levavasseur was another whose star was to wane even more quickly. He never recovered status in aeronautical circles after the failure of the *Société Anonyme Antoinette*. He, too, died in 1922, ending his days in straitened circumstances.

Latham's early rival, Blériot, was rather more fortunate than Levavasseur, despite a having a chequered career in aviation that saw many bad times as well as good. But nothing ever came to match the triumph of the 1909 Channel flight that made his name. He died in 1936. And fate was soon to catch up with Elise Deroche, daughter of a humble Parisian plumber, aka the Baroness Raymonde de Laroche. Although prevented from taking on any aviation exploits during the First World War, as soon as hostilities ceased she returned to flying and met her death in a fatal air crash the following year, 1919.

Jean and Léon Parmentier went on to achieve success in their lives, albeit in different ways. Jean's brilliant career in Paris as a senior civil servant in the French Department of Finance saw him rise to the pinnacle of his profession. He remained single to the end of his life and died in 1936. His brother Léon's accomplishments were to be no less fulfilling. In the years to come, he and his wife raised five children and, although his days were governed by the responsibility of running the family's country estate, his continued interest in the progression of agricultural science was to gain him many distinguished honours for dedicated service within French rural and local civic affairs. He died in 1948.

Eileen Gray continued to be haunted by a deep interest in the paranormal and, although distancing herself from the Crowley set, for many years she remained very attached to her friend, Jackie Raoul-Duval, whose husband, René, one of Latham's closest associates, had died during the First World War. Gray was almost airbrushed out of history until her reputation as an important *avant garde* artist was restored in the 1970s. She had several partners in life, but never married, and died in Paris, aged ninety-eight.

On 29 March 1912, Captain Robert Falcon Scott, Kathleen's husband, had written his final entry in his Antarctic Diary, but she was not to receive news of his death until the following year. Shortly afterwards, her long-time friend Isadora Duncan lost her two young children in a drowning accident and Isadora herself perished in an equally freak accident, strangled by a long scarf – a present given to her by one of Aleister Crowley's erstwhile mistresses – which had caught in the wheel of her car. In 1922, Kathleen Scott re-married a politician who later became 1st Baron Kennet. Lady Kennet died in 1947.

The rumours of Aleister Crowley's powers to cause tragedy may or may not have been true, but his own self-indulgence in pursuing an unorthodox lifestyle brought about no shortening of his own days. He was aged seventy-two when he, too, died in 1947.

There is one person who did not suffer adverse consequences in the aftermath of Latham's death. The distinguished army record of Captain Pierre Cros of the French Colonial Army Service, commandant of Fort Archambault in 1912, notes the award of a citation in late July 1912, followed by several more laudatory mentions in despatches and the bestowal of the *Légion d'honneur*. Recalled to France from Tchad for the duration of the First World War, Cros returned to serve in Africa where he rose to the rank of colonel and subsequently retired as an honorary lieutenant colonel. That embarrassing little incident involving the death of Latham in the Moyen-Chari region of French Equatorial Africa had caused no lasting damage to the success of this ambitious soldier's military career.

# Sources and Bibliography

## RESEARCH SOURCES

*Primary sources: private papers, archived material and unpublished papers:*

Hubert Latham Private Papers
The Parmentier Archives
Lucy M. White, unpublished typescript contemporary account of the 1909 Reims Aviation Meeting, RAS Library, London (undated, presented to the library in 1960); *The Delaroche Family History* (privately printed)

*Oral interviews and/or correspondence:*

Sylvie Armand-Delille and her late father, Lionel Armand-Delille; Matthew, Jeff and Oliver Murray and other members of the extended Armand-Delille family. Dr Guy Parmentier and his aunts Elizabeth and Odile (*née* Parmentier), and cousins Marie-France Parent and Matthieu Brard
Gordon Bruce, Mark Latham, Stephen H. King and his wife, Catherine
Ken Harman, Brian A. Elliott and the Royal Aeronautical Society's librarian, Brian Riddle
Jennifer Goff, researcher in the National Museum of Ireland, and Ruth Starr, researcher in the Department of History and Fine Art, Trinity College, Dublin

*Libraries and museum collections:*

The Royal Aeronautical Society Library, London; Le Centre de Documentation, Musée de l'air et de l'espace, Paris; Ministère de la Défence, Service Historique, Paris; Muséum national d'histoire naturelle, Paris; La Société de Géographie, Paris; The British Science Museum Library, Imperial College, London; The British Library, Newspaper Library, Colindale Avenue, London; The National Library, Dublin; The National Museum of Ireland; The Royal Irish Automobile Society archive, Dublin; The Clothworkers' Company, London; The Nelson Museum and Local History Centre, Monmouth; Gwent Record Office, Library and Museum, Wales

*Newspapers and journal articles:*

Published during 1909–12: *The Times, Evening Times, Times of India, Daily Mail, Daily Telegraph, Lancaster Guardian, North Mail, The New York Herald* (European edition), *New York Daily Tribune, San Francisco Chronicle, New York Journal of Commerce, Pall Mall Gazette, The Sketch, Westminster Gazette, The Car, The Motor Journal, Motor News, The Field, Flight Magazine, The Aeroplane, Paris Journal, Fémina, Le Figaro, Le Monde, Le Matin, L'Illustration, La Revue Aérienne, La Vie au Grand Air, Journal du Havre*

Newspaper cuttings contained in the Alexander Collection in the library of the Science Museum
    in the Imperial College, London under the ref. Arch: Alex. B103

Jean Parmentier, 'De Khartoum à Addis Ababa', in *La Géographie* XXV No.4, 15 Avril 1912,
    pp.231–46

Hubert Latham, 'Au Sidamo et chez les Gallas Aroussi', in *La Géographie* XXVI No.1, 15 Juillet
    1912, pp.1–4

*Bulletin de la Société de Géographie*, Vol.25, Paris, 1912

*Balliol College Register*, 1832–1914 (Oxford, 1914)

*The Listener*, 25 August 1955


## SECONDARY SOURCES

### AERONAUTICAL HISTORY:

Aspin, C., *Dizzy Heights* (Helmshore Local History Society: Lancashire, 1988)

Bacon, G., *Memories of Land and Sky* (Methuen & Co.: London, 1928)

Brett, R.D., *History of British Aviation 1908–1914: vol.1* (Air Research Publications (reprint) Kristall
    Productions: Surrey, 1934)

Bruce, G., *Charlie Rolls – pioneer aviator. Historical Series no.17* (Rolls-Royce Heritage Trust: Derby,
    1990)

Corlett, J., *Aviation in Ulster* (Blackstaff: Belfast, 1981)

Edgerton, D., *England and the Aeroplane* (Macmillan Academic & Professional: London, 1991)

Elliott, B.A., *Blériot: Herald of an Age* (Tempus: Stroud, Gloucestershire, 2001)

Farman, D. & H., *The Aviation Companion* (Mills & Boon: London, 1910)

Gollin, A., *No Longer an Island: Britain and the Wright Brothers 1902–1909* (Heinmann: London, 1984)
    *The Impact of Air Power on the British People and their Government* (Stanford University Press:
        Stanford, California, 1989)

Gastambide, R., *L'Envol* (Paris: 1932)

Gunston, B. (ed.), *Aviation Year by Year* (Dorling Kindersley: London and New York, 2001)

Harris, S., *The First to Fly: Aviators' Pioneer Days* (Macmillan: London, 1970)

Hallion, R.P., *Taking Flight* (Oxford University Press: Oxford and New York, 2003)

King, Stephen H., *Windkiller* (Word Association Publishers: Tarentum, Pennsylvania, 2004)

Kohri, K., Komori, I. and Waito, I. (Trans.), Ohyauchi, K., *Airviews: The Fifty Years of Japanese
    Aviation 1910–1960 Book 2* (Kantosha: Tokyo, 1961)

Lebow, E.F., *Before Amelia* (Brassey's Inc.: Washington, 2003)

Monday, D. (ed.), *Illustrated Encyclopaedia of Aircraft* (Hamyln: London, 1978)

Opdycke, L.E., *French Aeroplanes before the Great War* (Schiffer Publishing: Atglen, Pennsylvania, 1999)

Penrose, H., *British Aviation: The Pioneer Years* (Putman: London, 1967)

Riddle, B. and Sinnott, C., *Letters of the Wright Brothers* (Tempus: Stroud, Gloucestershire and
    Charleston South Carolina, 2003)

Taylor, J.W.R. (ed.), *Aircraft 1973* (Ian Allan: London, 1972)

Wallace, G., *Flying Witness: Harry Harper and the Golden Age of Aviation* (Putnam: London, 1958)

Wohl, R., *A Passion for Wings: Aviation and the Western Imagination 1908–1912,* (Yale University:
    New Haven and London, 1994)


### BACKGROUND HISTORY, POLITICS AND CONTEMPORARIES:

Adam, P., *Eileen Gray, Architect Designer: a biography* (Thames & Hudson, revised edition: London
    and New York, 2000)

Barney, Natalie, *Pensées d'une Amazone* (Emile Paul: Paris, 1920)

Bence-Jones, M., *The Catholic Families* (Constable: London, 1992)

Booth, M., *A Magick Life: A Biography of Aleister Crowley* (Hodder & Stroughton, Coronet paperback edition: London, 2001)

Blackwood, B.G., *The Lancashire Gentry and the Great Rebellion 1640–60* (Manchester University Press: Manchester, 1978)

Capstick, P. (ed.), Édouard Foà's *After Big Game in Central Africa* (St Martin's Press reprint of 1899 edition: New York, 1989)

Constant, C., *Eileen Gray* (Phaidon: London, 2000)

Danchen, A., *George Braque: a Life* (Hamish Hamilton: London, 2005)

Fleming, F., *The Sword and the Cross* (Granta, paperback edition: London, 2003)

Ferguson, N., *Empire* (Penguin, paperback edition: London, 2004)

Fyfe, H., *Northcliffe: an intimate biography* (Allen & Unwin: London, 1930)

Grand, C., *Trois Siècles de Banque de Neuflize, Schlumberger Mallet: 1667–1991* (Éditions E/P/A: Paris, 1991)

Greenwall, H.J., *Northcliffe: Napoleon of Fleet Street* (Allan Wingate: London, 1957)

Kennett, K., *Self-Portrait of an Artist* (John Murray: London, 1949)

Kynaston, D., *The City of London: a world of its own Vol.1* (Chatto and Windus: London, 1994)

Pakenham, T., *The Scramble for Africa* (Abacusm, paperback edition: London, 1992)

Roberts R. and Kynaston, D., *The Bank of England: 1694–1994* (Clarendon Press: Oxford, 1995)

Service, R.W., *The Spell of the Yukon and other verses* (Barse and Hopkins: New York, 1907)

Souhami, D., *Wild Girls* (Weidenfeld and Nicholson: London, 2004)

Thompson, J.L., *Northcliffe* (John Murray: London, 2002)

Young, L., *A Great Task of Happiness: the life of Kathleen Scott* (Macmillan: London, 1995)

# Endnotes

**Abbreviations:** Hubert Latham Private Papers: HLPP

## Introduction

[1] Robert W. Service, *The Spell of the Yukon and other Verses* (New York, 1907), p.36

## Chapter One

[1] In addition to oral interviews, data on family history is drawn from: The Clothworkers' Company archives in London; Christian Grand, *Trois Siècles de Banque de Neuflize, Schlumberger Mallet: 1667–1991* (Paris, 1991); *The Delaroche Family History* (printed privately), courtesy of Stephen and Catherine King; B.G Blackwood, *The Lancashire Gentry and the Great Rebellion 1640–60* (Manchester, 1978), p.139, and M. Bence-Jones, *The Catholic Families* (London, 1992)

[2] R. Roberts and D. Kynaston, *The Bank of England: 1694–1994* (Oxford, 1995), p.266, and David Kynaston, *The City of London: a world of its own* Vol.1 (London, 1994), pp.261 and 263. Alfred had entered merchant banking by a partnership with John Alves Arbuthnot in 1833 and remained a partner until 1866. His son George then followed from 1866–71

[3] *The Delaroche Family History*, page ref. C III

[4] Faure's mother, Marie Oberkampf, whose family came into prominence in the 1790s as the manufacturers of *Toile de Jouy* (speciality designed printed cotton or linen). The Oberkampf daughters married into the Mallet and Verne families. Additional data on Jacques Faure courtesy of Musée de l'air et de l'espace, Le Bourget, Paris. See also obituary notice in *The New York Herald* (European edition), December 1910

[5] Jacques Faure 'De Londres à Paris en Ballon' in Pierre Lafitte et Cie (ed.), *La Vie au Grand Air*, No.336, February 1909, pp.130–1

## Chapter Two

[1] Peter Adams, *Eileen Gray, Architect/Designer: a biography* (revised edition: New York, 2000), p.66

[2] Brian Elliott, *Blériot, Herald of an Age* (Stroud, Gloucestershire, 2000), p.37

[3] C. Dollfus and H. Bouche, *Histoire de l'Aéronautique*, (Paris, 1932), p.209, cited in Elliott, p.40

[4] Robert Gastambide, *L'Envol* (Paris, 1932), p.26

[5] Ibid, pp.28–9. The agent was named as M. Braunbeck, a director of the German published magazine *Motorwagen und Motorboat illustrierte Zeitung*

[6] HLPP

[7] Sir H. Rider Haggard, *King Solomon's Mines* (London, 1885). This author's most famous novel, set in this region of Africa, was followed by others in similar vein and published prior to 1906

[8] H. Weld Blundell, 'Exploration in the Abai Basin, Abyssinia', *The Geographical Journal,* Vol.XVII, No.6, June 1906, pp.529–53

[9] Winston Churchill, *My African Journey* (London, 1908)

[10] These reports were later published in Paris: Jean Parmentier, 'De Khartoum à Addis Abeba', in *La Géographie* XXV No.4, 15 Avril 1912, pp.231–46, and Hubert Latham, 'Au Sidamo et chez es Gallas Aroussi', in *La Géographie* XXVI No.1, 15 Juillet 1912, pp.1–4. Referred to later by Le Secretaire Général, in *Bulletin de la Société de Géographie* Vol.25, 1912, p.151

## Chapter Three

[1] Latham's letters (HLPP) together with Léon's notebooks and diaries, held in the Parmentier archives, log the progress of their expedition

[2] Gastambide, p.144

[3] HLPP

[4] Parmentier, pp.231–46

[5] 'Le Commerce à Addis Ababa' in *Bulletin du Comité de L'Afrique Française*, supplément Août 1908, pp.121–2

[6] HLPP: There was a young man of Kodok,
Who thought he would have a good f★★★
When the girl cried 'Dear me,
Get away with your knee',
Said 'that's not my knee, that's my cock'!

[7] Latham, 'Au Sidamo', p.3

[8] Graham Wallace, *Flying Witness: Harry Harper and the Golden Age of Aviation* (London, 1958), p.139

## Chapter Four

[1] Léon Delagrange, quoted in Robert Wohl, *A Passion for Wings: Aviation and the Western Imagination 1908–1912* (1994), p.33

[2] Alfred Gollin, *The Impact of Air Power on the British People and their Government* (Stanford, California, 1989), p.5, cites the author of this slogan to have been Major Baden-Powell, in an article written for the *Daily Mail* on 11 July 1909

[3] Elliot, p.29

[4] Gastambide, p.143. My thanks also to Brian Elliot for his letter which cites Louis Blériot's grandson's account: *L'Envol du XXe Siècle* (Paris, 1994), p.47

[5] Blériot, *L'Envol*, pp. 94–95

[6] Wohl, p.20

[7] David Edgerton, *England and the Aeroplane* (London, 1991), p.3. See also Alfred Gollin, *No longer an Island: Britain and the Wright Brothers 1902–1909* (London, 1984), pp.200–5

[8] Gollin, *No longer an Island*, p.202

[9] Gastambide, pp.124–8

[10] Ibid., p.148

[11] Ibid., p.149

[12] Elliott, p.77

[13] F.T. Marinetti, 'The Founding and Manifesto of the Future' in *Le Figaro*, 20 February 1909, Paris

[14] Principles cited by Wohl in his discussion of Kamensky, p.152

[15] Marinetti's Manifesto

[16] Adam, p.64

[17] Marinetti's Manifesto

[18] Ibid.

[19] Caroline Constant, *Eileen Gray* (London, 2000), p.11. A later lover was the architect, Badovici, fifteen years her junior, with whom she lived for several years

[20] Adams, p.44

[21] Ibid., p.65

[22] Gordon Bruce, *Charlie Rolls, pioneer aviator*, Rolls-Royce Heritage Trust Historical Series No.17 (Derby, 1990), *passim*

[23] Bruce, p.15

[24] Adams, pp. 27–8 and 31

[25] Martin Booth, *A Magick Life: A Biography of Aleister Crowley* (paperback edition: London, 2001) pp.185–7

[26] Ibid.

[27] Adams, pp.36–7. See also Booth, pp.270–4. Crowley's subsequently disastrous marriage to the sister of Eileen's friend, painter Gerald Kelly, ended in her alcoholism and suicide

[28] Louisa Young, *A Great Task of Happiness* (London, 1995), pp.32–3 and p.100. Also Booth, p.246

## Chapter Five

[1] J. Lee Thompson, *Northcliffe* (London, 2002), p.35

[2] *The Times*, 2 July 1909, p.5 (d)

[3] My thanks to their descendant, David Iron, for this information. Wing-Commander Eric D. Crundall, became an ace pilot in the First World War and later wrote about his exploits in *Fighter Pilots of the Western Front* (Kimber, 1975). One of the Iron family cousins became a naval pilot – probably the first Englishman to undertake a landing on a platform at sea and this man's brother, who was also a career pilot in the RAF, later founded the RAF's Royal Training Corps in the Second World War

[4] Elliott, p.89. See also see *European Nobility*, National Library, Dublin. His wife was Cordelia Consett of Brawith Hall, Thrisk, North Yorkshire, and Château Champ du Bataille, Eure. Her mother was the eldest daughter of Lord Kerr

[5] D. & H. Farman, *The Aviation Companion* (London, 1910)

[6] Elliott, p.87

[7] Adams, p.66

[8] Bill Gunston (ed.), *Aviation Year by Year* (London and New York, 2001), p.66

[9] Thompson, p.168 cites a letter dated 18 May 1909

[10] Wallace, p.106. See also my chapter one, p.20

[11] Gastambide, pp.158–9

[12] Adams, p.66

## Chapter Six

[1] *The Times*, 21 July 1909, p.8 (d)

[2] *Daily Mail*, 22 July 1909

[3] *The Times*, 21 July 1909, p.8 (d)

[4] HLPP

[5] Wallace, p.116

[6] Elliott, p.104, and *The Times*, 26 July 1909, p.8

[7] *Lancaster Guardian*, 31 July 1909, p.7 (a)

[8] *The Times*, 26 July 1909, p.8

[9] Elliott, p.108 cites M. Lhospice, *Match pour la Manche* (1964), p.129

[10] Letter held in the Clothworkers' Archive.

[11] Wohl. p.61

[12] Ibid.

[13] David Edgerton, *England and the Aeroplane* (London, 1999), p.6, cites the *House of Commons Debates* Vol.8, 2 August 1909, col.1566

[14] Harry J. Greenwall, *Northcliffe: Napoleon of Fleet Street* (London, 1957), p.95

[15] Ibid.

[16] Hamilton Fyfe, *Northcliffe: an intimate biography* (London, 1930), p.149

[17] Shackleton came from a County Kildare family with an estate near Athy. Alfred Harmsworth was born in Chapelizod in County Dublin

[18] *Flight*, 3 June 1911, citing a letter received from Latham in Paris, dated 21 May 1911

[19] *La Revue Aérienne*, 10 August 1909, p.467. Cited by Rénald Fortier in *1909 – An Illustrious Year*, The Canadian Aviation Museum Austro-Hungarian Collection, 2002, p.18

[20] The same doctor later reported a coincidental incident connected with the aviator in Africa, in 1912, *The Listener*, 25 August 1955. (See also reference in my chapter thirteen)

[21] *The Motor News*, Vol.X, No.32, 7 August 1909, pp.1392–4

[22] The Clothworkers' Company Archives. Memo dated 12 December 1980

[23] *The Times*, 31 July 1909

[24] HLPP

[25] HLPP

[26] HLPP

## Chapter Seven

[1] *New York Herald*, 4 July 1910, p.1

[2] *The Times*, 22 August 1909. See also Wallace, p.24

[3] Wallace, p.138

[4] Wohl, p.104

[5] Gertrude Bacon, *Memories of Land and Sky* (London, 1928), p.150

[6] Unpublished typescript account of Reims meeting by Lucy White (Lady Baldwin), the sister of Douglas White, an aviation engineer and partner in White and Thomson Ltd (taken over by Hadley Page in 1919). RAS Library, London

[7] Ibid.

[8] Eileen F. Lebow, *Before Amelia* (Washington, 2003), p.6

[9] Bacon, p.157

[10] Ibid., p.154

[11] Ibid., p.146

[12] *New York Herald*, August 1909

[13] Wohl, pp.111–2

[14] Ibid., p.115

[15] By May 1909 the Wright brothers had already established the Flugmaschine Wright-Gesellschaft Company to manufacture their designs in Germany. Brian Riddle and Collin Sinnott, *Letters of the Wright Brothers* (Stroud, Gloucestershire, 2003) p.37

[16] Richard P. Hellon, *Taking Flight* (Oxford and New York, 2003), p.268

[17] Unattributed contemporary newspaper cutting, Science Museum Library Special Collection, B105, reel 95, p.129

[18] Leonard E. Opdycke, *French Aeroplanes before the Great War* (Atglen, Pennsylvania, 1999), p.24

[19] *New York Herald*, 24 September 1909

[20] *Daily Telegraph*, 28 September 1909

[21] *The Times*, 11 October 1909

[22] *New York Herald*, 26 September 1909, p.2

[23] W. de B. Whittaker in his Memorial to Latham in *The Aeroplane*, 25 July 1912

[24] Chris Aspin, *Dizzy Heights* (Lancashire, 1988), p.9

[25] Gunston, p.88. Also John Corlett, *Aviation in Ulster* (Belfast, 1981), pp.12–5; Peter Lewis in (ed.)

J.W.R. Taylor, *Aircraft 1973* (London, 1972), pp.68–79; Lebow, pp.123–7

[26] Lebow, pp.103 and 109

[27] Ibid., p.9

[28] Kathleen Kennett, *Self Portrait of an Artist* (London, 1949), pp.42–4, 61–4 and 93

[29] Adams, pp.109–10, and Constant, p.9

[30] Natalie Barney, *Pensées d'une Amazone* (Emile Paul: Paris, 1920), cited in Diana Souhami, *Wild Girls* (London, 2004), pp.60 and 63

[31] Alex Danchen, *George Braque: a Life* (London, 2005), pp.7 and 9. Le Havre's most notable families – which included the Lathams – were know to be enthusiastic patrons of the arts. See also Wohl, pp.115–22 and 187

[32] Between 1909 and 1911 José de Charmoy was working on the famous Paris monument to Beethoven. He was killed in the First World War and the monument was never completed

[33] Adams, p.110

[34] Ibid., p.38

[35] Ibid., p.117, an observation about Eileen presented by her biographer.

[36] W. Somerset Maugham, *The Magician* (London, 1908; reprinted London, 2000). The introduction outlines how he based his book on Crowley, viii-x. See also Adam, p.40

## Chapter Eight

[1] *Flight Magazine*, 27 November 1909, p.766

[2] Thompson, p.187

[3] Lebow, p.67

[4] HLPP

[5] Ibid.

[6] *North Mail*, 9 August 1911

[7] HLPP

[8] Lebow, p.129

[9] Ibid., p.105

[10] Following acclaim for his construction of the Suez Canal, Ferdinand de Lesseps had been appointed chief engineer of the Panama Canal project. Work had continued for eight years and 22,000 workers had died from disease or accidents, before mismanagement and corruption led the company into bankruptcy in February 1889. De Lesseps and his associates were put on trial and sentenced to imprisonment in 1893 but none of the leading figures served their sentences. See Alan Palmer, *The Penguin Dictionary of Modern History 1798–1945* (second edition, London, 1963)

[11] *The Times*, 8 May 1910, p.7 (e)

[12] The first aerial crossing of the Atlantic from Newfoundland to Clifden in Ireland was made on 15 June 1919 by Alcock and Brown

[13] Gollin, *The Impact of Air Power*, p.199

[14] W.E. de B. Whittaker in *The Aeroplane*, 25 July 1912, p.78

[15] Thompson, p.188

[16] Ibid., p.191

[17] *Flight Magazine*, 13 August 1910, p.648

## Chapter Nine

[1] *New York Herald* (European edition) 21 October 1910, p.1

[2] HLPP

[3] Wallace, p.208

[4] Grahame-White's own account appeared in the *Evening Times*, 9 December 1910

[5] S. Harris, *The First to Fly: Aviators' Pioneer Days* (London, 1970), pp.197–8

[6] Ibid., p.209

[7] Stephen H. King, *Windkiller* (Tarentum, Pennsylvania, 2004), p.269, cited this quote from the *Baltimore Sun*'s society page

[8] *Journal of Commerce*, 11 November 1910

[9] *New York Herald* (European edition), 9 November 1910, p.1

[10] *New York Herald* (European edition), 24 December 1910, p.4, suggested either a Peruvian aviator, Carlos Tenaud, one of Blériot's pupils currently in training at his flying school in France, or an American pilot – Clifford B. Harmon

[11] *New York Herald* (European edition), 11 January 1911

[12] *New York Herald* (European edition), 5 December 1910, p.1

## Chapter Ten

[1] *Paris Journal*, 3 October 1910

[2] *Morning Post*, 28 December 1910. See also F. Fleming, *The Sword and the Cross* (2004), p.267

[3] Gunston, pp.97 and 298. Santos-Dumont fulfilled his vow as a 'global ambassador', but took his own life in 1932, by then utterly depressed by the futility of his cause and the severity of his illness

[4] HLPP

[5] The Bohemian Club was founded in 1872 by five newspaper men, a Shakespearean actor, a vintner and a local merchant. (Oddly, in later years journalists were barred for fear of secrets being leaked.) The new club house had been opened on 13 November 1910

[6] *Sketch*, 14 December 1910

[7] *Daily Telegraph*, 2 January 1911, quoting Charles Hamilton

[8] *San Francisco Chronicle*, 16 January 1911, p.2 (d)

[9] *Westminster Gazette*, 27 December 1910

## Chapter Eleven

[1] Booth, pp.297–8

[2] *The Field*, Vol.117, 11 March 1911

[3] Thompson, p.206

[4] *The Field*, Vol.117, 11 March 1911

[5] Ibid.

[6] Thompson, p.199

[7] Booth, p.275 – many believed Crowley retained power over people he had been close to

[8] *The Field*, 12 December 1911

[9] HLPP

[10] *L'Aviation: aux colonies*, December 1911

[11] Thomas Pakenham, *Scramble for Africa* (paperback edition: London, 1991), chapters 32 and 35 cover the past history of Belgian and French exploitation of this region. See especially pp.635–40

[12] Ibid., p.636

[13] Ibid.

[14] Ibid., chapter thirty-two

[15] *The Aeroplane*, Vol.2, January 1912, p.6

[16] HLPP

[17] David Monday (ed.), *Illustrated Encyclopaedia of Aircraft* (London, 1978)

[18] Whittaker in his Memorial to Latham in *The Aeroplane*, 25 July 1912

[19] HLPP

## Chapter Twelve

[1] HLPP: Latham kept a neat, pencil-written daily account of his last journey in the Congo from 22 January to 24 June 1912. There are no gaps in the narrative. In conjunction with his letters home, they provide an authentic record of the last six months of his life

[2] Translated by Stephen H. King

[3] HLPP: Latham used a small 'lady's' diary for 1912, to list stores and check supplies

[4] HLPP: African Journal, 1912. Entered on back page – no date

[5] Pakenham, p.632

[6] HLPP

[7] Quotations cited by Terence Ranger, writing on Casement in *History Ireland*, Vol.14, No.4, July/August 2006, pp.47–8

[8] Pakenham, pp.639–40. See also André Gide, *Voyage to the Congo* (1927) and *Le Retour du Tchad* (1928)

[9] HLPP

[10] HLPP

[11] Military record of Pierre Cros: Ministère de la Défense, Service Historique

[12] HLPP

## Chapter Thirteen

[1] HLPP

[2] HLPP

[3] With acknowledgement of Stephen H. King's researches

[4] *The Listener*, 25 August 1955. Letter from broadcaster Collinson Owen (real name Hugh Addison 1882–1956) citing Dr J.C. Ridgway's letter to him. Courtesy of the Clothworker's Archives

[5] Ibid. The *Daily Mail* had originally reported five stitches, three in his forehead and two in his nose.

[6] HLPP

[7] HLPP

[8] Léon Parmentier, 'Hubert Latham Chasseur' in *L'Illustration*, 31 August 1912, p.113

[9] Bangui is now capital of the present-day Central Republic of Africa

[10] HLPP

[11] I acknowledge with thanks the help of Guillaume Moustey's daughter, Sister Thérèse, Catholic Mission, République Centrafricaine, for this information

## Epilogue

[1] Thompson, p.209

[2] Ibid., p.396

# Index

If you are interested in purchasing other books published by Tempus,
or in case you have difficulty finding any Tempus books in your local bookshop,
you can also place orders directly through our website

**www.tempus-publishing.com**